THE PRESIDENT'S DAY

MATTHEW N. BECKMANN

THE PRESIDENT'S DAY

Managing Time in the Oval Office

COLUMBIA UNIVERSITY PRESS

NEW YORK

Columbia University Press
Publishers Since 1893
New York   Chichester, West Sussex

Library of Congress Cataloging-in-Publication Data
Names: Beckmann, Matthew N., 1975– author.
Title: The president's day : managing time in the Oval Office /
Matthew N. Beckmann.
Description: New York : Columbia University Press, 2024. | Includes
bibliographical references and index.
Identifiers: LCCN 2024003318 | ISBN 9780231215862 (hardback) |
ISBN 9780231215879 (trade paperback) | ISBN 9780231561013 (ebook)

Subjects: LCSH: Presidents—United States—Time management. |
Presidents—United States—Decision making. | United States—Politics
and government—1945–1989. | United States—Politics
and government—1989–
Classification: LCC JK516 .B389 2024 | DDC 973.92092/2—
dc23/eng/20240508

Cover image: Wikimedia Commons

To Kenya, my incredible (and funny) wife

CONTENTS

ACKNOWLEDGMENTS

THE FIRST PRESIDENTIAL DAILY DIARY I recall seeing was displayed in the Nixon Library's Apollo 11 exhibit. It was for July 20, 1969. Among its minute-by-minute rundown of Nixon's activities was a highlighted entry: 11:45 to 11:50 P.M., "The President held an interplanetary with the Apollo 11 Astronauts, Neil Armstrong and Edwin Aldrin on the Moon." I naively asked a docent about this so-called diary, and, well, more than a decade later, this book culminates the scholarly voyage that ensued.

As that timeline hints, this study proved far more complex than I envisioned. The journey from diaries to data included many unexpected turns, good and bad, and required rerouting from numerous dead ends. I have been lucky to have so many talented, generous people helping me through it all. I am not confident I can articulate the depths of my gratitude, but I will certainly try.

My first thank you goes to the hundreds of University of California, Irvine students who joined this project over the years. The first undergraduate research assistants helped me imagine, test, revise, and retest the coding scheme until we all agreed that it faithfully captured the archival content. Subsequent crews located archives, coded diaries, entered data, and smartly navigated one hitch after the next.

More recent groups helped me fill gaps, resolve discrepancies, audit outliers, and otherwise ensure that our data were as accurate as possible. To my students who invested their talents on my behalf, I cannot thank you enough. You not only made this book possible; you also made the work fun and rewarding.

On that score, I lucked into working with a fantastic bunch of graduate students. Ken Chaiprasert, Neil Chaturvedi, Jenny Garcia, Sierra Powell, and Kelly Rivera helped me resolve design and deployment issues when this project was in its early phases. I also want to thank Jenny for locating, copying, and transporting critical records from various presidential libraries. Jenny's effectiveness was as impressive as it was invaluable.

That gets to the National Archives and Records Administration (NARA). Like so many others, I am indebted to the professionals who perform an amazing public service: the staff who processed my voluminous requests; the Freedom of Information Act (FOIA) coordinators who answered my obscure questions; the archivists who tracked down supplementary information; and the experts who proactively steered me to useful records. Several current and former NARA employees also granted me interviews, which helped me understand the people and protocols behind the archives I was using. I promise everyone anonymity, so I will not thank them by name, but I will say that NARA is a national treasure, and I will always be grateful for its officials' expertise, assistance, and thoughtfulness.

Then there are the diarists themselves, Susan Yowell and Ellen McCathran. It would have been easy to ignore emails from an unfamiliar academic inquiring about work from decades before, yet both Susan and Ellen could not have been more generous with their time or insights. I learned so much from both, and I greatly enjoyed meeting each. I hope appendix A faithfully relays those lessons and, in turn, highlights their legacy. I also want to thank various assistants who served in the diarist office at different points, all but one of whom granted me an extended interview.

When it comes to understanding the modern presidency, nothing compares to interviewing West Wing alumni. More than a dozen former staffers who joined different administrations, filled different roles, and held different ranks let me pry into seemingly mundane details about their daily work. A few shared forms. Most shared advice. All shared stories. To the extent that this book affords real-world insights into White House work patterns, it is because these insiders generously allowed me to sit on their shoulders. Their names are unspecified, but their lessons are ubiquitous.

Turning to the academic world, I profited from numerous colleagues' questions, suggestions, and encouragement. Chuck Cameron, Matt Dickinson, Brendan Doherty, Lindsey Gailmard, Rick Hall, Alex Hirsh, Will Howell, Karen Hult, Jeff Jenkins, Joseph Jenkins, Doug Kriner, John Matsusaka, Jim Pfiffner, Paul Quirk, Jon Rogowski, Brandon Rottinghaus, Andy Rudalevige, Brook Thomas, and Charles Walcott all influenced my thinking at different points, and I thank each for their efforts on my behalf. I also appreciate the anonymous referees who combined astute comments with generous assistance.

At University of California, Irvine, I am blessed to be surrounded by fantastic scholars whom I'm lucky to have as friends and colleagues. Graeme Boushey, Simone Chambers, Marek Kaminski, Jeff Kopstein, Davin Phoenix, Michael Tesler, Danielle Thomsen, and Marty Wattenberg have assisted me in ways big and small, from start to finish. Marty, in particular, has been a mentor since I arrived in Irvine some twenty years ago. My version of a "book conference" entailed me sending Marty chapters (one by one at random intervals) and him returning constructive, reassuring reviews within 48 hours.

With drafting nearly done, I turned to publishing, which is when I recalled meeting an editor who saw an early presentation and offered to help connect me to her colleagues when I was ready. True to her word and selfless beyond measure, Cindy Rast pointed me toward Columbia University Press (CUP). After scouring CUP's list, I was keen to meet the American politics editor, Stephen Wesley. I could not have gotten a better break. Stephen was not just enthusiastic about my project, but he also deftly led me through reviews, boards, and revisions. I will always appreciate Stephen's talents and style, and even more how he generously invested both on my behalf. Kat Jorge and Wren Haines shared editorial expertise that improved my prose and this book, which I greatly appreciate.

That leads to my family, starting with my parents, Bob and Mary Lou. That I love and appreciate and admire you is obvious. Less evident is how those feelings grew deeper and stronger with time. These last few decades together have been so fun, so fulfilling. As much as I appreciate your readiness to serve as chauffeur or chaperone, my main sentiment is gratitude that your lives have been so interwoven with mine and my family's.

On that score, what can I say about the Beckmann kids? Charlotte, Brooks, and Weston, being your dad will always be my life's "high point." Char, you are as intelligent and creative as you are interesting and fun. Your sparkle and spirit brighten every day. Brooks, you are caring and empathetic, a genuinely independent thinker, and funnier than anyone I know. To be with you is to be happy. Weston, I so admire your curious soul and your analytic mind, the way you build people up, and the kindness you show everywhere you go. Weston was the first person I asked to read working drafts, and his suggestions are sprinkled within each.

Finally, Kenya. When we met twenty-five years ago, I was charmed by your intelligence and empathy and creativity and generosity, your laugh, your smile, your heart - you. Everyone you meet sees the extraordinary light you shine into the world, but nobody gets to see it as clearly as I do, and nobody else gets to experience how wonderful it is to be your husband. I love you more than you can imagine, and it is impossible to express how lucky I feel that we get to do this together.

THE PRESIDENT'S DAY

INTRODUCTION

VIEWED ACROSS PENNSYLVANIA AVENUE, the White House is a model of neatness. Inside the West Wing, however, things rarely appear so tidy. Infinite demands, limited time, high stakes, and hard problems conspire to make presidents' work extraordinarily difficult, not to mention exhausting. Theirs is an awesome burden, one Lyndon Johnson felt acutely when he said that "only in the White House can you finally know the full weight of this office."[1]

Presidents' foremost quandary is that they are asked to resolve the unsolvable. After (relatively) straightforward tasks get handed off and (relatively) consensual matters get signed off, it is the president who is left to wrangle with the obstinate items that remain. As presidents experience it, the workday brings an endless stream of unprecedented questions, intricate dilemmas, and intractable problems. Barack Obama explained the predicament: "By definition, if it was an easily solvable problem, or even a modestly difficult but solvable problem, it would not reach me, because, by definition, somebody else would have solved it. So the only decisions that came were the ones that were horrible and that didn't have a good solution."[2]

The presidential decision load is complicated further by its variety and volume. Any given day can bring some constellation of military operations, diplomatic overtures, legislative negotiations, bureaucratic snafus, political exigencies, press inquiries, disaster preparations, emergency declarations, executive appointments, judicial nominations, and on and on. The scope is arresting; the flow is relentless; the pace is absurd.

Then there are the public demands. The leading performer on the global stage, presidents are expected to play—in fact, must play— a myriad of public-facing parts: answering before a hostile press; pleading before a stubborn Congress; being charming before a wealthy donor; speaking before a global audience; bowing before a fallen soldier. Requests for the president's company are as varied as they are numerous, and every invitation accepted is yet another item that devours time, demands focus, and drains energy.

Edmund Morris, Ronald Reagan's official biographer, once asked to shadow his subject for a couple of days. The president agreed, and years later Morris recounted the experience:

> Within a couple of hours I was so emotionally exhausted that I could hardly stand. It was not that Mr. Reagan, 30 years my senior, set the pace that some hyperactive presidents have kept. What drained me was my writer's tendency to feel what people in the room are feeling. The hundreds who shook his hand (he told me that he averaged 80 new acquaintances a day, for eight years) were avid to make the most of the window granted them in the president's schedule, whether it was an interview, conference, ceremony, drop-by, or photo opportunity.[3]

This extraordinary-as-ordinary workflow led historian Richard Reeves to call the presidency *sui generis*. He is right. Nothing compares to the presidency, each presidency is unique, and no president can foresee the trials ahead. Presidents can plan but never truly prepare. When Robert McNamara warned John Kennedy that he was ill-prepared to be defense secretary, Kennedy had a compelling rejoinder: "Look, Bob, I don't think there's any school for presidents either."[4]

Herein lies a fundamental insight into presidential work: for all the attention given to dramatic moments, a president's performance is mostly seeded in the daily grind of doing the job. On the ground, matters of leadership manifest as questions of time. What meetings should the president take? What events should the president attend? What people should the president see? This book is about the seemingly pedestrian but ultimately fascinating rudiments of presidents' daily work: time, people, and process. It builds from a modest premise—that the presidency's *organization* and the president's *operation* are distinct systems that intersect at the president's calendar—into an extended argument about how presidents define the job by doing their work.

I begin theoretically, conceptualizing presidential schedules as investment portfolios spread over two domains—"speaking" and "thinking"—that are subject to scarce time. This analytic exposition reveals that although *absolute time* is fixed for all presidents, the *relative time* available to each depends on a president's stamina, priorities, and efficiency. Disparities in relative time supply, in turn, have spillover effects on a president's *distribution of time*. Interestingly, these differences are less noticeable when presidents perform on the public stage but become readily apparent as we peer behind the scenes.

Alas, it is one thing to theorize about how presidents work; it is quite another to study that work systematically. Most presidential activities are carefully concealed from public inspection, and those activities that are disclosed tend to be both unrepresentative and unreliable. And while presidential libraries provide tantalizing glimpses behind the curtain, even those archival holdings vary dramatically in form and substance from president to president, aide to aide, issue to issue, and even day to day.

This book provides a new, systematic look with an eclectic array of granular evidence about presidents' daily work practices from 1961 to 2008, John F. Kennedy to George W. Bush. These data come from a myriad of sources, culled from a myriad of methods: elite interviews and archival records, small-*n* case studies and large-*n* quantitative analyses. The heart of the research is a comprehensive dataset of 37,781 distinct presidential work activities (on stage *and* behind the scenes), spread over a representative sample of 1,781 days, spanning forty-eight years, and covering nine presidencies.

At one level, this evidence offers an unprecedented look at how postwar presidents have tackled the nation's hardest job; at another it lets me test why presidents operate the office as they do. Controlling for national conditions, political circumstances, and daily exigencies, I find that each president plots signature paths in terms of how long they work, how many tasks they perform, how quickly they process those tasks, which tasks they prioritize, and the number and type of people they engage along the way. In other words, we cannot understand *how* without also understanding *who*.

Having built a multifaceted case—theoretical and empirical, logical and historical—that presidents reveal themselves in the ways they work, I conclude this book by considering the implications—and possibilities. I thus conclude my study by defining the first principles of "everyday leadership."

To those ends, let me begin.

INFINITE INBOX

Charles Pinckney spurred debate among his fellow constitutional conventioneers by asking a deceptively simple question: "Shall the blank for the number of the Executive be filled with a single person?"[5] A few delegates worried about creating an executive with kinglike features; others worried that an unsavory character could exploit such features.

Ultimately, though, the framers decided that a singularity would create accountability within the executive branch and induce "energy" in its chief. The first sentence of the Constitution's second article therefore resolved: "The executive Power shall be vested in a President of the United States of America."

The choice to funnel government operations through a single person places an incredible workload on the president. Whether it is signing laws or issuing vetoes, receiving foreign leaders or delivering military orders, nominating federal judges or granting criminal pardons, declaring national emergencies or negotiating international agreements, not to mention countless other executive actions presidents must perform, the nation's chief executive is personally responsible for the federal government's vast scope.

Nevertheless, few presidents have limited themselves to performing constitutional duties. Teddy Roosevelt's expansive interpretation of the presidential purview was controversial in his era, but it now reads as little more than conventional wisdom: "I declined to adopt the view that what was imperatively necessary for the Nation could not be done by the President unless he could find some specific authorization to do it. My belief was that it was not only his right but his duty to do anything that the needs of the Nation demanded unless such action was forbidden by the Constitution or by the laws."[6]

If the first President Roosevelt advocated an activist presidency, it was the second who actuated it. Franklin drafted legislation and lobbied lawmakers, fashioned agencies and appointed officials, and spearheaded a nonstop, multifaceted public relations campaign. His initiative did not only change the nation; it also launched the modern presidency. Thomas Cronin and William Hochman summarized: "Franklin Roosevelt's virtuoso performance permanently redefined the presidency as a central leadership post for nation and world."[7]

In the generation between Roosevelt's inauguration and Eisenhower's farewell, Clinton Rossiter marveled at how much work now flowed to the Oval Office: "If there is any one thing about [the president] that strikes the eye immediately, it is the staggering burden he bears for all of us."[8] Among the "many hats" presidents had come to wear, Rossiter cited chief of state, chief executive, commander in chief, chief diplomat, chief legislator, chief of party, voice of the people, protector of the peace, manager of prosperity, and world leader.[9]

No doubt, the presidency's "staggering burden" has only grown larger over time. Today Americans expect their chief executive to manage the government and solve assorted public policy problems while simultaneously leading the country through all manner of crises: wars, recessions, disasters, riots, tragedies, and more. Each president must also perform as the nation's foremost representative, attending multifarious ceremonies, speeches, memorials, and summits, not to mention obliging an extensive array of political demands—including the requisite pictures, dinners, rallies, speeches, fundraisers, interviews, and debates.

In short, the framers purposefully designed the Constitution to induce "energy" in the executive, and, for better or worse, it worked. America's political universe now has a presidential core. The question for political scientists is the same one that presidents themselves must answer: How can an all-too-human president handle the presidency's superhuman workload?

SCAFFOLDING THE OVAL OFFICE

As hinted, Franklin Roosevelt entered a White House that his successors would recognize but a presidency that they would not. Roosevelt's first team included about fifty staff, most custodial or clerical, plus a couple dozen reinforcements culled from around the executive branch. This was Roosevelt's so-called brain trust, an entourage that included few people, fewer levels, and less structure.[10] That Missy LeHand, Roosevelt's personal secretary and companion, performed many duties that now fall to the White House chief of staff (COS) exemplifies how loosely "roles" were defined.[11]

Keenly aware that his ambitions outpaced his assistance, Roosevelt recruited an expert panel to envision ways to overhaul his office. The President's Committee on Administrative Management—chaired by Louis Brownlow and colloquially called the Brownlow Committee—returned with a clear verdict: "The president needs help. His immediate staff assistance is entirely inadequate." Going forward, they proposed that the president "should be given a small number of executive assistants who would be his direct aides in dealing with the managerial agencies and administrative departments of the Government. These assistants, probably not exceeding six in number, would be in addition to his present secretaries, who deal with the public, with the Congress, and with the press and the radio."[12]

President Roosevelt gladly endorsed his handpicked panel's advice and urged lawmakers to do the same, which they did in the spring of 1939. A few months later the Executive Office of the President (EOP) opened as a small shop serving at the president's pleasure.[13] Figure 0.1 displays the EOP's initial components.

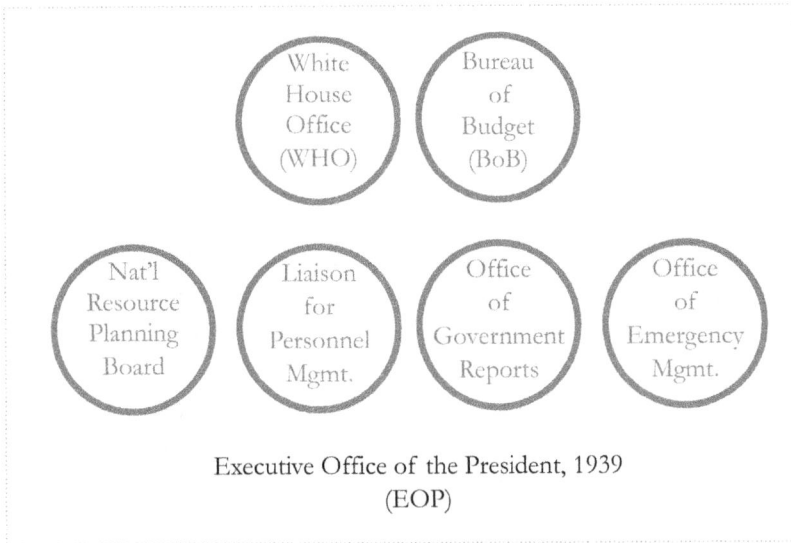

Executive Office of the President, 1939
(EOP)

FIGURE 0.1 Original Executive Office of the President.

Modest roots notwithstanding, the EOP quickly grew more ornate.[14] The White House Office (WHO)—the unit within the EOP that includes the president's closest advisors—grew from sixty-one staffers to more than two hundred during Harry Truman's first year. Truman also revamped the EOP, launching the National Security Council (NSC) and Council of Economic Advisors (CEA) as subunits. By the time Truman moved out of 1600 Pennsylvania Avenue, the EOP counted more than one thousand positions scattered across a half-dozen offices.

Where Truman added manpower, Eisenhower imposed structure.[15] This was no coincidence; Dwight Eisenhower's abiding faith in organizational discipline ran deep: "Many people are always saying the Presidency is too big a job for any one man. When I hear this assertion, I always try to point out that a single man must make the final decisions that affect the whole, but that proper organization brings to him only the questions and problems on which his decisions are needed."[16]

In pursuit of "proper organization," the White House COS position was an Eisenhower innovation. Eisenhower gave Sherman Adams the job and tasked him with managing the office. According to Bradley Patterson Jr., it largely worked as intended: "It is to Dwight Eisenhower and to Sherman Adams that the nation owes this debt of innovation: helping bring orderly administration to the very apex of government."[17]

Naturally, not everyone appreciated Eisenhower's methods. To his detractors, Eisenhower was less a model of efficiency than of passivity. John Kennedy (then the junior senator from Massachusetts) was among the critics. Kennedy panned Eisenhower's "detached, limited concept of the Presidency" before advocating a more hands-on approach: "Whatever his views may be on all the issues and problems that rush in upon us, he must above all be the Chief Executive in every sense of the word. . . . He must master complex problems as well as receive 1-page memorandums. He must originate action as well as study groups. He must reopen channels of communication between the world of thought and the seat of power."[18]

Kennedy's belief that the presidency required the president's direct involvement was more than a personal conviction; it also reflected Richard Neustadt's professorial counsel. Neustadt advised Kennedy, "It would be well to avoid reminders of [Sherman] Adams, not only for public relations but because . . . Adams was a terrible bottleneck."[19] This sentiment helps explain why Kenneth O'Donnell, as vital as he was, held neither the title nor the authority of a White House COS. The result: Kennedy's structure was loose, his process fluid, and access direct. Figure 0.2 stylizes the Kennedy model, which Richard Tanner Johnson characterized as "collegial,"[20] and Roger Porter characterized as "adhocracy."[21]

Like John F. Kennedy, Lyndon B. Johnson was loath to be layered. In Johnson's White House, the president played all parts—producing and directing, starring and supporting. Although W. Marvin Watson was certainly a valued member of Johnson's inner circle, titling his memoir *Chief of Staff* was quite a stretch. Watson's own account exposes the reality: after meeting the president in the residence, "I then continued my day at my desk adjoining the Oval Office. My 'normal' working hours were spent carrying out his instructions

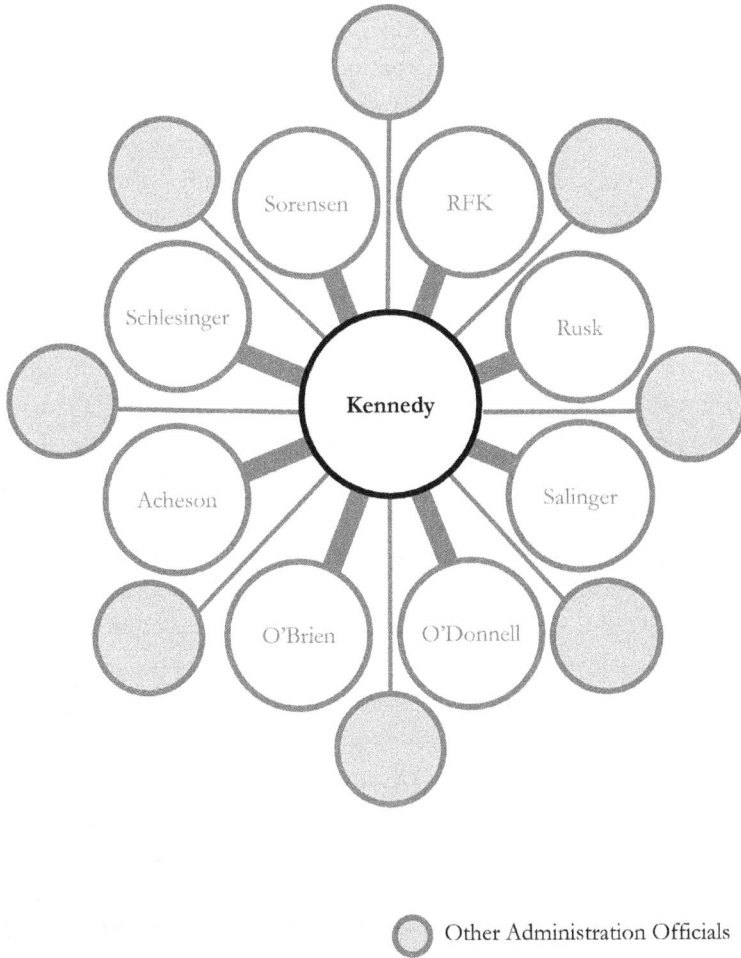

FIGURE 0.2 Stylized version of the Kennedy White House organization.

through seemingly endless telephone calls and meetings."[22] In other words, Johnson was chief; everyone else was staff.

Then came Richard Nixon, the rare politician who liked to be alone. Nixon wanted a buffer between himself and (almost) everyone else. To that end, Nixon made H. R. Haldeman his COS and urged him to apply his title zealously. Haldeman did, famously proclaiming, "Every President needs an S.O.B.—and I'm Nixon's."

The Nixon model, meticulously mapped by Charles Walcott and Karen Hult,[23] included several defining features: a hierarchical, formalized decision-making process that was led by the president, managed by a strong COS, informed by domain-specific experts in the White House and Cabinet, and implemented by scores of executive branch officials. A few senior aides had "walk-in" privileges to see the president directly. For everyone else, the path to Nixon ran through Haldeman, the S.O.B. who limited access to those with a written agenda, coordinated responses, and a scheduled meeting. Figure 0.3 sketches the Nixon model. Interestingly, Walcott and Hult found that Nixon's structure evolved from an organizational template into something of a normative standard. The "once-lively debate over the proper size and organization of the president's White House staff seemingly has been settled. Where once Democrats and Republicans hewed to distinct views, now there appears to be a consensus."[24]

That is not to say that Nixon's successors always embraced his design—Presidents Ford, Carter, Clinton, and Trump all sought to jettison Nixon's system in favor of something more like Roosevelt, Kennedy, or Johnson's—but rather that defectors eventually returned to a more (Nixonian) formal, hierarchical structure. The exception is Donald Trump, the one president who unfailingly eschewed structure and embraced bedlam. Of course, Trump's counterexample only helped cement the Beltway consensus: the modern presidency tends toward chaos without the discipline the Nixon model imposes.[25]

In sum, the postwar era was when the presidency professionalized. It commenced when Roosevelt spearheaded America's response to the Great Depression and World War II. It gained traction when Roosevelt founded the EOP. It increased capacity when Harry Truman added manpower. It grew sturdier when Eisenhower formed and Nixon fortified clear organizational order. And it gained legitimacy as Nixon's successors adopted his blueprint as their own. President Trump's four years notwithstanding, the same basic organizational model has proven remarkably durable for almost a century.

In light of the presidency's institutional hardening, the obvious follow-up question is about the president: Does a standard organization impose a standard operation?

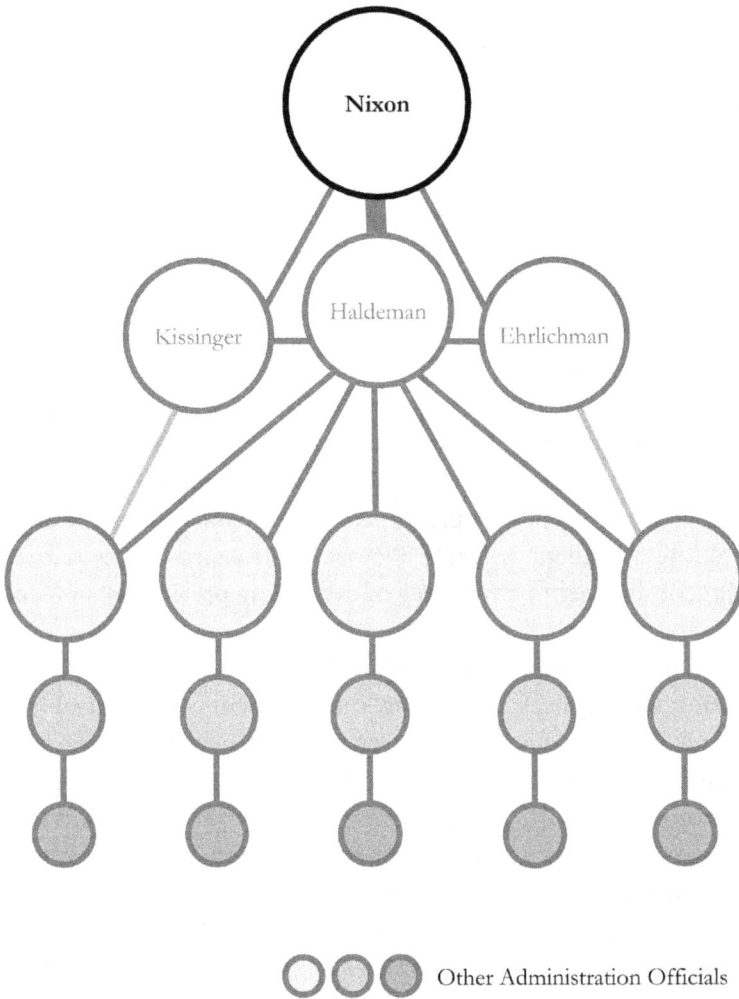

FIGURE 0.3 Stylized version of the Nixon White House organization.

ORGANIZATIONAL THEORY

Bill Clinton once cited the White House as "the crown jewel of the federal penitentiary system,"[26] an echo of Harry Truman's "great white jail" reference decades before.[27] It was in that same spirit that Ronald Reagan confided to one audience: "And now I know that my time is up, and I'm going to have to leave, and I don't want to. But I don't have much choice. They tell me I'm the most powerful man in the world. I don't believe that. [Laughter] Over there in that White House someplace there's a fellow that puts a piece of paper on my desk every day that tells me what I'm going to be doing every 15 minutes. He's the most powerful man in the world."[28] These are self-deprecating quips to be sure, but they are not merely self-deprecating. As presidents know well, many of their office's trappings are quite literally trappings.

In his groundbreaking book, *Presidential Power*, Richard Neustadt explained how the presidency encroaches on its tenants. "However much [the president] knows, however sharp his senses, his time remains the prisoner of first things first. And almost always something else comes first. . . . The net result may be a far cry from the order of priorities that would appeal to scholars or to columnists— or to the President himself."[29] That is, the presidency's *institutional* commitments have a way of overriding presidents' *individual* inclinations.

Richard Neustadt's diagnosis stood in stark contrast to Woodrow Wilson's famous declaration that "the President is at liberty, both in law and in conscience, to be as big a man as he can. . . . His capacity will set the limit."[30] Whereas Wilson imagined the presidency as autonomous and almighty, Neustadt saw the president as but one among many actors within a broader system, purposive but far from independent, let alone omnipotent.

In this clash of professorial perspectives—Neustadtian versus Wilsonian—contemporary political scientists' verdict is unanimous: Neustadt's *Presidential Power* remains the subfield's canonical text.[31] In fact, building on the notion that presidents are responsive to incentives and constrained by institutions, succeeding scholarly generations increasingly developed abstract, generalizable theories to explain presidential behavior.[32] The point is not that presidents have the same aims and traits—certainly, they do not—but rather that different presidents will nevertheless converge to what works, thereby muting interpersonal differences.

It was in this spirit that Terry Moe urged his colleagues to adopt institutional theories of presidential behavior, especially but not exclusively rooted in rational choice. "It's perspective is entirely *impersonal*, based on conceptual building blocks—structure, authority, incentive, and other institutional variables—that treat presidents and other actors as *generic* types rooted in an institutional system" (emphasis in original).[33] In essence, "Presidents are not individual people, by this reckoning."[34]

That idea gets back to the modern presidency. The fact that the West Wing's organization settled into a standard institutional mold seemingly squares nicely with Moe's "presidency-centered" perspective. Modern presidents share systemic goals—such as maintaining popularity, winning elections, enacting legislation, securing peace, and promoting prosperity—and adhere to battle-tested methods to help achieve them. From this perspective, presidential behavior reflects institutionalized protocols more than individual capabilities.

This "generic" thesis has a logical corollary: presidents understand the job similarly and, facing similar circumstances, act similarly. This is a point William Howell and Terry Moe state forcefully: "They may well be very different people, but they are all presidents. And in the pulling and hauling of American politics, they think and act in ways that are distinctly presidential."[35]

But do they? Just as theory is not practice, organization is not operation, and elegant ideas often fall prey to inelegant realities. That was Helmuth Karl Bernhard Graf von Moltke's lesson from war—"No battle plan ever survives contact with the enemy"—and Mike Tyson's lesson from boxing: "Everybody has a plan until they get punched in the mouth." The modern presidency is nothing if not a punch in the mouth.

OPERATIONAL REALITY

In theory, when the presidency serves the president, it matters little whether the president acts directly or indirectly, doing or delegating. There is more than one way to shine a penny. So long as decisions reflect the president's preferences, operational particulars are more matters of style than substance.

In practice, however, there are good reasons to suspect that decision-making processes and products differ when a president becomes personally involved. After all, rich literatures across psychology, economics, and political science find that deliberative paths and players affect decision destinations, especially when the situation includes complex problems, fluid circumstances, uncertain information, limited time, intense pressure, or various distractions—that is to say, the very conditions that mark modern presidents' work environment.[36]

After "hanging around" President Obama for several months, what struck author Michael Lewis was the unrelenting inflow of hard problems that demanded a presidential decision, in short order, so that it could be announced to the impatient reporters waiting outside. "Many if not most of his decisions are thrust upon the president, out of the blue, by events beyond his control. . . . They don't order themselves neatly for his consideration but come in waves, jumbled on top of each other."[37]

So as convenient as it may be to relegate daily logistics to a metaphorical "black box," the truth is that decisions require deliberation, and deliberation takes time. As Johnson said, "Doing what's right isn't the problem. It is knowing what's right." How do presidents choreograph their schedule to get the information needed, in the format needed, at the time needed, amid the job's other inexorable demands?

Presidential "operations" are the means by which the presidency's workload is translated into the president's workday. The label is innocuous; the implications are not. When the office's unlimited possibilities bottleneck at the occupant's limited hours, choices about what the president does, with whom, and for how long are quite literally job defining. Richard Neustadt expressed this point well: "He makes his personal impact by the things he says and does. Accordingly, his choices of what he should say and do, and how and when, are his means to conserve and tap the sources of his power."[38]

To be sure, there are no easy answers. Andy Card, George W. Bush's first and longest-serving COS, flagged the problem: "The biggest challenge is time-management. Almost everything else has an infinite opportunity. There's lots of good ideas, wonderful people to meet, places to go. . . . But one thing you have no control over is how many days there are in a week, or hours in a day, or minutes in an hour."[39]

Again, Card's insight is easy to appreciate but also underestimate. The temptation is to assume that strict time constraints mean that presidents must *really* lean on staff, *really* depend on process. That is true as far as it goes, but it mostly falls short. Constitutional design dictates practical reality: the president must personally step in precisely when the staff disagrees or the process stalls—which is often.

This lesson has been most apparent to those with the closest view. Asked what he learned during his time as Gerald Ford's COS, Dick Cheney did not hesitate: "You have to have somebody disciplined running the calendar because the president's time is the most valuable thing there is."[40]

This is not to say that the president's time is wholly (or even mostly) discretionary. There is always something that *needs* the president's attention, whether or not the president *wants* to give it. Jimmy Carter's private diary entry on June 1, 1977, is illustrative: "The backlog of paperwork was mountainous. . . . It doesn't stop when I'm not here; just piles up deeper."[41]

But not always . . . and not equally. My thesis is that presidential scheduling is the mechanism by which presidents wrest operational control from organizational protocols. Indeed, in discovering how presidents allocate their time, we gain a new perspective about how presidential differences can generate performance differentials.

In a nutshell, while it is certainly true that the presidency binds presidents in many ways, it is equally true that presidents are never generic, their individuality becomes infused into their office, and this inevitability affects how each president translates an impossible workload into a manageable workday.

LOOKING AHEAD

The rest of this book examines the theory and practice of presidential operations—that is, how presidents translate their job into work. Chapter 1 develops an analytic model to explain the political economy of presidential time. As foreshadowed, I posit presidential scheduling as the mechanism by which presidents wrest operational control from organizational protocols.

For a first test of my thesis that presidents' work is president derived, chapter 2 compares two dissimilar presidents who served sequentially: Jimmy Carter and Ronald Reagan. Drawing on a detailed audit of their public and private work patterns from Carter's first day through Reagan's first term—January 20, 1977, to January 19, 1985—I show that Carter and Reagan were not merely different people with different outlooks, but also very different presidents. They differed in stamina; they differed in priorities; they differed in efficiency. These differences are substantively striking and statistically significant, leaving no doubt that standard organization does not induce standard operation.

Chapter 3 probes whether the presidency has something like a standard shift—an institutionalized schedule that structures presidential workdays—or whether each president decides for himself what constitutes a good day's work. The verdict is clear. Not only is there a lot of variation in how long presidents work—ranging from Kennedy on one end (about 10 hours per day) to Carter on the other (more than 15 hours per day)—but those variations are highly correlated with each president and not at all correlated with national conditions or political circumstances. To the extent that the old saw holds true that a president's time is the most valuable commodity in Washington, some presidents are clearly richer than others.

Having interrogated the duration of presidents' workdays, chapter 4 considers the obvious follow-up: composition. In terms of quantity (the number of activities), pacing (the number of activities per hour), distribution (the time invested in different activities), and engagements (the assortment of people that presidents encounter along the way), how do presidents fill their workdays? And, just as importantly, what explains the variation? Are presidential time allocations driven by policy demands, political context, presidents themselves, or the unpredictable pull of "first things first"? Once again, systematic analyses corroborate the overriding lesson: the only way to understand how the presidency functions is to understand how each president works.

For the penultimate chapter, I circle back to the vital case of Richard Nixon, the president who forged the organizational model that has structured the White House ever since. Here I consider whether Nixon's organizational model kept the president's workflow on track even as the president himself strained under the weight of Watergate. Analyzing Nixon's daily contacts with top government officials, in person or by phone, I show that the Nixon model was only as strong as its creator, which is to say more fragile than it appeared. Both man and model buckled more than half a year before Nixon resigned from office.

Lastly, the conclusion. After acknowledging that presidential leadership sometimes entails fateful actions in dramatic moments, chapter 6 considers more common, practical principles to guide presidents' daily work—something I call everyday leadership. Everyday leadership speaks to the ways that presidents approach the work that only a president can do, recognizing the extraordinary opportunities presidents enjoy, given the limits of time and information that each president must confront. My account does not produce a universal prescription, but it does clarify guiding principles for presidents aspiring to "faithfully execute the Office of President of the United States."

1

TIME, PEOPLE, AND PROCESS

COMMENCING HIS SECOND TERM AS PRESIDENT, Richard Nixon gave his Cabinet secretaries and senior staff a special gift: a customized desk calendar that enumerated how many days remained in the Nixon presidency. The cover included a personal message: "Every moment of history is a fleeting time, precious and unique. The presidential term which begins today consists of 1,461 days—no more, no less. Each can be a day of strengthening and renewal for America; each can add depth and dimension to the American experience. The 1,461 days which lie ahead are but a short interval in the flowing stream of history. Let us live them to the hilt, working every day to achieve these goals."[1]

That President Nixon's "moment of history" proved more fleeting than scheduled only underscores his message: a president's term passes quickly; each day is a precious resource; harnessing every moment is crucial.

Of course, appreciating the president's time is one thing; extracting its value is quite another. The ends are obvious; the means are not. How can presidents invest their "fleeting time, precious and unique"? What options are available? What constraints are unavoidable? And do answers depend on who is president, or does each president follow well-worn paths?

At first glance, pursuing a parsimonious theory of presidential operations may seem a fool's errand. A truism among experienced White House hands is to expect the unexpected. Problems are always emerging, circumstances are always evolving, and the schedule is always in flux. That is why Ted Sorensen, John Kennedy's trusted counselor and speechwriter, warned that "to be preoccupied with form and structure . . . is too often to overlook the more dynamic and fluid forces on which Presidential decisions are based."[2]

While it is certainly true that every day is a new day and no two days are alike, there are compelling reasons to suspect that a clear, portable theory of presidents' work behavior is achievable. Because presidents have specific goals, limited hours, and expert counsel, if the president's time has value, then there ought to be a logic to allocating it. And if I can map that logic, then I ought to be able to analyze presidents' options, deduce their choices, and predict their actions.[3] Such is where this chapter plans to go—and aims to finish.

STAFFING THE OVAL OFFICE

Presidents have two basic means to increase productivity: work faster or get help. They embrace both, clearly, but because there are only so many ways to quicken a president's own pace, far more effort goes into staffing, organizing, and managing the president's people.

Presidency scholarship has mirrored presidents' practice. I draw on this literature to highlight the modern presidency's key organizational features, noting each feature's intended benefits and unintended risks.[4]

The sea change came with Franklin Roosevelt. When Roosevelt realized that borrowing various executive branch officials was insufficient for his needs, he proposed adding a coterie of personal staff—the White House staff. Roosevelt's initiative spawned the Executive Office of the President (EOP), an institutional innovation that quickly and profoundly changed the presidency.

Figure 1.1 shows staffing levels in the White House Office (WHO), the EOP's nerve center, from its inception in 1939 through George W. Bush's presidency. Whereas Roosevelt's WHO had 50 people, Truman

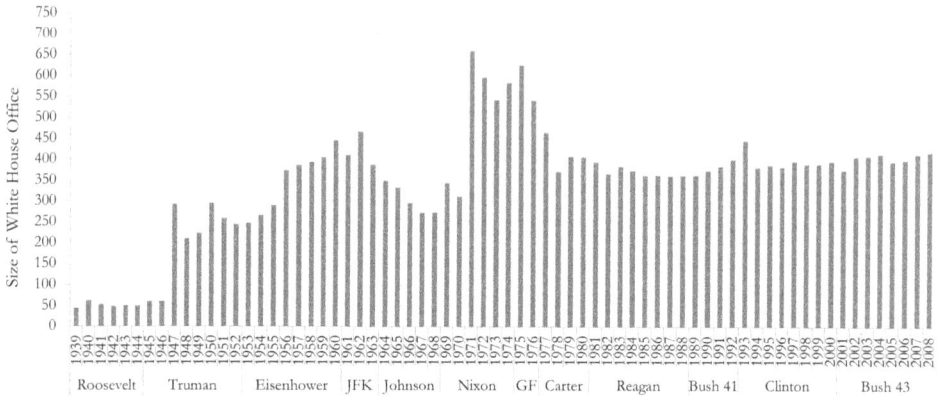

FIGURE 1.1 Number of staff in the Executive Office of the President's White House Office (WHO), 1939–2008.

Source: Lyn Ragsdale, *Vital Statistics on the Presidency: The Definitive Source for Data and Analysis on the American Presidency*, 4th ed. (Washington, DC: CQ Press, 2014).

grew it more than fivefold, and then Eisenhower nearly doubled it again. After some ebbs (e.g., during Johnson's presidency) and flows (e.g., during Nixon's presidency), the WHO's staffing settled around 400 positions under Jimmy Carter—and since.

The two conspicuous takeaways about WHO staffing are how much it grew beyond Roosevelt's initial design, and then how steady it has remained for the last half century.

STAFF ASSETS

What makes White House staffers different from other executive branch officials is that they tend to be presidential loyalists, especially at the highest levels. A president's "assistants" have typically logged years working in his service, through the campaign and across the various offices and elections that preceded it. In a very real sense, the president is *their* president.

Consider Ted Sorensen, the aforementioned aide Kennedy hired when he was elected to the Senate. Despite different backgrounds and personalities, the two quickly became friends and colleagues. On everything from substance to strategy, campaigning to governing,

Kennedy sought Sorensen's counsel. So extensive were their interactions that they eventually could—and did—finish each other's sentences. "By the time our postconvention travels began in September 1960, I had worked with [Kennedy] on so many speeches, long and short, important and routine, and spent so much time traveling and talking with him about every issue, that I knew what he wanted to say and how he wanted to say it on virtually every topic, and probably could not determine then—and certainly cannot now—which words in the final draft had originally been his and which were mine."[5]

As I say, Sorensen's trajectory into the White House is distinct in details but typical in general. Every president assembles a cadre of assistants whom he trusts specifically because they have proven their mettle in many ways, through many trials, over many years. What makes these staffers so valuable from the president's perspective is partly that they know the president's preferences (and peccadilloes) and, just as much, that they have demonstrated their commitment to the president given that knowledge.

Yet staff loyalty is more than a personal leap of faith. It also reflects professional ambition. The most prestigious West Wing positions are filled at the president's will, fired at the president's whim. When a reporter asked one longtime Obama aide if she planned to stay in her post through the president's second term, she offered the prototypical response: "I serve at the pleasure of the President. If he wants me to stay, I will."[6]

Given this selection and structure, it is no wonder that scholars often distinguish the "presidential branch" (i.e., the EOP generally and the WHO in particular) from the broader executive branch.[7] The president's people really are the president's people in a manner and to a degree that other executive branch officials are not.[8]

But if loyalty helps presidents trust their staff, it is the staffers' competencies that presidents ultimately need. By hiring an array of domain-specific experts—in public relations, congressional affairs, Cabinet administration, budgets, laws, regulations, economics, security, and diplomacy—presidents can increase both the quantity and quality of their work. Franklin Roosevelt wanted the EOP so he could do more—and better.

The Brownlow Committee (short for the President's Committee on Administrative Management, recruited by Roosevelt) envisioned the EOP as a resource to help presidents grip the presidency. On the potential usefulness of the EOP, the committee could not have been more accurate; on the number of staff who would fill it—"probably not exceeding six"—it could not have been more wrong. As I say, the White House staff grew so large, so discrete, that political scientists came to understand the presidential branch as an institution unto itself, part of the executive branch but distinctive in principle and practice.

STAFF LIABILITIES

Growing the White House staff greatly expanded the presidency's capacity, but it introduced a myriad of liabilities as well. Packing scores of smart, ambitious aides into the West Wing's cauldron of policy, power, politics, and publicity creates an explosive mix. Personal animosities, institutional rivalries, petty jealousies, professional slights, inadvertent insults, intellectual clashes, and simple misunderstandings greatly complicate a president's work. Infighting and backstabbing can spur everything from yelling in the Roosevelt Room to leaks in the *Washington Post*.

Tevi Troy's *Fight House* shows how easily relationships can fray, and how often they do.[9] Beyond the iconic cases—such as Bobby Kennedy and Lyndon Johnson—is a broader reality: interpersonal friction is a staple of the modern presidency. Sometimes the tensions are within the Cabinet (e.g., Caspar Weinberger and George Schultz under Reagan), sometimes they are within the West Wing (e.g., Dick Morris and George Stephanopoulos under Clinton), sometimes they span both (e.g., Condoleezza Rice and Donald Rumsfeld under Bush 43), and sometimes it is *bellum omnium contra omnes*—war of all against all (e.g., under Donald Trump).

Occasionally the menace is not too much internal strife, but rather too little. This ailment arises when collegiality prompts presidential aides to overlook uncomfortable truths: problems, errors, conflicts, risks, contradictions, uncertainties, or hubris. The canonical case is Kennedy's 1961 "Bay of Pigs" operation to overthrow Fidel Castro.

Although Kennedy surrounded himself with shrewd advisors, they were keen to support the president and one another. In the run-up to the Cuban operation, several people had doubts about the Central Intelligence Agency's plan yet pulled those punches during meetings.[10]

After the Cuba operation failed as thoroughly as it did quickly, Kennedy kicked himself: "How could we have been so stupid?" It was more or less the same question that the sociologist Irving L. Janis sought to answer years later, which led him to analyze Kennedy's decision-making process.[11] Janis concluded that the Bay of Pigs operation suffered from "groupthink"—"a mode of thinking that people engage in when they are deeply involved in a cohesive in-group, when the members' strivings for unanimity override their motivation to realistically appraise alternative courses of action."[12] In other words, President Kennedy's team was so invested in consensus and collegiality that it inhibited their—and Kennedy's—critical thinking.[13]

Through lessons learned from these kinds of trials and errors, the modern presidency evolved. Managerial innovations forged over time sought to maximize the upsides and minimize the downsides associated with a large organization. In fits and starts, as the presidency added staff, it developed structure.

STRUCTURING THE OVAL OFFICE

The U.S. Constitution has many ambiguities but is unequivocal about one thing: "The executive power shall be vested in a President of the United States" ("Constitution of the United States," art. 2, sec. 1). When George Washington formed a Cabinet by hiring a "team of rivals," there was no doubting that the rivals were not equals. Upholding the chief executive's primacy has remained the executive branch's overriding organizational principle, even as it grew larger and more complex than its creators ever imagined.

Below the president, however, the constitutional order blurs. Lines of authority quickly become bones of contention. In the president's absence, who speaks on the president's behalf? And who takes precedence when many make the claim?

Lacking constitutional guidance, defining roles within the growing presidential branch thus fell to the boss, the president. This organizational groundwork was seeded by Roosevelt, shaped by Eisenhower, and strengthened by Nixon. Through the years, a suite of organizational features became institutional fixtures, and a particular complement hardened into what Charles Walcott and Karen Hult called the standard model for structuring the modern White House.

Figure 1.2 illustrates the standard model and its three signature elements: (1) a hierarchical structure, (2) "honest brokers" at pivotal positions, and (3) institutionalized protocols to facilitate "multiple advocacy." In the following sections I review these pillars of the presidency's organization.

HIERARCHY

When daily exigencies arise, as they inevitably do, they implicate a vast ensemble within the executive branch. Economic news, for instance, implicates the president's economic and budget advisors, political and legislative teams, and press and communications aides. Teams within the Commerce, Labor, or Treasury departments might get pulled in, as could some mishmash from Energy, Education, State, and Transportation. The vice president and the first lady may want to be looped in too.

Economics is hardly unique in this way. Whether it is national security, domestic policy, budgets, speeches, scandals, or hearings, daily events reverberate throughout the executive branch. Considering the vastness of the presidential portfolio—subjects and subordinates— it is easy to imagine presidents drowning as frenzied crosscurrents converge at the Oval Office.

Seeking order amid commotion spurred the modern presidency's first key organizing feature: hierarchy. Although there are countless ways to slice and sort executive officials, one clean cut separates White House officials from the rest. As already noted, building the presidential branch within the executive branch helped launch the modern presidency, and the ascendance of the former relative to the latter quickly became critical to understanding both.[14]

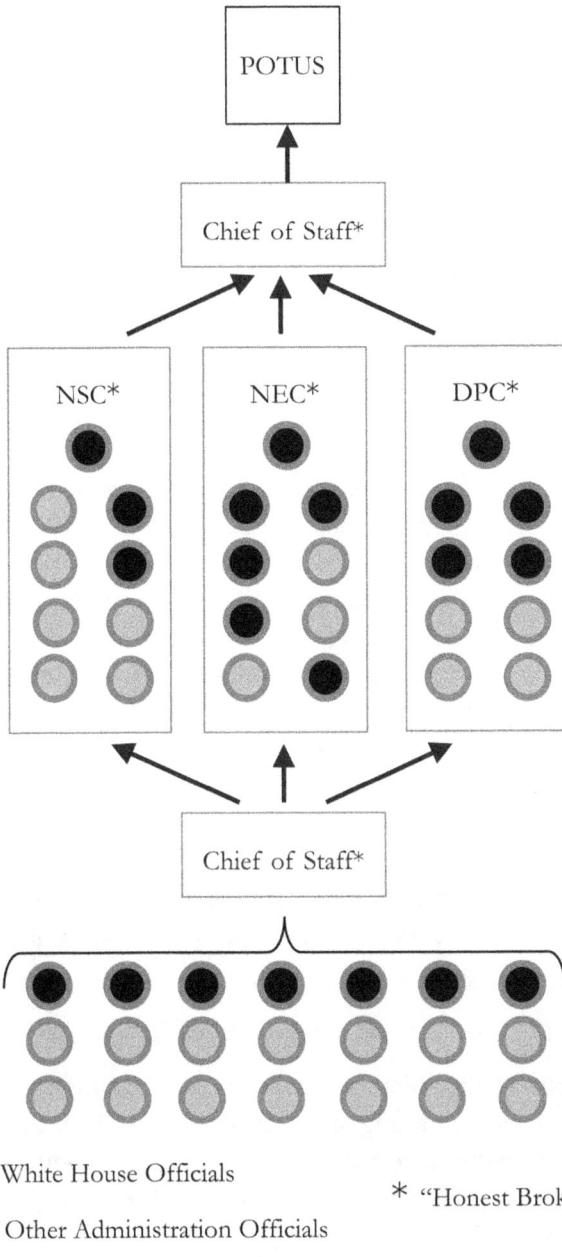

FIGURE 1.2 "Standard model" of organizing the modern White House;
NSC = National Security Council, NEC = National Economic Council,
DPC = Domestic Policy Council.

For presidents, the White House staff are more than a support system; they are also a buffer zone. On any given day there are thousands of advisors, formal and informal, who would love the opportunity to bend the president's ear. Layering White House staffers between the president and everyone else helps limit the president's exposure. That Robert Reich, President Clinton's labor secretary, entitled his memoir *Locked in the Cabinet* revealed more candor than humor.[15]

No doubt, the executive branch hierarchies are far more intricate than a simple White House/Cabinet divide. Peeling back any executive branch office reveals layers within layers within layers. The White House has the chief of staff over assistants to the president over deputy assistants over special assistants and so on. Cabinet departments have secretaries over deputies over directors and so on. Elaborate "org charts" map officials' relative positions vis-à-vis one another and the president, and the lesson that stands out for most is not the notional line between themselves and the president, but rather how many boxes clutter the route.[16]

In short, the Constitution established that the nation has one chief executive at a time, the president of the United States. That was sufficient guidance when the entire executive branch could fit in one room, but it became inadequate when thousands of officials were spread across hundreds of offices with innumerable titles, roles, and responsibilities. The modern presidency codified the relative status of "White House officials" and "other administration officials," with the former layered above the latter and additional levels within each.

HONEST BROKERS

Richard Nixon liked hierarchy because it helped maintain order and minimize contact. Adding layers also allowed Nixon to reduce irrelevances and redundancies while increasing focus and efficiency. An "open door" policy may sound inspiring, but really it means that presidents hear half-baked ideas from whoever pops in.

On the other hand, hierarchies also introduce a myriad of well-known vulnerabilities. Perhaps the most common is informational. As information moves up or down an organization, critical pieces can get lost or distorted, if not stuck or blocked, along the way.

These problems can reflect carelessness, cunning, incompetence, zealousness, or any number of other impulses. Whatever the root cause, the effects of signal-to-noise problems can range from irritating to deadly given the presidential purview.

Inaccuracies are not the only problem associated with a large, hierarchical structure. When stakeholders feel they are not being heard, understood, and appreciated, the impulse to end-run gatekeepers is natural. This might mean cultivating backchannels to key players, leveraging encounters with the president, skewing information at meetings, or leaking details to outsiders. Indeed, Beltway wags know well that officials who feel stymied make great sources. For it is the jilted who are most willing to reveal internal debates and, better still, mix in juicy morsels of palace intrigue—the story behind the story.

To mitigate the perils of hierarchy, the modern presidency developed a second key organizational device: "honest brokers." The idea, advanced by experts such as Alexander George and Roger Porter, is to make specific officials responsible for cultivating a fair decision-making process.[17] Honest brokers ensure that discussions include relevant stakeholders, develop a range of options, and hear a diversity of opinions. The honest broker also pledges that the president's briefings faithfully reflect the group's deliberations. In these ways, honest brokers do not advocate; they facilitate.

Several White House positions now include honest broker responsibilities. The foremost is the White House chief of staff (COS).[18] Returning to figure 1.2, we see this dynamic early in the process when the COS organizes officials via advisory teams—for example, the National Security Council (NSC), the National Economic Council (NEC), and the Domestic Policy Council (DPC). Though each council has standing members, the COS can adapt invitation lists for certain issues or specific stages, formally or informally. In this capacity as an honest broker, the COS privileges procedural legitimacy over personal relationships, policy preferences, or any other partialities.

There are also other ways and other times when a COS dons honest broker duties. A critical point is the deliberative process's penultimate stage, when officials' expansive contributions get winnowed to the subset reaching the president (i.e., the top of figure 1.2). Here the COS, having nurtured a fair deliberative process, must now ensure that the president's briefing fairly conveys its contents—the most encouraging estimate as clearly as the most stinging critique.

Over the years, the White House developed an additional layer of honest brokers. The directors of the policy councils—the NSC, the NEC, and the DPC—fill the space between the COS and other executive officials. These council directors serve as domain-specific versions of the COS—senior staffers who coordinate the people and process within their issue area. Like the COS, council directors can (and do) offer the president advice or engage in public outreach, but their primary responsibility is managing a fair deliberative process.[19]

The NSC was the first formal policy "council," created to bring intentionality and rationality to the president's security policy for the nuclear era. Specific institutional arrangements have changed over the years—such as membership and protocols—but the NSC's core auspices remain. The president's national security advisor leads the NSC with the explicit expectation that he or she will facilitate deliberations as the group's honest broker. President Joe Biden's organizing order is representative: "In reporting to the President, the National Security Advisor will represent attendee views and differences faithfully."[20]

Seeking a similar structure in other realms, Nixon fashioned the Office of Policy Development to handle domestic policy (just as the NSC ran foreign policy). Eventually, Clinton separated economic policy from other domestic issues, a partition that continued through other presidents. Nowadays, appointees who lead the National Economic and Domestic Policy councils are akin to the national security advisor, tasked with organizing officials, coordinating schedules, sharing information, and dependably conveying "views and differences" to the president.

The honest brokers' location within the standard model—near the top, next to the president—signifies their importance. When it works as intended, honest brokers' commitment to process qua process lets everyone trust that their input will not be unfairly impeded or distorted before reaching the president. Likewise, the president can trust that skipping meetings does not mean missing essential information. From top to bottom, forward and backward, having honest brokers orchestrate deliberations instills confidence that presidential decisions reflect informed preferences rather than office politics.

That said, it is crucial to recognize that there is no objective method for implementing honest broker ideals. However earnestly the president's top aides strive to apply honest broker principles, someone will always feel slighted, sidelined, undervalued, or misunderstood. Some losing factions will inevitably suspect that their recommendations were felled by strategic cabals, surreptitious meetings, devious distortions, or other dark arts of less-than-honest brokering. (And the fact that it is impossible for the honest broker to prove otherwise only highlights the predicament.)

For better or worse, honest brokers are situated at the crossroads of the modern presidency. The White House COS, working in concert with the president's policy council directors, must direct traffic without playing favorites—or getting overrun. Indeed, given that there are too many issues and too many people for presidents to manage directly, they *need* honest brokers to help metabolize an unremitting inbox.

MULTIPLE ADVOCACY

The other side of the honest broker coin is a policy process characterized by a range of advisors, a diversity of views. As noted, Alexander George believed presidents perform best within a marketplace of ideas; therefore, he argued honest brokers should "structure and manage the policy-making system to ensure that there are advocates to cover the range of interesting policy options on a given issue."[21] George called this deliberative method multiple advocacy.

The multiple advocacy objective pairs nicely with rational models of decision-making. The explicit goal is to have experts detect problems, gather information, generate alternatives, and analyze options. Presidents, drawing on this collective wisdom, can identify their preferences and make good decisions—hopefully in short order. What is more, to the extent the presidential perch affords its occupants unique "vantage points," as Richard Neustadt put it, the president can utilize a rich information environment in ways other officials cannot.

That is not to say that actual deliberations will always (or routinely) achieve the rational ideal. There will constantly be hitches in the process, just as there will often be errors by the president. Nevertheless, the bent toward rationality remains the animating goal because there is no feasible alternative. Even when problems do not submit to a standard optimization analysis, the president's most dependable search strategy is to proceed as if they do. This is why the modern presidency's third signature feature is institutionalized multiple advocacy vis-à-vis the policy councils.

SUMMING THE PARTS

Two final points about these "standard" organizational features deserve mention. First, because the Nixon-like staff system has become so familiar, presidential aides tend to know their role and are eager to play their part. They understand that the president was on the ballot, is behind the desk, and will be judged by history. They empathize with the burdens the president must carry, and they grasp the difficult choices the president must make. So as much as officials surely hope that the president will follow their advice, the vast majority are also quick to subordinate their own views to the views of the president. The modal staffer does not only serve at the president's pleasure; it is their pleasure to do so.

That idea highlights the importance of the process itself. Even as numerous aides toil tirelessly on the president's behalf, far fewer see the president on any given day (or week, or month). The value in combining hierarchy, honest brokers, and multiple advocacy lies less in form than in function. But there is also value in the form, which fosters something like Sam Kernell's notion of a "legitimizing creed." To the extent that officials believe that "standard" decision-making protocols are fair, they are more willing to play by those rules. In this fashion, the modern presidency's standard organizational model is as much an evolved equilibrium of perceived legitimacy as it is a functional theory of executive management.

In broad strokes, then, I have sketched the institutional presidency's evolution into a standard organizational model. The president's handpicked aides, including a set of honest brokers adhering to the principles of multiple advocacy, coordinate numerous officials who are institutionally attentive to a range of presidential objectives. Domain-specific working groups vet their issues systematically before winnowing their discussions to the essentials: the essential options; the essential arguments; the essential evidence. Their charge is not forging consensus, necessarily, but clarifying the decisions the president must make.

That gets us to the Oval Office, the spot where a president weighs the options—and makes the call.

REACHING THE OVAL OFFICE

Having traced the modern presidency's philosophical underpinnings, it is important to note that the standard organizational model's initial virtue is more prosaic: the only ship ready to sail is the one in the dock. Presidents may get transition memos that delineate the EOP's auspices and roles, which include extant organization charts and job descriptions,[22] but the reality that incoming presidents already know or quickly discover is that trying to fill the existing EOP structure is hard enough. Trying to overhaul it would fall somewhere between perilous and impossible.

But inertia is not the only factor at play. Another reason presidents have good reason to assume a standard organization is that they can always customize operations. When it comes to schedules, agendas, meetings, and speeches, those filling key posts can tailor their ways of working to fit themselves—and the president.

In truth, customization is less a possibility than a necessity considering that virtually all West Wing positions change hands at noon on Inauguration Day. Dan Pfeiffer, President Obama's communications director, described the stark reality: "Most people don't understand how the actual handover of power works. We all sit in the freezing cold. We watch the final culmination of years of effort to see our friend and boss become President of the United States. Then for the senior team, you get on a bus and they take you to the White House. They drop you off, and someone shows you your office. You walk in and there's a computer there with a Post-it note with your password, and you're in charge of the government."[23] Transition by transition, then, the presidency's organizational design can remain intact even as the operational protocols get reconstructed anew.

This distinction between organization and operation has not been lost on political scientists. In analyzing the COS position, for instance, David Cohen and George Krause noted that "we are not interested in explaining the formal organizational chart of the White House, but rather we are concerned with how the organizational structure works in practice."[24] In a similar vein, Andrew Rudalevige maintained that the true test of the White House's structure is not its design per se, or even its results, but "whether it brought the president the information he needed." [25]

Continuing along the "how it works" path, I now introduce a model that weaves presidential operations into the presidency's organization. Assuming that a president's primary role is decision-making, the model explicitly builds on the rational model tradition while hewing to the presidency's organizational features previously summarized. As we shall see, clarifying the president's role vis-à-vis other key players helps nail down the sequence of their play, the nature of their options, and, ultimately, the operational impossibility they must confront.

To start, imagine the presidential workflow has three basic phases: agenda-setting, discovery, and decision-making. The first two—agenda-setting and discovery—comprise the *organizational* system, that is, processes that occur *without the president*. The last phase defines the *operational* system by *engaging the president directly*. Let me now trace this model's key players and key junctures, detailed in Figure 1.3, to reveal how scheduling serves as the bridge connecting the presidency and president.

PHASE 1: AGENDA-SETTING

The president wears many "hats," as Clinton Rossiter famously put it. As mentioned at the outset, part and parcel of the presidency's staggering purview are the exceptional burdens levied on each president—ranging from ceremonial events to natural disasters, foreign leaders to

Phase 1: Agenda-Setting	Phase 2: Policy Discovery	Phase 3: Decision-Making

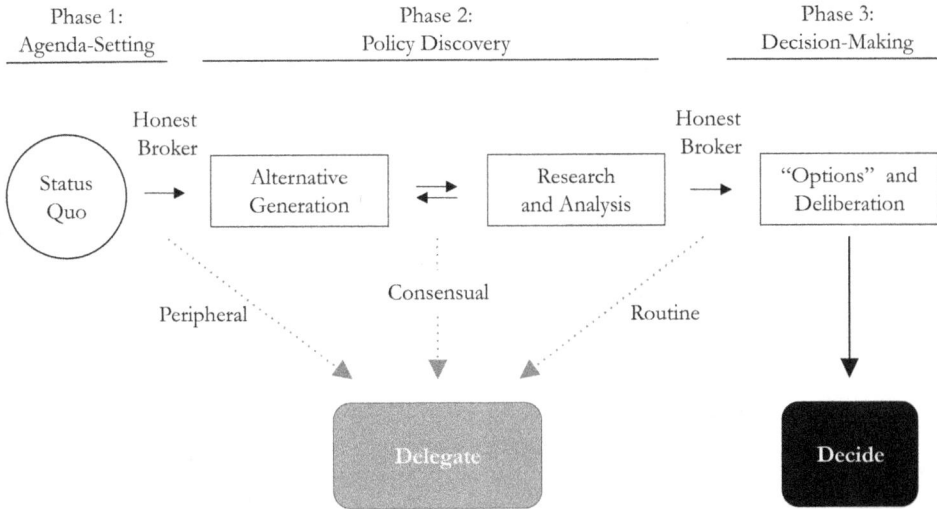

FIGURE 1.3 Integrated model of the presidential workflow.

fallen soldiers, graduation addresses to military orders, and reporters to donors, not to mention an endless array of meetings, briefings,
greetings, rallies, interviews, and photos. Witnessing the daily tor-
rent of unrelenting demands, President Obama's final COS, Denis
McDonough, shared a deceptively simple lesson: "Don't overload
[the President] with decisions he doesn't need to make."[26]

The model's first phase captures McDonough's sage counsel. As
potential tasks arise—whether within government, from external
events, in news reports, on the road, or wherever else—an honest broker (serving in the role already described) must decide whether they
merit White House staffers' time and attention. Precious few tasks
clear this "importance" hurdle, as topics that would be momentous
in other arenas are run-of-the-mill inside the West Wing.

"Agenda-setting" may thus sound rather pedestrian, but its implications are in fact significant. Presidents have a stake in many issues
and are responsible for vastly more. Delegating decisions like federal judgeships or veto threats can be a hard pill to swallow—for
the staff and president alike. Staffers want to cover their butts by

checking with the president, just as presidents want to cover their butts by checking on the staff. From both ends, then, the temptation is to bring everything to the president.

Seeing this situation while serving as Gerald Ford's COS, Donald Rumsfeld formulated one of his famous rules: "If a matter is not a decision for the President or you, delegate it. Force responsibility down and out. Find problem areas, add structure and delegate. The pressure is to do the reverse. Resist it." Another of Rumsfeld's rules declares, "If in doubt, move decisions up to the President." This tension between forcing responsibility "down and out" except "if in doubt" explains the eternal desire to loop in the president.

One possible solution seems obvious: sort by significance and save the president for the most important issues. Alas, this is not as straightforward as it seems, in no small part because "importance" is an ever-shifting standard. A high-stakes budgetary showdown that dominates deliberations one day can be readily sidelined by new or unexpected events.

Consider 9/11 as an especially vivid example. On the day terrorists attacked the United States, President George W. Bush's staff canceled all existing plans—literally, everything. The idea was that post-9/11 planning needed to start anew, as issues that had been significant for months (e.g., federal funding for stem cell research) suddenly became ancillary.

Likewise, it is impossible to know how nascent issues will evolve. The Federal Emergency Management Agency's preparations for the looming Hurricane Katrina took on new importance when the levies guarding New Orleans were breached, the city flooded, the power grid failed, citizens died, and help was nowhere to be found. That President Bush had delegated authority to his subordinates (and state officials in Louisiana) appeared reasonable until it did not. Because the presidency's responsibilities are far greater than a president's bandwidth, agenda-setting is a necessity—and a liability.

As I conceive it, then, the organizational system's first phase begins when honest brokers triage among countless tasks a president could perform to select the precious few status quos that will proceed to alternative generation. These choices are hard because information is uncertain and deadlines are unforgiving. Most tasks are deemed "peripheral" to the president and thus get steered else-where in the executive branch. A smaller set deemed "vital" proceeds into the White House, into phase 2 of Figure 1.3.

PHASE 2: POLICY DISCOVERY

Having decided that some issue might merit presidential attention, the follow-up question is easy to ask but hard to answer: What can the president do? After all, the public always expects the president to "do something." William Howell described the demand: "In every policy domain, presidents must not only demonstrate involvement, they must act—and they must do so for all to see, visibly, forthrightly, and expediently."[27]

Earlier I explained how the responsibility for developing alterna-tives typically falls to a White House council—that is, the National Security Council, the National Economic Council, or the Domestic Policy Council—whose director operates (primarily) as an honest broker coordinating relevant officials to (a) identify and (b) analyze various recommendations.[28]

Because the stakes are high but the implications ambiguous, policy discovery is the nucleus of presidential decision-making. Figure 1.3 includes two-way arrows between the alternative genera-tion and research/analysis processes in recognition that this work is iterative, with proposals spurring research and vice versa. For as much as presidents aspire to textbook rationality, phase 2 practice often repairs to what Charles Lindblom called "the science of mud-dling through" or what Michael Cohen, James March, and Johan Olsen characterized as a "garbage can model."[29]

Part of the difficulty is that the administration's research and analysis are not limited to legal edicts, programmatic effects, or budgetary implications. Presidential deliberations also demand cal-culating how various combinations will play on Capitol Hill, in the press, with key interest groups, and among donors, not to mention at the polls. Uncertainty associated with this sort of multidimensional dynamic forecasting is pervasive, which is why policy discovery pro-cesses typically include "consultation" with key players in and out of government, including those with dissenting voices.[30]

Tracking the policy discovery phase through Figure 1.3 reveals three distinct deliberative paths among items deemed important enough to consider. The first and easiest opens when internal consensus emerges (see "consensual" arrow). Here the honest broker will almost always accept the group's advice. To the extent that the group's collective recommendation reaches the Oval Office at all, it typically arrives as a quick update rather than a detailed explanation.

A second lane guides routine deliberations toward a routine solution (see "routine" arrow), which does not require the president to partake more than marginally—signing off rather than weighing in. Whether it is executive appointments or party business, legislative dealing or speech drafting, a myriad questions that implicate the president may not achieve consensus, but the differences fall into familiar categories that do not warrant presidential time and attention. Staffers do not know exactly what the president will do, and they disagree about what the president should do, but when such differences are small or likely to be rendered moot, the COS can either decide the matter personally or designate who should.

President Obama entered office while the United States was waging two wars and mired in the deepest depths of the Great Recession. Jason Furman, a White House economic advisor, recalled how staffers were not initially calibrated about what differences were sufficiently "routine" so as not to warrant the president's input.

> There were times in 2009 when we didn't agree on the technical design of a small business lending program. Because we couldn't resolve it ourselves, we brought that disagreement to the President. In retrospect, it's pretty embarrassing that we were bothering him with details as small as that. Big disagreement on philosophy on how to deal with autos? Bring that to a President. Should you do a 10 percent or 15 percent matching rate for your new tax credit for such-and-such? Probably worth figuring that out on your own.[31]

For the "big disagreements," as Furman labeled them, there is a third path, the one that leads to the Oval Office. It is these cases, the ones where the president's closest advisors have core differences on critical matters, that only the president can resolve.

PHASE 3: DECISION-MAKING

Amid numerous proposals and supplementary analyses, the final stage of the decision-making process moves to winnowing options and curating arguments for the president ("Options and Deliberation" in figure 1.3). The overriding objective is to give the president *focused analyses* about *specific options* on *critical issues*. This information typically reaches the president via a nightly briefing book, and then again at an in-person meeting with implicated officials shortly thereafter.

It is here we pinpoint the president's unenviable (yet inevitable) dilemma: with "peripheral," "consensual," and "routine" matters already delegated (figure 1.3), the president is left with the "vital," "controversial," and "intractable" problems that remain. This was President Kennedy's point when he wrote that "no one in the country is more assailed by divergent advice and clamorous counsel. . . . Still, in the end, he is alone. There stands the decision—and there stands the President."[32]

Researchers have long studied effective methods for resolving hard problems, which itself has proven a hard problem.[33] Horst Rittel and Melvin Webber's conception of "wicked problems" captures the gist: "In a pluralistic society there is nothing like the undisputable pubic good . . . policies that respond to social problems cannot be meaningfully correct or false; and it makes no sense to talk about 'optimal solutions.' . . . Even worse, there are no 'solutions' in the sense of the definitive and objective answers."[34]

Such is the president's reality. From the president's point of view, the "standard model" is less a decision-*making* process than it is a decision-*sorting* process, and what it sorts to the president is a steady stream of "wicked problems" that lack straightforward options, analyses, or implications. The president's hardest challenge is not optimizing over alternatives but making decisions when no optimal option exists.[35]

This is where the operational system kicks in—and takes over. The first operational hurdle is also one of the highest: finding time on the president's calendar.

INSIDE THE OVAL OFFICE

Before punching out, Ronald Reagan liked to jot down a few notes about his day. These offerings were rarely profound or poetic, but they do capture Reagan's private reflections in real time. On Wednesday, October 14, 1981, the president wrote: "Another busy day. Ive [*sic*] discovered I hate those days where I have one meeting right after the other with no time to collect my thoughts between meetings & Im [sic] supposed to make remarks or a short speech at every one."[36]

Reagan's exhaustion and exasperation are understandable. "Another busy day" with "one meeting right after the other with no time to collect my thoughts" is the rule rather than the exception. When Clinton felt similarly overworked, he did not blow off steam in a private journal; instead, he complained directly to his aides: "You're working me like a mule."

To be fair, what else are staffers to do? After all, constitutional decrees and organizational designs purposefully funnel significant but unresolved matters to the president, and it turns out there are many, many matters that are as important as they are hard to solve. How could one *not* pack the president's schedule?

Such is a paradox of the modern presidency. Having reached the nation's highest office, the view is not of someone sitting atop an organizational pyramid so much as someone surviving under an operational avalanche. Questions, proposals, concerns, requests, updates, meetings, guests, aides, press, and problems come flooding in. The calendar fills quickly. The schedule overflows easily.

To illustrate the point, consider a suite of work streams like those depicted in figure 1.4. Some streams map onto the policy councils introduced previously—NSC, NEC, DPC—while others process a myriad other tasks within the presidential purview: meeting requests, speech drafts, press queries, personnel choices, and political exigencies. As discussed, each working group churns through

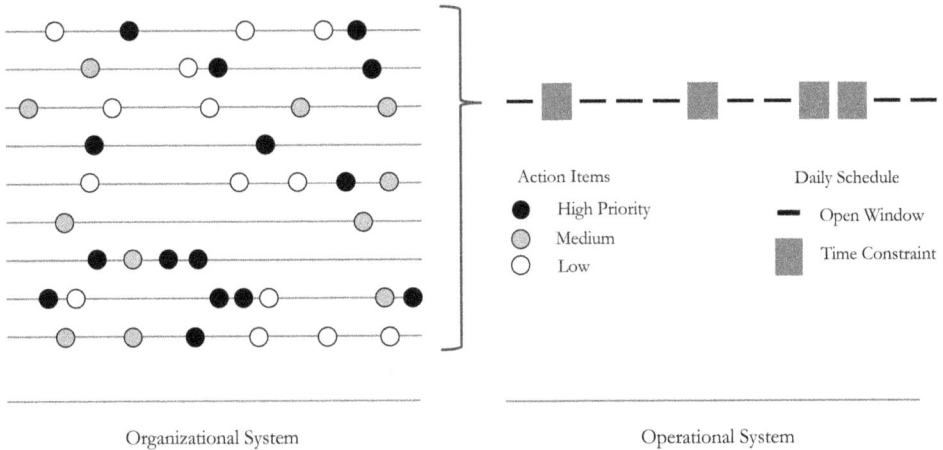

FIGURE 1.4 Transition from organizational system to operational system.

its respective stream's agenda, resolving whatever it can and preparing the president to handle whatever it cannot. The latter become potential "action items," depicted here as dots or circles in each stream.

For the myriad action items awaiting the president, the puzzle is finding time to give attention. The cruel reality is that presidents cannot get to most items, even ones flagged as "high priority." If anything, such designations only underscore how much the president's workload overruns the president's workday. Action items that would be career defining in any other realm—such as hiring a Cabinet secretary or declaring a national emergency—are a dime a dozen inside the White House.

Again, a critical aggravating factor is that much of the president's calendar is beyond his control. There are basic needs—food and family and sleep—that consume precious time, and then there are the countless obligations that come with the office: ceremonial functions; historic traditions; global summits; political exigencies . . . the list is endless. Richard Neustadt called these impositions "first things first" and noted that "a president's priorities are set not by the relative importance of the task, but by the relative necessity for him to do it."[37]

In figure 1.4, I label these sorts of impositions on the president's schedule "time constraints."

Taking presidential time seriously stresses the mismatch between supply and demand, which introduces the political economy of presidential time. For when decisions require deliberation and deliberation takes time, scheduling becomes more than a matter of survival; it is also a matter of strategy.

THINKING VERSUS SPEAKING

Clearly, action items clamoring for the president's time fill a broad spectrum. To get analytic traction, however, we can consider two broad activity classes in which presidents can invest their time. The first is *thinking time*—the time presidents need to learn issues, understand options, weigh arguments, ask questions, and, ultimately, make decisions. In practice, thinking time can include reading or writing and meeting or talking, as well as thinking itself.

A second class of time-consuming behaviors is *speaking time*. This category includes press inquiries and political rallies, formal ceremonies and commencement addresses, congratulatory notes and condolence calls, photo sessions, fundraising dinners, travel, handshakes, rehearsals, and so on. These sorts of performative obligations are very much part of the modern president's job, even as they are not part of the presidency's constitutional duties.

To be sure, thinking and speaking activities can be complementary. Speechwriting, for instance, demands some combination of thinking and speaking. Nevertheless, I will model the two tasks as two independent dimensions. For this project I assume that editing a speech is thinking time and that delivering a speech is speaking time.[38]

To help unravel the logic underlying presidential operations, consider a simple model in which a president (P) can allocate time between aforementioned activity classes—"thinking" (T) and "speaking" (S)—subject to a limited time budget (B). The president appraises the value of investing time between the two options with a standard indifference curve, which determines his optimal scheduling distribution (P_t, P_s). Figure 1.5 integrates these components within a standard constrained-optimization setup.

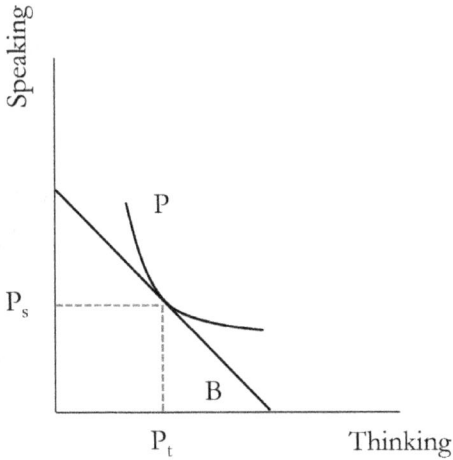

FIGURE 1.5 Speaking versus thinking time allocation: generic president.

With the basic elements in place, what rapidly becomes clear is that different presidents will do the job differently—and must. For when the presidency's infinite inbox bottlenecks at the president's desk, differences in each president's stamina, priorities and conditions, and efficiency affect (a) the relative time supply a president can allocate and (b) how each president allocates the time he has. Let me explain.

Stamina

According to the laws of nature and man, each president's "time" is fixed and equal. There are 24 hours in a day, 365 days in a year (+1 in leap years), 1,461 days in a term—and one president at a time. This is what President Nixon noted on his gift calendars, and it is what President Clinton's first COS had in mind when he declared, "The president's time is, in many ways, his most valuable commodity because it's finite."

Yet if absolute time is immovable, the relative time available to each president is not. Figure 1.6 illustrates how shifting the time budget constraint affects presidents' scheduling.

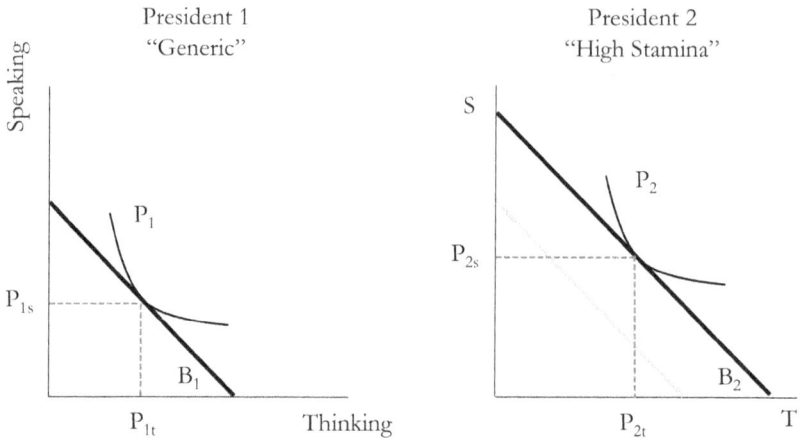

FIGURE 1.6 Speaking versus thinking time allocation: different stamina levels.

There are any number of reasons that presidents could have variable stamina. It could be that one president needs a lot of sleep, another is a workaholic, a third loves golf, a fourth falls ill, a fifth is simply lazy, and so on. Whatever the underlying cause, the key theoretic question is what happens if presidents are willing and able to work different hours (all else being equal).

Figure 1.6 depicts two presidents with different work stamina levels, one high (P_1) and one low (P_2), as indicated by their time budget constraints, B_1 versus B_2, respectively. For simplicity, let me play out a case in which P_2 is willing or able to work 1.5 times as long as P_1.

Here we get our first glimpse at why different presidents necessarily perform their work differently. Casting stamina as an individual budget constraint, B, which binds differently for two presidents: one (relatively) low-stamina president, P_1 subject to B_1, and one (relatively) high-stamina president, P_2 subject to B_2. If P_1 works a 10-hour workday and splits time equally between "thinking" and "speaking" activities, the daily workload is 5 hours of thinking, 5 hours of speaking. By contract, P_2 is able to work 1.5 times as many hours (but is otherwise identical to P_1), which enables him to invest comparatively more time on thinking activities (7.5 hours) *and* speaking activities (7.5 hours).

To be sure, the insight here is simple but important: the greater a president's stamina, the more work the president can process (all else being equal). Because these extra hours are unrestricted, they do not necessarily affect a president's scheduling breakdown—speaking versus thinking—but rather increase the time available for either – or both. Inasmuch as "first things first" always infringe on the president's schedule, the extent of the inconvenience depends on how many hours the president has to accommodate the imposition.

This is my *stamina hypothesis*—presidents who work longer hours will process more tasks. But what if presidents do not merely have different amounts of time to spend but also vary in how they prefer to spend it? In other words, what if presidents have different priorities and conditions?

Priorities and Conditions

Some presidents enjoy the presidency's public-facing aspects—crowds and cameras—or at least see a relative advantage in prioritizing them. Kennedy privileged press conferences; Reagan pushed his made-for-television events; Clinton pressed his "message of the day." And then there is President Trump, who, by all accounts, fixated on publicity, polls, press, and tweets. Ronald Reagan's quip from decades back feels just as apt today: " 'How could an actor be president?' I've sometimes wondered how you could be president and not be an actor?"[39]

But if all presidents must perform for the public, not all are equally eager to play the role. Here again, Richard Nixon's example is instructive. Nixon preferred a pen and paper to people and press, which shaped how he channeled his time. Henry Kissinger reflected: "Paradoxically, Nixon's abhorrence of face-to-face meetings enabled his administration to deal with one of the most important challenges of modern government: to husband the President's time—his most precious resource."[40]

Moving beyond casual conjecture, we can see how this impulse plays out vis-à-vis the theoretic model. To illustrate, as shown in figure 1.7, imagine two presidents, P_1 and P_2. The first prefers to spend more time "speaking," while the latter prefers to allocate more time to "thinking." Whereas P_1 would assign approximately 80 percent to

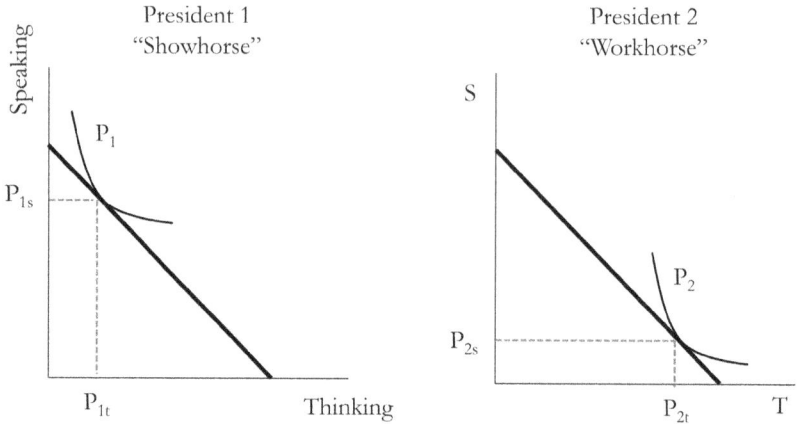

FIGURE 1.7 Speaking versus thinking time allocation:
different priorities and/or conditions.

"speaking time" and 20 percent to "thinking time," P_2 would do the opposite, allocating time 20 percent to speaking and 80 percent to thinking. Such vast differences are merely instructive, but they make a more general point: different priorities can affect how presidents allocate their time.

This is my *priorities hypothesis*—presidents will choose to spend their time differently, all else being equal.

Importantly, there is an alternative interpretation for this same analytic intuition. Rather than conceptualizing P_1 and P_2 as two different individuals, it is also possible to imagine them as the same president under dissimilar conditions. For example, P_1 could reflect conditions that privilege "speaking" (e.g., proximity to the president's reelection date), while P_2 could indicate situations that put a premium on "thinking" (e.g., war or recession). From this perspective, variations in presidential scheduling would track external conditions, which would induce more speaking time through some intervals, more thinking time during others.

This is my *conditions hypothesis*—conditions will dictate how presidents spend their time, all else being equal.

The priority and conditions hypotheses are not mutually exclusive. It could very well be—in fact, is likely to be—that presidents respond to both internal priorities and external conditions. The analytic model is agnostic regarding the relative importance of priorities vis-à-vis conditions, leaving that as an open question for the empirical chapters to follow.

EFFICIENCY

Unpacking how stamina and priorities/conditions affect how presidents handle the presidency's workload is useful, as is explicating how national conditions and political circumstances could override those factors. It is the model's final deduction, however, that strikes me as most interesting and important: variability in presidents' efficiency does not just affect the quantity of their work; it can also alter its composition.

As I conceive it, a president's work efficiency indicates how much work a president processes *during a workday*. It is not about time or tasks alone but rather about speed—action items per hour worked. All else being equal, a president who completes 30 tasks in a 15-hour day does more and works longer than a president who does 25 tasks in a 10-hour workday, but the latter is more efficient (2.5 tasks per hour for the latter versus 2 tasks per hour for the former).

Here again, the reasons to expect efficiency differentiation are manifold. Each president enters the presidency with different expertise, experience, intelligence, style, personality, and so on, and each president's particular constellation is directly relevant to how they process the presidency's workload. It is easy to imagine that a legislative question that Lyndon Johnson could answer instinctively might take Jimmy Carter considerably longer to navigate, just as we would expect a foreign policy issue that George H. W. Bush knew cold could take Donald Trump far longer to comprehend.

A few months into the Biden presidency, the *New York Times* reported on Biden's approach to decision-making: "Quick decision-making is not Mr. Biden's style. His reputation as a plain-speaking politician hides a more complicated truth. Before making up his mind, the president demands hours of detail-laden debate from scores of policy experts, taking everyone around him on what some in the West Wing refer to as his Socratic 'journey' before arriving at a conclusion."[41]

Even discounting staffer-sourced puffery, it is likely that Biden's deliberative "journey" has not followed Trump's, just as Trump's did not follow Obama's, just as Obama's did not follow Bush 43's.

That speaks to an important point: I model efficiency as related to "thinking time" but not "speaking time." I do so because presidents' information-processing capacity can vary dramatically, while there is no comparable means to streamline travel, speeches, press conferences, or photo ops. Put differently, the flight from DC to LA takes about 5 hours regardless of who is president, but how many meetings the president holds during the flight is malleable. Likewise, a presidential rally takes about the same amount of time for each president, but the amount of time the president puts into drafting and editing his speech can vary considerably.

Figure 1.8 considers efficiency differentials within the model by comparing a typical president (P_1) to one with greater efficiency (P_2), holding the presidents' speaking-thinking indifference curves constant. As illustrated here, although P_1 and P_2 have identical preferences

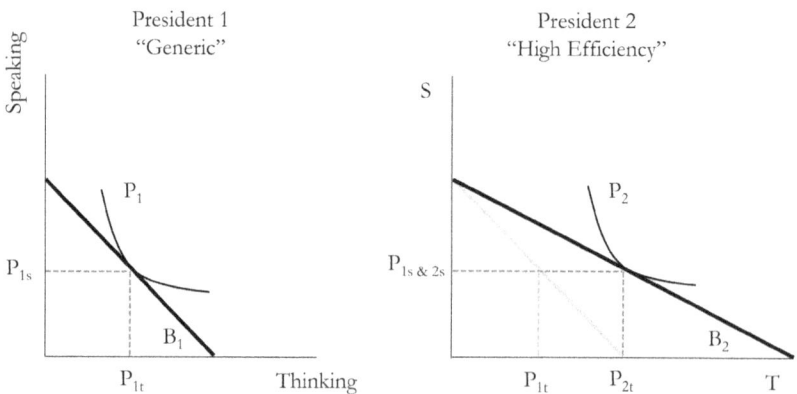

FIGURE 1.8 Speaking versus thinking time allocation: different efficiency levels.

about how to allocate their time, the latter processes decisions twice times as fast, as indicated by the different slopes between B_1 (slow) and B_2 (fast).

Conceptualizing efficiency in this way turns out to be instructive in myriad ways. When P_1 is half as efficient as P_2 within some time interval, the corollary is that P_2 effectively has twice as much thinking time as P_1 during that window. So while time is constant in an absolute sense (and appears as such from the outside), inside the Oval Office time is effectively moving twice as fast for one president (P_1) compared to the other (P_2).

Importantly, the differences need not be so dramatic to be significant; even a 5 percent efficiency difference between two presidents is the equivalent of the efficient president having an extra 2 months of thinking time per term. This "fleeting time, precious and unique," as Nixon put it, is time that the more efficient president can use to tackle extra issues, ask extra questions, hear extra voices—or simply rest, read, write, and think.

Having exposed the stark differences in their relative "thinking time," it is worth reiterating that both P_1 and P_2 are able to maintain an equivalent public schedule—that is, $P_{1t} < P_{2t}$, $P_{1s} = P_{2s}$. This is why a president's processing power is so valuable. Increased efficiency permits a president to focus on personal priorities while still attending to "first things first."

This is my *efficiency hypothesis*: presidents differ in how many thinking tasks (but not speaking tasks) they process per hour worked, all else being equal.

EXECUTIVE ACCOMMODATION

Having argued that presidential differences will produce different work patterns, I hasten to add the final piece to the theoretical puzzle: the institutional presidency often, if not eagerly, accommodates individual presidents. Such adaptations reflect pragmatic reality as much as a constitutional design, though the latter certainly buttresses the former. So rather than compel presidents into standardized routines, I expect that the office will routinely adapt to accommodate each chief.

Take the presidential daily brief (PDB)—the intelligence product the Central Intelligence Agency (CIA) famously called "the family jewels." As John Helgerson and David Priess expose in exquisite detail, the intelligence community carefully tailors the PDB to fit each president.[42] When it comes to the nation's most valuable secrets, the package is not delivered *to* each president so much as it is developed *for* each president.

The change from President Obama to President Trump is a case in point. After the election, intelligence officials decided that the PDB would need a substantial reboot on January 20, 2017. In the chapter "Donald J. Trump—A Unique Challenge," John Helgerson describes how intelligence officials purposefully redesigned (and kept refining) the PDB for Trump by including fewer items, less text, more figures— and a greater emphasis on Trump himself.[43]

It may be tempting to discount Trump as unique—because he was. But so was Obama. And so is every president. The insight here is not that each president is distinctive; rather, it is how enthusiastically the executive branch adapts in response. In the daily practice of presidential work, each president's preferences, annoyances, habits, and methods are not so much frivolous eccentricities as guiding principles.

To the extent that presidential operations are tailored to presidents' stamina, priorities and conditions, and efficiency, it thus becomes easy to extrapolate the indirect effects. In prepping for their moment with the president, for example, officials will surely sync their work style to the president's. This sort of strategic anticipation can be both conscious and unconscious. In short order, things like start times and end times, what gets done and what gets delegated, and who gets looped in and who gets left out, can feel self-evident—a natural practice rather than an intentional choice—when they are anything but.

This is not to say that the institutional presidency is simply derivative of individual presidents.[44] As already detailed, the institutional presidency has evolved into a robust institution, with features and protocols that create opportunities and impose constraints on all executive branch officials, up to and including the president.[45]

But not always, not everywhere. While it is certainly true that the presidency constrains presidents in many ways, it is also true that the presidency is not an exogenous, immovable force. As I see it, the modern presidency cannot help but accommodate each president, formally and informally, especially regarding the presidents' own daily operations. Each president adapts to the presidency and the presidency adapts to each president.

In short, differences between presidents emerge in the first instance because daily operations necessarily depend on each president's stamina, priorities, and efficiency. Those presidential particulars get routinized in the second instance because the institutional presidency configures itself to each president. This is why the presidency can have a standard organization *as well as* nonstandard operations.

CONCLUSION

That the presidency entails an awesome workload is hardly an original idea. Practitioners, pundits, and political scientists have long known that presidents must brave long hours and heavy burdens. But even that does not convey the full weight of an impossible job. Perhaps no words can, though Lyndon Johnson's reflections are certainly evocative: "But if I was seldom lonely, I was often alone. No one can experience with the President of the United States the glory and agony of his office. No one can share the majestic view from his pinnacle of power. No one can share the burden of his decisions or the scope of his duties."[46]

This chapter examined the nature of presidential work by theorizing the nature of presidential workloads and the political economy of presidential time. Situating presidential operations within the broader context of the presidency's organization, I then modeled presidential scheduling as time investments across two domains— "speaking" and "thinking." The underlying question was whether the presidency could have a standard organization *and* nonstandard operations. The answer, I argued, is less that it can than that it must.

My theory of presidential operations generated several predictions about how (and why) different presidents will necessarily do the job differently—day to day, month to month, year to year. Whereas some presidents will work from dawn to dark, others will not let the workday last all day. Whereas some presidents will disproportionately invest their scarce time in public outreach, others will prioritize policy deliberations. And, perhaps most importantly, whereas some presidents will find that external obligations crowd out personal priorities, others will discover that they can handle both.

To be sure, the idea that individual presidents animate the institutional presidency may seem obvious. That is certainly White House staffers' view. For those who have been "in the room," the president's preeminence within the presidency is self-evident; the thesis that executive branch officials eagerly adapt their work to fit the president's interests and abilities is but common sense.

Yet this is precisely why a clear theory of presidential operations is so valuable. Absent an explicit model and concrete hypotheses, it is easy to discount presidential differences as matters of form rather than function. In fact, the "presidency-centered" perspective underlying so much contemporary scholarship explicitly postulates that presidents' interpersonal differences are readily apparent but not especially important.

Clearly, I take a different tack. As this chapter makes clear, differences in presidents' stamina, priorities and conditions, and efficiency are not stylistic; rather, they implicate core presidential functions: agenda-setting, deliberation, and decision-making. Such analytic insights thus complement Richard Neustadt's essential thesis: "He makes his personal impact by the things he says and does. Accordingly, his choices of what he should say and do, and how and when, are his means to conserve and tap the sources of his power."[47]

Having unpacked the logic underlying presidential operations, in the next few chapters I strive to test these ideas against extraordinary data, with careful analyses, across myriad settings. Chapter 2 delves into a critical test case: Jimmy Carter versus Ronald Reagan.

2

JIMMY VERSUS RONNIE

MERE WEEKS AFTER JIMMY CARTER lost to Ronald Reagan in the 1980 election, the outgoing president welcomed the incoming president to the White House. The stated itinerary was transition planning, but reporters suspected that the occasion was more ceremonial—a courteous nod to democratic unity. The *New York Times* lede said as much: "A minute ahead of schedule, at 1:59 P.M., Ronald and Nancy Reagan arrived at the back door of the White House today for a social call and a visit to the building that will serve as home and office after Jan. 20."[1]

In fact, Carter's agenda was hardly ceremonial. During the 90-minute meeting between president and president-elect, Carter briefed Reagan about twenty handpicked topics. Carter explained himself in his memoirs: "I considered the visit very important, and had carefully prepared a list of the most significant issues that needed to be discussed—issues which only a President could ultimately resolve."[2]

Reagan listened but did not appear especially engaged, polite if not interested. When Carter asked Reagan "if he wanted a pad so that he could take some notes," the president-elect declined.[3] And when Carter cautioned, "We've both been governors, but let me tell you, it's different in the White House. The day begins early. A C.I.A. officer briefs you at 7 A.M.," Reagan offered a cheeky retort: "Well, he's sure going to have to wait a long while for me."[4]

No doubt, presidential transitions are awkward under the best of circumstances. James Pfiffner's terrific book on the topic exposes how "the potential for friction and bitterness" is more a probability than a possibility.[5] From both sides and across all levels, snark flows and eyerolls abound. This is especially true when switching presidents includes switching parties, and it is particularly acute when the arriving president defeated the departing president.

For my purposes, however, what makes the Carter-Reagan transition so interesting is not the transfer of power itself. Rather, it is that the two presidents had such different conceptions about the job and their role. Whereas Carter believed that the presidency required that presidents maintain long hours and personal involvement in programmatic details, Reagan believed that he could focus on the big picture—messaging as much as managing—and handle the presidency's workload within a standard workday. Theirs was not a difference in ambition; it was a difference in approach.

These interpersonal differences make Jimmy Carter and Ronald Reagan a critical test for the preceding chapter's core hypotheses. If, as I argue, differences in presidents' stamina, priorities, and efficiency compel each to operate the presidency differently, the difference ought to show up in the duration, density, and composition of Carter's and Reagan's work. On the other hand, if Jimmy Carter and Ronald Reagan worked similar hours and filled them similarly, this finding will firmly corroborate the thesis that individual presidents must submit to the presidency's institutional constraints.

This chapter thus investigates the pivot from Carter to Reagan as a first test of my theory's core hypotheses. Were presidential operations under Carter and Reagan meaningfully distinct, and, if so, did those differences correspond to the presidents' relative differences in stamina, priorities, and efficiency?

DIFFERENT PRESIDENTS

In *The Unfinished Presidency*, Douglas Brinkley scrutinizes Jimmy Carter's presidency in rich detail. The portrait that emerges is now familiar: Carter was a smart, earnest man who was loathe to delegate important tasks or, for that matter, any tasks.[6] Brinkley wrote, "Carter approached the presidency like a family farmer: plow the fields, spread the fertilizer, harvest the crop—and keep an eye on every detail the whole way. You hire help, of course, but sharecroppers, migrants, or day-wagers just don't have the same stake in the work as the farmer; a good harvest depends on his devotion and God's will."[7]

Brinkley's analysis corroborates reports by Carter's own assistants—not to mention the president himself. In fact, Carter's diary entry after his first week in office signaled his mentality: "I have tried to hold down drastically the ceremonial events that Presidents ordinarily attend and to let my sons and their wives and Rosalynn . . . and others substitute for me. The time pressures are so tremendous that every minute's valuable."[8]

Carter's method stands in stark contrast to Ronald Reagan's. Reagan enjoyed the grand stage of the modern presidency far more than granular details about the federal government, in part because he believed that a president's highest and best use was in the lights, not the weeds. Lou Cannon aptly titled his Reagan biography *The Role of a Lifetime*. There Cannon explained, "But eight years as [California] governor had taught Reagan he performed best when he attended to larger visions. . . . What he wanted to be, and what he became, was an accomplished presidential performer."[9]

One may quibble about details or degrees, but there is no doubt that Carter's and Reagan's differences ran deeper than party or ideology. Indeed, Carter and Reagan were very different people who brought very different traits and styles to the same office. Carter was high-stamina, policy-focused, and fast-paced. Reagan was (comparatively) low-stamina, public-focused, and slower-paced.

CONTINUITY OF CHANGE

Per the U.S. Constitution's Twentieth Amendment, "The terms of the President and Vice President shall end at noon on the 20th day of January." ("The U.S. Constitution," Amend. 20, sec. 1). So it was that midday on January 20, 1981, Jimmy Carter's 1,461 days as president ended and Ronald Reagan's first 1,461 days as president began.

The fact that the interval between 1/20/77 and 1/19/85 was divided on a predetermined date and time helps us compare presidents across this divide.

Before elaborating on why Carter's and Reagan's first terms form an opportune interval to study, I hasten to acknowledge the difficulties to making *any* presidential comparisons. After all, because the issues, people, events, and circumstances are always unique to a particular time, the eternal question is whether presidency scholars can ever make comparisons that satisfy the experimental ideal of holding "all else equal."

The short answer is that we cannot. There is but one president at a time, and both the president and time are distinctive to their moment. The business of comparing presidents always involves confounds, and there is no cure for that basic ailment. More to the point, when it comes to presidents, there is no random assignment, and there is no control group.

But just as the perfect is not the enemy of the good, the fact that presidency research is complicated does not render it impossible. That presidency scholars cannot impose experimental control does not mean that we must forsake scientific standards; it simply means we must be especially careful, especially vigilant, and especially candid about how well those standards fit—or do not.

While it is true that change is the only constant, it is also true that change can be more or less constant. Even as the details are ever-changing, some days (and years) are more comparable than others. Presidents are most comparable when they inhabit similar vectors in the historical arc, occupy a similar space on the global stage, and face similar issues on the home front.

By contrast, for presidents who served before and after the presidency modernized, the contexts are so dissimilar as to render presidential comparisons somewhere between dubious and ludicrous. To a lesser degree, the same problem arises if one president takes office after an election and the other after an assassination, one during peace and the other during war, or if one presidency transpires during an economic boom and the other amid an economic bust.

For the eight years from 1/20/77 to 1/19/1985, there are countless differences at the microlevel, but I submit that this eight-year window was a relatively stable period at the macrolevel. This was a transition when one newly elected first-term president was replaced by another newly elected first-term president.[10] Such a pairing—newly elected, first term, back to back—is relatively uncommon, partly because some presidents assumed office without an election (Johnson, Ford) and partly because other presidents left office after two full terms (Reagan, Clinton, Bush 43). The fact that Presidents Carter and Reagan won back-to-back elections and then served back-to-back first terms makes them comparable in ways that few other presidential pairs have been.

That Carter and Reagan served consecutively also bolsters confidence regarding the relative continuity of their circumstances. The overlap is not complete, but it is comparable. For unlike so many postwar presidencies, this eight-year window from 1977 through 1985 did not experience any major shift in ongoing trends, no critical juncture that upended the established order. There was no Great Depression, no Korea, no Vietnam, no Iraq, no fall of the Soviet Union, and no 9/11. If anything, the interval from the start of Carter's presidency till the start of Reagan's second term showed that the United States and Soviet Union had settled into a fairly stable geopolitical equilibrium.[11]

Similarly, though domestic conditions are always churning, the basic issues and dynamics held their form throughout this era. While the economy was certainly in flux—from income and budgets to inflation and unemployment—the prominence of economic issues was consistent. Likewise, even as congressional agendas changed from day to day—sometimes it was a nominee, other times a bill, occasionally a treaty—the basic contours of the legislative battlefield were mostly entrenched. The late 1970s and early 1980s was an era of strong committees, (many) conflicted partisans, and a familiar suite of policy debates.

An additional point is worth reiterating: by the mid-seventies, the modern presidency had already settled into its "standard" form. Well before Jerry Ford left the White House, the Executive Office of the President's key offices and positions, roles, and norms had hardened into a prevailing mold. Inasmuch as succeeding presidents (e.g., Carter or Reagan) adopted or rejected the standard organizational model, it was not because the office was unfinished; rather, it was because that president had designs on how to structure and run *his* White House.

In a nutshell, because there is one president at a time, conditions are always shifting, and issues are always evolving, presidency research never submits to the experimental ideal. Nevertheless, the relative continuity of political circumstances, global setting, and national issues makes Jimmy Carter's and Ronald Reagan's first terms an especially good pairing for study. Put differently, if we could magically switch Carter's and Reagan's order in the presidential lineage, there is good reason to suspect that how each would behave is comparable to how each did behave.

ARCHIVING THE PRESIDENT

Given the potential insights to be gained by studying how Jimmy Carter and Ronald Reagan operated their office, the task becomes how to translate what is potential into what is tangible. The key is a specific archival record, one largely unknown to the public but highly prized by academics: the presidential Daily Diary. In appendix A, I detail the Daily Diary's history to assess its virtues and vices as a data source. Here I will just reiterate a few points that are particularly relevant to the Carter and Reagan years.

First, there is an essential distinction between the daily schedule and the Daily Diary. Whereas the daily schedule anticipates what the president plans to do (*ex ante*), the diary logs what the president actually did do (*ex post*). March 30, 1981, epitomizes the difference; see figure 2.1. While Reagan's schedule anticipates that Reagan will "return to White House" at approximately 2:30 and then meet with Republican Ways and Means Committee members at 3:10, the Daily Diary's third page captures what really happened: 2:25, "The President was shot in the left side leaving the hotel during an assassination attempt."

Importantly, this sort of archival precision is not reserved for dramatic days or notorious moments. The diaries log the president's behavior for slow days, busy days, boring days, and historic days, when the president was on stage or behind the scenes, and whether

THE WHITE HOUSE

WASHINGTON

UNPUBLISHED
March 27, 1981
5:00 pm

THE PRESIDENT'S SCHEDULE
Monday, March 30, 1981

Time	Activity	Location
8:30 am (60 min)	Leadership Breakfast (Craig Fuller)　(TAB A) Press Photo Pool	East Room
9:30 am (15 min)	Staff Time (Baker, Meese, Deaver)	Oval Office
9:45 am (30 min)	National Security Briefing (Richard V. Allen)	Oval Office
10:15 am (15 min)	Meeting with James Baker, Edwin Meese, Michael Deaver, Max Friedersdorf, James Brady and David Gergen	Oval Office
10:30 am (15 min)	Meeting with Hispanic Supporters (Lyn Nofziger)　(TAB B) Press Photo Pool	Cabinet Room
11:00 am (2½ hrs)	To Residence for Lunch and Speech Preparation Time	Residence
Approx. 1:45 pm	Depart for Washington Hilton Hotel to address General Session of the National Conference of the Building & Construction Trades Department, AFL/CIO	Washington Hilton Hotel
2:00 pm (20 min)	Remarks by the President　(TAB C)	
Approx. 2:35 pm	Return to White House	Oval Office
3:10 pm (20 min)	Meeting with select GOP Members of House Ways and Means Committee (Bill Gradison, Guy Vander Jagt, Phil Crane and Jim Martin) (Max Friedersdorf) Dick Darman (TAB D) No Press Coverage	Oval Office
3:30 pm (60 min)	Personal Staff Time	Oval Office
4:30 pm (15 min)	Courtesy Visit by Messrs. David Rockefeller, George Berthoin and Takeshi Watanabe (Joseph Canzeri)　(TAB E) White House Photographer	Oval Office
4:45 – Drew Lewis 5:00 pm (30 min)	Staff Time (Baker, Meese, Deaver)	Oval Office
5:30 pm (30 min)	Haircut	West Basement
6:00 pm	Return to Residence	
7:00 pm	The President and Mrs. Reagan will have dinner with Secretary and Mrs. Schweiker and Secretary and Mrs. Regan	Residence

FIGURE 2.1A Presidential schedule for the afternoon of March 30, 1981.

THE WHITE HOUSE · THE DAILY DIARY OF PRESIDENT RONALD REAGAN

LOCATION	DATE
THE WASHINGTON HILTON HOTEL WASHINGTON, D.C.	MARCH 30, 1981
	TIME 2:25 p.m. / DAY MONDAY

Time		PHONE P = Placed R = Rec'd	
2:25			The President was shot in the left side leaving the hotel during an assassination attempt.
2:30	2:44		The President motored from the Washington Hilton Hotel to the George Washington University Hospital.
			The President went to the emergency room at the hospital.
2:51		R	The President was telephoned by Senator Edward M. Kennedy (D-Massachusetts). The call was not completed.
4:00?			The President went into surgery for removal of the bullet, which penetrated his left lung.
?	?		The President met with the First Lady.

EJ

FIGURE 2.1B Presidential Daily Diary for the afternoon of March 30, 1981.

the president was riding high or falling flat. The Reagan Library's holding description makes the point best:

> The President's Daily Diary is a day-by-day record of Ronald Reagan's eight years as President. It chronicles such activities as meetings, briefings, press conferences, telephone calls, photo sessions, meals, travel, and recreation. Presidential Diarist Ellen Jones (McCathran), a National Archives employee detailed to the White House, had chief responsibility for creating the Diary, based on documents provided by various White House units.
>
> The primary Diary document for most days is a log, entered on a standard form. The logs list starting and ending times for activities, brief descriptions for activities which require explanation, and information on persons or groups involved. Some log entries refer to appendices which provide full participant lists, and other additional information, for certain meetings, air travel, and social affairs.[12]

This is not to say that the diaries are perfect. Some activities are not recorded (e.g., impromptu run-ins in the West Wing hallways), and some days do not have any accompanying diary at all.

Happily, missing data are reasonably rare, and better still, typically correspond to presidential travel (e.g., vacations) or archivist overload (e.g., not finishing the last diaries before a new president's inauguration, whereupon source materials get boxed up and hauled off). I found no evidence of strategic censorship, by presidents or archivists, across the period of my study.[13] To the contrary, the stated goal of the National Archives and Records Administration (NARA) for the diary is ensuring the "consistency, completeness, and accuracy of the record,"[14] and by all accounts it seems to have succeeded to an extraordinary degree, with remarkable reliability, for more than half a century.

MEASURING WORK

To capitalize on this research opportunity, I endeavored to code every Daily Diary from the start of Jimmy Carter's presidency (January 20, 1977) through the end of Ronald Reagan's first term (January 19, 1985).

I did so by randomly assigning diaries among a large team of trained undergraduate research assistants (RAs).

The first measure gets at my first hypothesis—the stamina hypothesis, which presumes that presidents have different capacities for work. We thus measured the *duration* of work during each day. Each RA would scour the Daily Diaries in their sample to classify the start of the first work activity and the end of the last work activity, from which we calculated the duration between the two.[15] The threshold for deciding a work activity was to appraise whether it mainly reflected the president's personal or professional interests. So, for example, the president and first lady eating breakfast together would not count as a work activity, but hosting a dinner for Cabinet officials would.

My next measures aimed to operationalize thinking and speaking time. For *thinking activities*, we measured the president's contacts with key administration officials whose purview emphasizes governance (rather than communications or campaigns) to sharpen the speaking/thinking distinction. RAs thus counted the total number of 5+ minute contacts, in person or by phone, that the president had with seven key officials: the vice president; the secretaries of state, defense, and treasury; the attorney general; the national security advisor; and the CIA director. Carter's daily contact count was 0 to 33 while Reagan's was 0 to 25.

We measured *speaking activities* by counting how many "interviews," "news conferences," "spoken addresses and remarks," "oral addresses," and "miscellaneous remarks" the president totaled during each day. These data come from John Woolley and Gerhard Peters's invaluable *The American Presidency Project*, a comprehensive database for the Public Papers of the Presidents.[16] I chose these categories because they entail presidential remarks personally delivered rather than press releases issued under the president's name. The daily count was 0 to 9 for Carter, 0 to 8 for Reagan.

Having pointed out many ways the presidency complicates comparisons across presidencies, I hasten to note that while I cannot escape those basic realities, the design and measures thus introduced were designed to mitigate familiar inferential pitfalls. By drawing on the presidential Daily Diary and the Public Papers of the Presidents,

I compiled a new, granular dataset of President Carter's and President Reagan's daily work activities throughout their first terms in office. With these interpersonally comparable data across two interpersonally dissimilar presidents during a relatively contiguous eight-year window, I now test whether who was president explains how the president's work got done.

ON THE CLOCK

Every president must impose limits on a job that has none. It is a matter of survival as much as philosophy. Amid an onslaught of legislative meetings, conference calls, security briefings, global summits, public speeches, press conferences, ceremonial photos, and this and that from near and far, presidents must find time to eat, to sleep, and to relax.

In the preceding chapter, I theorized that variation in presidents' work stamina will affect their work patterns—in some ways that are straightforward, others not so much. Before getting there, however, I should first probe that premise. Is presidential stamina variable? That is, do presidents meaningfully differ in how long they work, or do all presidents adhere to something of a standard shift—the White House version of 9 to 5? As I say, if there are meaningful differences in presidents' work capacity, Jimmy Carter and Ronald Reagan should reveal as much, and if they do not, there is good reason to suspect that institutional structures override individual stamina—not just here but in general.

For a first look into presidents' days, I begin by putting new evidentiary meat to old anecdotal bones. Specifically, figure 2.2 plots President Carter's and Reagan's typical starting and ending time across their first terms.

Clearly, the Carter and Reagan divergence starts early and persists late. Whereas Carter typically punched in around 6:30 A.M., Reagan got going closer to 9:00 A.M. And whereas Carter typically finished his last work activity after 10:00 P.M., Reagan tended to wrap up by 7:30 P.M. These initial results, which exclude weekends and holidays to improve precision, underscore how demanding a president's day can be.

12a
9
6
3
12p
9
6
3

77.1 77.2 77.3 77.4 78.1 78.2 78.3 78.4 79.1 79.2 79.3 79.4 80.1 80.2 80.3 80.4 81.1 81.2 81.3 81.4 82.1 82.2 82.3 82.4 83.1 83.2 83.3 83.4 84.1 84.2 84.3 84.4

Carter   Reagan

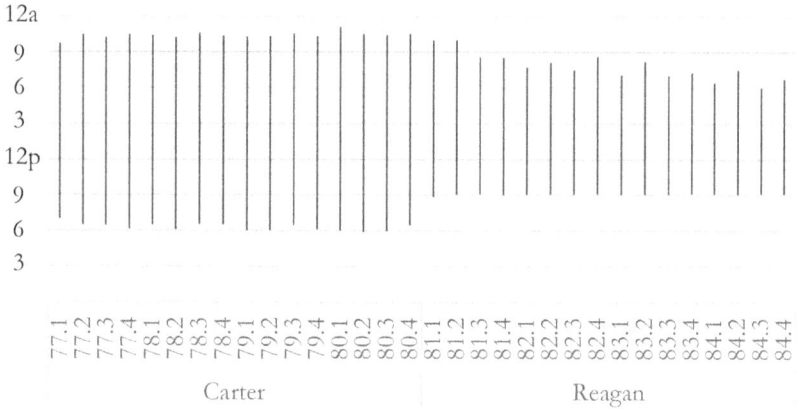

FIGURE 2.2 Median start and end times of the president's workday, by year and quarter.

They also illustrate how differently Carter and Reagan approached the workday.

If their specific starting and ending times are interesting, more insightful is the duration between the two. In my theory, stamina's impact depends on how long presidents work, not whether they do it early or late. On this score several points stand out, as illustrated in figure 2.3. The first is the most obvious: Carter and Reagan both worked a long day, yet the difference is still vast. Carter's median workday duration (excluding weekends and holidays) was a tick under 16 hours *per day*. For Reagan it was 10 hours, 55 minutes. In other words, for every hour Reagan was on the clock, Carter averaged 1 hour and 27 minutes—each hour, every day, for four years.

Beyond the sheer magnitude of their workday duration difference, another fascinating feature is the relative steadiness of each president's daily grind. The overall standard deviation in workday duration (3.7 hours) is greater than the standard deviations within each presidency (Carter = 3.0 hours, Reagan = 3.0 hours). As it turned out, that 1980 transition meeting did foreshadow a bigger lesson: Carter and Reagan had different definitions of a good day's work.

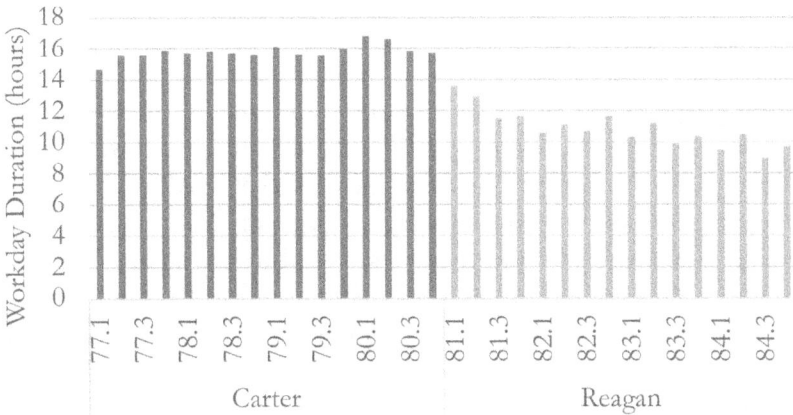

FIGURE 2.3 Duration of the president's typical workday (hours), by year and quarter.

The final noteworthy discovery concerns how Carter's and Reagan's workdays evolved over time. While Carter's daily work hours remained quite consistent (r = 0.11 between weeks in office and workday duration), Reagan's days became somewhat shorter as he moved through his first term (r = −0.23). So whether one analyzes the whole period, the period nearest the inauguration, or equivalent periods within their respective terms, the conclusion is the same: Reagan's days were long, but Carter's workdays were longer—substantially, consistently, and reliably.

SPEAKING, THINKING, AND BEING

Having seen that Carter and Reagan differed in work *hours*, I now turn to whether they also differed in work *activities*. That is, did Carter's and Reagan's daily tasks differ in quantity or quality? And, if so, why? Was their workday tied to national conditions and political circumstances (or random chance), or did their work patterns reveal something about the presidents themselves?

Clearly, I expect the latter. Carter's and Reagan's daily work should reflect each president's stamina, priorities, and efficiency—above and beyond their respective contexts, above and beyond the idiosyncrasies of daily events. Compared to Jimmy Carter, Ronald Reagan's lower stamina should result in fewer activities overall (all else being equal); his emphasis on publicity should result in a mix of activities that skews toward public events (all else being equal); and his lower efficiency should result in fewer policy meetings (all else being equal).

Before turning to the results, I should note that these hypotheses are falsifiable given these data. For example, I could not reject the null (i.e., Reagan and Carter worked similarly) if Reagan (compared to Carter) performed an equivalent:

- number of work activities (refuting the stamina hypothesis);
- mix of speaking/thinking activities (refuting the priorities and conditions hypothesis);
- number of thinking activities controlling for workday duration and speaking activities (refuting the efficiency hypothesis).

This is no minor point. Even if one stipulates that Jimmy Carter and Ronald Reagan were different people, that alone does not mean they worked differently, however "obvious" such inferences may seem. The road from conjecture to conclusion is littered with truths that initially appeared self-evident. What is more, even when some idea ascribed to conventional wisdom survives careful testing, the journey almost always sharpens our resolution, clarifies our caveats, and advances our understanding.

In that spirit, I now test whether differences in Carter's and Reagan's relative stamina, priorities and conditions, and efficiency manifested themselves in their daily practices as president of the United States. I start with their "thinking activities" (i.e., policy meetings) before turning to their "speaking activities" (i.e., public events).

THINKING ACTIVITIES

Many people meet the president; few are confidants. So even as innumerable people have a picture with the president—usually prominently displayed—the president's inner circle tends to be a small cadre of top government officials. Most presidential "thinking" occurs in meetings with a handful of the administration's key policymakers.

To investigate each president's thinking activities, we counted his 5+ minute contacts with seven top government officials whose responsibilities emphasized governance (rather than messaging or campaigns): the vice president; the secretaries of state, defense, and treasury; the attorney general; the national security advisor; and the CIA director. Figure 2.4 shows each president's average monthly contacts with these officials through their first term in office.

Before sifting through the differences, it is first interesting to note the similarities. Specifically, it is intriguing that Carter's and Reagan's contact patterns across positions were analogous. Both presidents met with the national security advisor and vice president far more often than with the CIA director and attorney general, for instance. Even their contact distribution is similar. Among the officials studied, 39 percent of Carter's contacts were with the national security

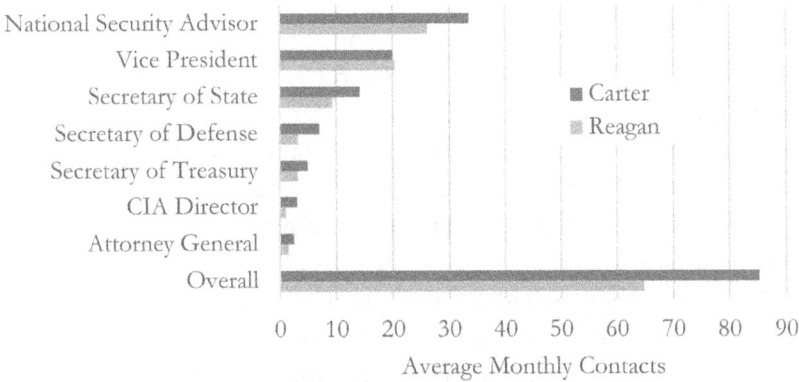

FIGURE 2.4 President's average monthly contacts with key officials, Carter versus Reagan.

Dependent variable: average number of 5+ minute contacts per month, in person or over the phone, between the president and seven top administration officials: national security advisor; vice president; secretaries of state, treasury, and defense; attorney general; and CIA director. Data are for first terms and exclude weekends, holidays, and days with missing records.

advisor, which is equivalent to the 40 percent for Reagan. The modest exception is the vice president, who comprised 23 percent of Carter's contacts but 31 percent of Reagan's.

But if their ranking and percentage of contacts are comparable, the absolute number is not. Both Carter and Reagan averaged 20 contacts per month with their vice presidents through their first term, yet when it came to the other six offices studied, Carter averaged more monthly contacts than Reagan: national security advisor (Carter +12); secretary of state (Carter +5); secretary of defense (Carter +4); secretary of treasury (Carter +2); CIA director (Carter +2); attorney general (Carter +1).

Given that Carter had more contacts with key officers than did Reagan, the follow-up question is whether this difference reflected Carter's relative priorities, stamina, or efficiency, dissimilar circumstances, some combination of each, or something else altogether (e.g., the opportunity cost of public events). To adjudicate among rival hypotheses, I develop a multiple regression model as detailed in table 2.1.

The model includes a dummy variable for the president, a set of variables that capture circumstances that could increase demands for meetings about governance (during the first 6 months in office) or decrease those demands (during reelection campaigns or the lame duck period after a loss). I also include a measure of the president's public activities during each day to account for the time tradeoffs presidents must make. Against that baseline (model I), I then add the variable to test the significance of the president's stamina (model II).[17]

The table includes both models for completeness, but I focus on model II because its tests are more precise. When I control for the president's workday duration (i.e., "stamina") and the day's number of public events (i.e., "speaking"), the fixed effect for the president tests whether Reagan's thinking activities (i.e., "priorities") meaningfully differed from Carter's given how long each worked and what else each did (all else being equal).

The lesson is unmistakable. When it came to daily contacts with top officials, Presidents Carter and Reagan differed substantially and consistently. They diverged in the first instance because Carter's days

TABLE 2.1 Negative binomial regression of the president's contacts
with key officials

	POLICFFY CONTACTS COEFFICIENT (SE)	
	MODEL I	MODEL II
Reagan (compared to Carter)	−0.28* (0.06)	−0.17* (0.08)
Honeymoon (January–June, first year)	−0.01 (0.05)	−0.01 (0.05)
Reelection period (August—election day, fourth year)	−0.32* (0.15)	−0.30* (0.15)
Lame duck period (post-loss, Carter fourth year)	−0.76* (0.10)	−0.76* (0.10)
Duration of workday (hours)	—	−0.02* (0.01)
Number of public events during day	0.01 (0.03)	0.00 (0.03)
Constant	1.52* (0.06)	1.16* (0.17)
Natural log, alpha	−1.14 (0.16)	−1.16 (0.16)
Log likelihood	−4,239.57	−4,232.47
N	1,868	1,868

Note: Dependent variable: the president's total number of 5+ minute contacts (in person or by phone) with seven key officials in his administration—national security advisor; vice president, secretaries of state, treasury, and defense; attorney general; and CIA director—during workdays from January 20, 1977, through January 19, 1985. Analysis excludes weekends, federal holidays, and days with missing records. The models also control for days the president was traveling outside Washington, and standard errors are adjusted for clustering on month.
*p < 0.05.

lasted so much longer than Reagan's, and those extra hours helped Carter include more interactions with key players in his administration (b = 0.02, SE = 0.01, p < 0.05). The predicted values plotted in figure 2.5 illustrate the lesson clearly: if Carter and Reagan both worked a 12-hour day, the predicted monthly contact differential would be Carter +15. The fact that Reagan worked a typical 11-hour day while Carter worked a typical 16-hour day bumps that predicted discrepancy to Carter +25 (contacts per month).

But Carter did not just have extra policy contacts per day; he also had extra policy contacts per hour. Set to equivalent conditions (non-honeymoon, non-election, non–lame duck period), Carter had 21 percent more contacts than Reagan (b = −0.17, SE = 0.08, p < 0.05), holding their workday duration constant. Assuming they worked the same number

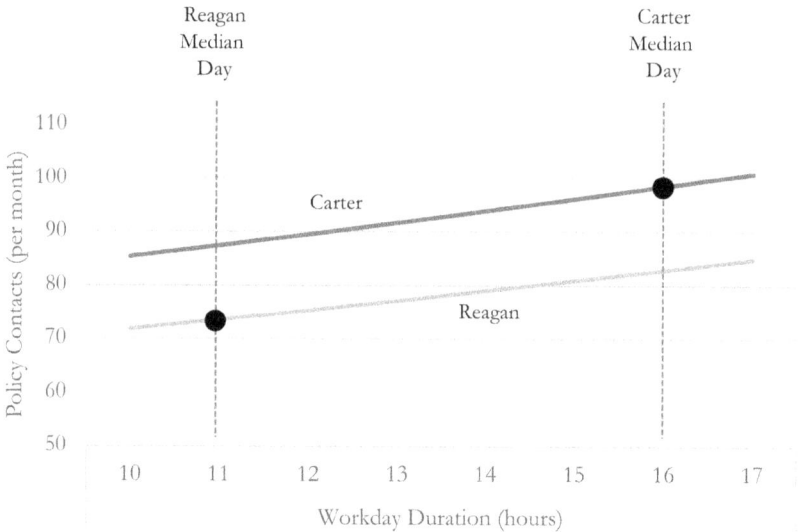

FIGURE 2.5 Predicted number of contacts with key officials per month (first term), Carter versus Reagan.

of days in a month and the same number of hours per day, Carter would be predicted to engage the top administration 90 times, which compares to Reagan's 75.

To be clear, just because presidents themselves matter does not mean their circumstances are irrelevant. If anything, it is important to recognize the ways presidents adapt to various circumstances. Both the reelection campaign (b = −0.30, SE = 0.15, p < 0.05) and lame duck period (b = −0.76, SE = 0.10, p < 0.05) saw a significant reduction in the presidents' deliberations with key administration officials. Substantively, president-official contact fell by 26 percent during the reelection campaigns and 53 percent after Carter became a lame duck (holding all else equal).

SPEAKING ACTIVITIES

Having just observed that President Reagan, compared to President Carter, worked shorter hours per day and had fewer meetings per hour even when accounting for their broader political context, I now

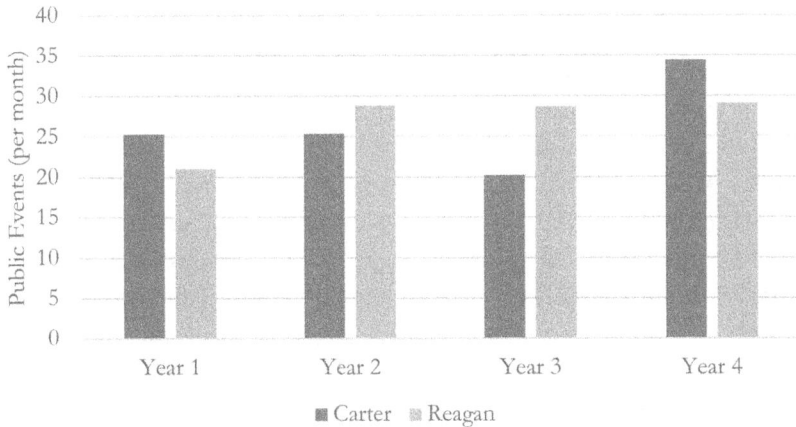

FIGURE 2.6 President's average monthly public events by year,
Carter versus Reagan.

Dependent variable: count of the president's "interviews," "news conferences,"
"spoken addresses and remarks," "oral addresses," and "miscellaneous remarks"
per John Woolley and Gerhard Peters, *The American Presidency Project*
(www.presidency.ucsb.edu). Figure displays monthly average for each year,
excluding weekends, holidays, and days with missing records.

turn to the public side of presidential work. Did Presidents Carter
and Reagan operate differently in terms of "speaking" activities as
they did in terms of "thinking" activities?

Figure 2.6 indicates the average number of public events during a
typical month through Carter's only term and Reagan's first. Unlike
the "thinking" results, these "speaking" results make the two presidents appear more or less equivalent. Overall, both presidents
averaged 26 public activities per month (assuming 21 workdays).
Carter's yearly average ranged from 20 (in 1979) to 34 (in 1980); for
Reagan it went from 21 (in 1981) to 29 (in 1984). At the descriptive
level, then, Carter and Reagan were analogous in speaking activities, and the year-to-year variation is greater than the president-to-
president differences.

However, because their workday durations were so different,
the fact that Carter and Reagan maintained an equivalent stage
presence suggests that Reagan put a premium on such endeavors.

To help disentangle the various factors at play, I now analyze the presidents' daily public activities using the same model specification discussed previously.

Table 2.2 reports results for a negative binomial regression model including a dummy variable for president (Reagan); variables related to the honeymoon, reelection campaign, and lame duck periods; measures of the day's work duration; and the daily count of the president's contacts with top officials. As before, I emphasize the comprehensive model (model II) except for the purpose of comparison.

To start, notice that background circumstances mapped onto presidents' public activities just as expected. The presidents were more likely to seek publicity during their reelection campaign ($b = 0.60$, SE = 0.20, $p < 0.05$) and less likely to do so in the interval between

TABLE 2.2 Negative binomial regression of the president's public events

	PUBLIC EVENTS COEFFICIENT (SE)	
	MODEL I	MODEL II
Reagan (compared to Carter)	0.00 (0.05)	0.31* (0.08)
Honeymoon (January–June, first year)	−0.04 (0.12)	−0.05 (0.10)
Reelection period (August—election day, fourth year)	0.59* (0.22)	0.60* (0.20)
Lame duck period (postloss, Carter fourth year)	−0.63* (0.16)	−0.60* (0.17)
Duration of workday (hours)	—	0.07* (0.01)
Number of policy contacts during day	0.01 (0.01)	0.00 (0.01)
Constant	0.07 (0.09)	−1.00 (0.23)
Natural log, alpha	−2.41 (0.48)	−3.14 (0.77)
Log likelihood	−2,699.53	−2,657.82
N	1,868	1,868

Note: Dependent variable: count of the president's "interviews," "news conferences," "spoken addresses and remarks," "oral addresses," and "miscellaneous remarks" per John Woolley and Gerhard Peters, The American Presidency Project (www.presidency. ucsb.edu) from January 20, 1977, through January 19, 1985. Analysis excludes weekends, federal holidays, and days with missing records. The models also control for days the president was traveling outside Washington, and standard errors are adjusted for clustering on month.
*p < 0.05.

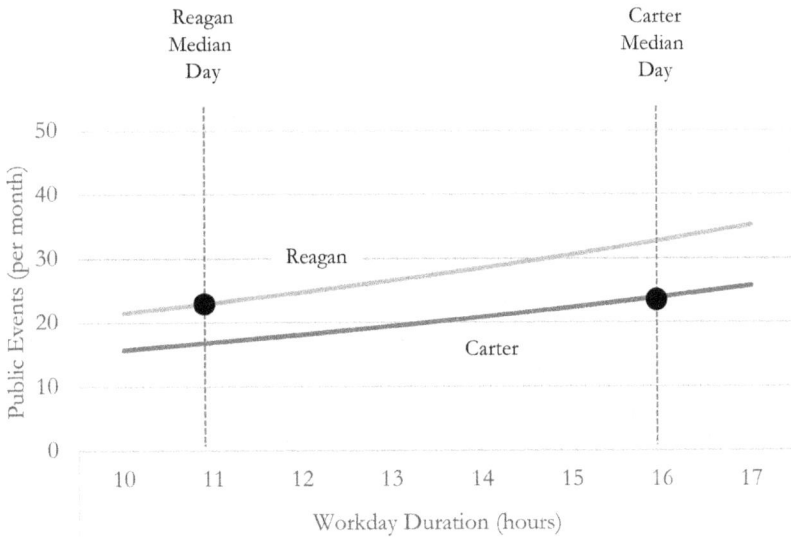

FIGURE 2.7 Predicted number of public events per month (first term), Carter versus Reagan.

losing reelection and the corresponding inauguration (b = –0.60, SE = 0.17, p < 0.05). Interestingly, the honeymoon period was not reliably related to the presidents' speaking frequency after controlling for the president, the duration of their workdays, and the circumstances in which they worked.

But highlighting how context shapes presidents' publicity-facing behavior is not to undersell each president's role therein. Indeed, the surface appears calm precisely because of the presidents' efforts beneath the surface.

Take the presidents' stamina. The length of the presidents' workdays is correlated with how many public activities each executed during that day (b = 0.07, SE = 0.01, p < 0.05). Though I cannot tell whether presidents extended the day because of public activities or whether the extra time simply allowed the presidents to squeeze more in, in many ways that is a distinction without a difference. Longer days correspond to more public activities. In this way Carter's stamina allowed him to keep pace with Reagan in terms of public speeches and remarks while also having far more contacts with key government officials.[18]

The role of presidential stamina is interesting in itself—and also how it gets masked. Without accounting for stamina explicitly, the presidents appear equivalent ($b = 0.00$, SE $= 0.05$, p $=$ n.s.); however, accounting for their workday duration shows that Reagan only kept up with Carter by putting a premium on public activities ($b = 0.31$, SE $= 0.08$, p < 0.05). This explains why such different presidents who allocate time so differently can still appear so similar. Carter's and Reagan's public activities per day were equivalent; per hour they were not. The difference would not be obvious day to day, but as we can see in figure 2.7, if each worked 12-hour weekdays for a month, that would correspond to Reagan having 25 public activities versus Carter having just 18.

CONCLUSION

Ronald Reagan loved to tell jokes, including ones where Reagan was his own punchline. At the 1986 White House Correspondents Dinner, the president deadpanned: "I don't know about you, but I've been working long hours. I've really been burning the midday oil."[19] The next year Reagan returned to the same well: "It's true hard work never killed anybody, but I figure why take the chance?"[20]

Yet popular impressions are not systematic evidence. This chapter sought to test the behavioral foundations underlying presidential operations by capitalizing on the striking contrast between Jimmy Carter and Ronald Reagan. To start, I argued that Presidents Carter and Reagan were not merely different people with different philosophies; they also approached their work as president differently. When it came to work stamina, they differed. When it came to work priorities, they differed. When it came to work efficiency, they differed.

The key question, then, is not whether Carter and Reagan were different people—they certainty were—but whether the institutional presidency rendered their differences moot. When it came to doing the job, did Presidents Carter and Reagan serve as more or less "generic" actors playing a well-defined organizational role, or did their interpersonal differences manifest in the ways they performed the job?

Situating Jimmy Carter's and Ronald Reagan's first terms as a critical test case—two very different people, holding the same office, in sequence, switching on a predetermined date—and then analyzing comprehensive archival records about their daily work behaviors, from start to finish, on stage and behind the scenes, I tested whether (and how) who is doing the job affects how the work gets done.

The results were clear, consistent, and compelling: Carter worked differently than Reagan; Reagan worked differently than Carter. Carter worked longer hours, packed more in, and put greater emphasis on interacting with top administration officials; Reagan worked shorter hours, at a lower rate, and put a premium on public relations. Neither my theory nor these results speak to which approach was more effective, but they do establish that just because presidents inherit a "standard" organization does not mean they adhere to a "standard" operation. Far from it.

Having emphasized the strength of these data and the clarity of these results, I hasten to note their limits. My decision to focus on Jimmy Carter and Ronald Reagan reflected a purposeful choice to maximize internal validity by minimizing confounding factors as much as practicable. This served its intended purpose, but it leaves open the issue of external validity. In particular, do Carter and Reagan signal a general pattern, or are they merely the extreme ends of a normal distribution? Chapter 3 takes up this question.

3

MAKING TIME

DURING THE 1960S, PROFESSOR CARROLL Quigley taught Georgetown students about the rise and fall of civilizations. Among his lessons was the tantalizing observation that history's great leaders seemed to need less sleep than ordinary men. The evidence was shaky, but one student's conviction was not. Bill Clinton concluded that sleepiness was weakness and committed to sleeping no more than 5 hours per night.

The habit became a hallmark. Clinton's long hours and late nights were well publicized during his presidential campaign, and sleeplessness quickly became a distinguishing feature of Clinton's presidency. Barely an hour into his first day, President Clinton began his remarks at the Statuary Hall Inaugural Luncheon with a confession: "I'd like to begin by saying I didn't get much sleep last night, and if I get through this, it will be tour de force."[1]

For aides, obliging President Clinton's late-night work habits came with the job. John Podesta, Clinton's final chief of staff, described the experience: "One of the things that would drive me crazy the most was that Clinton is a total night owl and I'm an early-morning person. So the phone would ring at 2:30 in the morning and I would shoot out of bed . . . I'd think, 'Oh, s—t, something bad must have happened.'

But most of the time, he was watching C-SPAN and wanting me to call some senator and correct what he said."[2]

Bill Clinton's successor, George W. Bush, preferred a different schedule—one with an early start, a hard stop, and a good night's sleep. A few months after the inauguration, the *New York Times* reported that "[President Bush] usually arrives at the Oval Office by 7 A.M. and is out the door by 6:30 P.M., often for dinner at the residence."[3] Nearly eight years later, the *Times* reaffirmed that "Mr. Bush has always been an early-to-bed, early-to-rise kind of guy."[4]

That Presidents Clinton and Bush 43 favored distinct schedules is hardly remarkable. Some people are night people; some people are morning people. What is more surprising is that the nation's most important job did not demand concessions. Clinton was not compelled to arrive for the early shift; Bush was not compelled to stay for the late shift. On the contrary, it seems that the respective presidents set their respective schedules, and their respective aides adapted in response.

To be sure, public portraits tend to caricature presidents. Unique features are enhanced. Distinctive habits are embellished. Idiosyncratic tics are exaggerated. So even though I showed in chapter 2 that Carter and Reagan worked differently, and there is good reason to believe that Clinton and Bush 43 did as well, the general question remains: Is there something of a standard work shift in the modern presidency from which some presidents occasionally (but conspicuously) deviate, or do presidents really define for themselves what constitutes a good day's work?

Clearly, I expect the latter. In chapter 1, I showed how presidents' stamina differences affect the amount of work they do and also the types of work they do. The presumption, naturally, is that some presidents are more willing to, or more capable of, working long hours.

This chapter maps theory to history. More precisely, I investigate whether different presidents have, in fact, worked different hours. I begin by introducing an innovative dataset of presidential work during a representative sample of days from 1961 to 2008, Kennedy to Bush 43, which affords an unprecedented look into when presidents work, for how long, and what explains the variations.

MARKING TIME

The White House has long produced two versions of the "president's schedule." The first, released publicly, discloses basic information about the next day's docket, as well as guidance for reporters, such as which press credential is required at each event.

The second schedule, distributed among a small cadre of staffers, tenders a minute-by-minute rundown of the president's planned activities for that day, including public events *and* private meetings. This version also includes a stern warning: "This schedule contains sensitive information and is provided for your information only. It may not be distributed, forwarded, or printed without the express written permission of the Director of Scheduling."[5]

There are good reasons that White House officials screen presidential activities from public view: security precautions, diplomatic delicacies, privacy protections, political cover, deliberative candor. Nevertheless, this sort of pervasive screening complicates academic research. Whereas presidents' public activities are easily analyzed, the vital work occurring behind the scenes remains hidden from public view, shielded from scholarly scrutiny.

It is no coincidence that research on the presidency's inner workings remains mostly impressionistic, stylized renderings sketched from an assemblage of insider interviews, contemporaneous reports, retrospective memoirs, or archival materials. John Hart's reflection from a prior generation remains just as apt today: "The most obvious and by far the most important constraint on presidency research is that access to the object of study is severely restricted."[6]

As I introduced in the preceding chapter and explicate further in appendix A, there is one archival record that defies the White House's standard practice of studied censorship: the Daily Diary. Unlike schedules, which anticipate the president's day, the Daily Diary is compiled after the fact to record the president's actual activities and interactions. Again, presidential libraries make the point better than I can, as epitomized by the Richard Nixon Presidential Library and Museum's holding description: "The Daily Diary of files represents a consolidated record of the President's activities. The Daily Diary chronicles the activities of the President, from the time he left the private residence until he retired for the day, including personal and private meetings, events, social and speaking engagements, trips, telephone calls, meals, routine tasks, and recreational pursuits. For any given meeting, telephone call, or event, the Daily Diary usually lists the time, location, persons involved (or a reference to an appendix listing individuals present), and type of event."

Because the Daily Diary approximates a comprehensive record of presidents' work, the question becomes how best to extract those contents faithfully. Seeking to navigate the nearly 18,000 Daily Diaries in the public domain (1961–2008), I fashioned a sampling strategy that satisfied two objectives: the first and foremost was generating a representative sample within each year; the second was permitting valid comparisons across years (and, in turn, presidents).

Befitting these dual aims—reliability and comparability—I employed a random sample, stratified by month (4 days per month), but defined by *day* rather than *date*. My sample does not include September 3 each year; rather, it contains every "first Wednesday in September." This random sample coupled with a quasi-matching design produces a representative sample of days within each year, and it also better ensures that comparisons across presidents (or years) reflect real behavioral differences and not merely variations in the mix of days sampled. Appendix B details the full sample frame and audits the sample of days and data it yielded.

To appraise presidents' stamina—defined here as how long a president is willing and able to work—research assistants scoured each sampled Daily Dairy to code the minute when the first work activity began and the minute when the last work moment ended.[7] Computing the interval between the two yielded each day's work duration.[8]

Measuring stamina this way has several advantages. Instead of trusting popular reputations or journalistic reports, this measure builds from presidents' concrete behaviors in the context of actual work for a representative sample of days. Constructing a behaviorally derived estimate of "stamina" thus allows me to examine each president's variations and make presidential comparisons. Furthermore, because the unit of analysis is the day (rather than the president), I can test whether variations move with national conditions, political imperatives, individual inclinations, or the unpredictable pull of idiosyncratic events.

PUNCHING IN

During the 2008 Democratic primary campaign, Hillary Clinton put out a spot entitled "3 A.M." Over pictures of children sleeping and the sound of a phone ringing, a narrator intones the following:

It's 3 A.M. and your children are safe and asleep.
But there's a phone in the White House and it's ringing;
Something's happening in the world.
Your vote will decide who answers that call,
Whether it's someone who already knows the world's leaders, knows
    the military—someone tested and ready to lead in a dangerous world.
It's 3 A.M. and your children are safe and asleep.
Who do you want answering the phone?[9]

Such ominous imagery plays to a popular narrative: the presidency as the site where leaders must make fateful decisions at a moment's notice. The world is a stage, and the president is its star.

Mercifully, the movie version of presidential work is fundamentally fiction. After reviewing presidents' crisis management through history, Tevi Troy concluded, "I have to say that it's mostly myth to think that any president is ever asked to make such critical decisions in the middle of the night . . . even if there is a crisis, the wakeups are often unnecessary."[10] The reality, which advisors know well, is that when the president needs to make a tough decision, it is far better if he does so after a good night of sleep, a strong cup of coffee, and a methodical review of information.

Protecting the president's downtime, especially sleep, is an instinct all White House workers internalize. Former White House officials say that waking the president is a provocative step, partly because the president needs sleep, but mostly because it would be odd for an issue to arise for which the president has not already provided sufficient guidance to make it through the night.[11] As one former senior administration official told me, "Almost nothing goes exactly as planned, but if you do a good job of planning, almost nothing catches you completely off guard."

The glaring exception would be an attack. That is the exceptional circumstance in which only the president can act *and* only has a few minutes to act. A version of this situation materialized in 1980 when, a few hours before dawn, a military aide woke National Security Advisor Zbigniew Brzezinski with news that two hundred missiles had just been launched from the Soviet Union toward North America. As Brzezinski processed the report, defense officials reviewed the data. Within a few minutes—and literally moments before Brzezinski placed a wakeup call so President Carter could decide the U.S. response—military officials realized their warnings were wrong. It was a false alarm.

This sort of destructive slipup exemplifies why presidential aides strive to give their boss vigilant analyses, not raw intelligence. When news breaks—day or night—subordinates' impulse is not to disturb the president so much as it is to dive into the work good staffers do: gathering information, developing options, honing analysis, and crystallizing arguments.[12] The "3 A.M. calls" are far more likely to wake staffers than the president.

Dipping into systematic data confirms this intuition. Excluding travel, only 5 of 904 days studied here saw the president start work before 5 A.M. Four of those were Lyndon Johnson. One (April 6, 1965) occurred just after Johnson decided to escalate the U.S. military operation in Vietnam; another (June 5, 1968) was the morning Robert Kennedy was assassinated in Los Angeles. The only non-Johnson instance came on June 12, 2005, when George W. Bush's workday began at 4:25 A.M. Although the contents of that specific diary entry remain redacted, the likelihood is that it covered breaking news from Iraq: that day four U.S. soldiers were killed by roadside bombs, and twenty Sunni Arabs' bodies were discovered (bound and shot) in a shallow grave just outside the city.

For the other 99 percent of days, the presidents' work did not start in the wee hours. Figure 3.1 displays the distribution of presidential start times between 1961 and 2008 (excluding travel days). From the early 1960s into the early 2000s, presidents' typical start time fell between 7 and 9 A.M., with the overall median start time coming just after 8 A.M. Simply put, typical workdays started at typical worktimes, and very few days started before dawn.

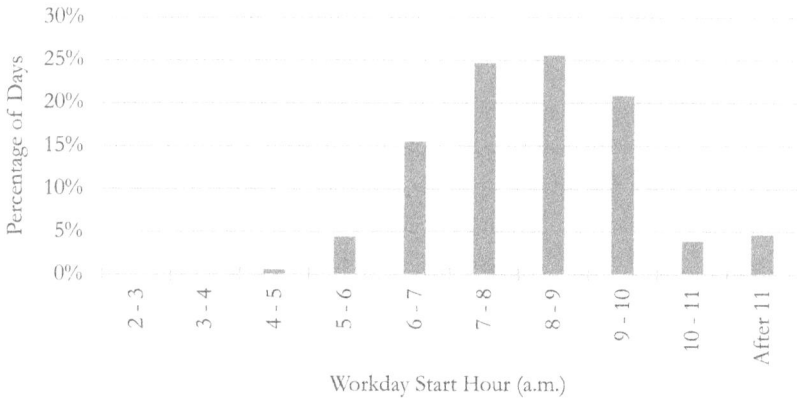

FIGURE 3.1 Start times for presidential workdays (excluding travel), 1961–2008.

Dependent variable: start time of the president's first work activity during a representative
sample of days each year, 1961–2008

The fact that overnight interruptions rarely rouse presidents to work raises the question of what does. It turns out the answer is mostly the presidents themselves.

Figure 3.2 illustrates each president's median start time during nontravel days. At one end of the spectrum are the early birds, starting with Carter, the president whose average workday began around 6:30 A.M. The second-earliest presidential start times were the Bushes, 41 and 43, at approximately 7 A.M. The other president who punched in earlier than the average was Gerald Ford. The median Ford workday started at 7:45 A.M.

Those presidents who were a slower to move from the residence to the Oval Office include Johnson and Clinton, who started around 8:30 A.M., as well as Nixon and Reagan, who typically got to work at 9 A.M. John Kennedy usually hit the Oval Office a few minutes before 9:30 A.M.

The details about when presidents punched in are fascinating on their own, but for my purposes, the more interesting discovery is the variation. The fact that some presidents tended to start early, some presidents tended to start late, and some presidents adopted something of a "typical" start time provides the first clue that

Median Workday Start Time

	5a	6	7	8	9	10	11	12p

Carter

Bush 43

Bush 41

Ford

Johnson

Clinton

Nixon

Reagan

Kennedy

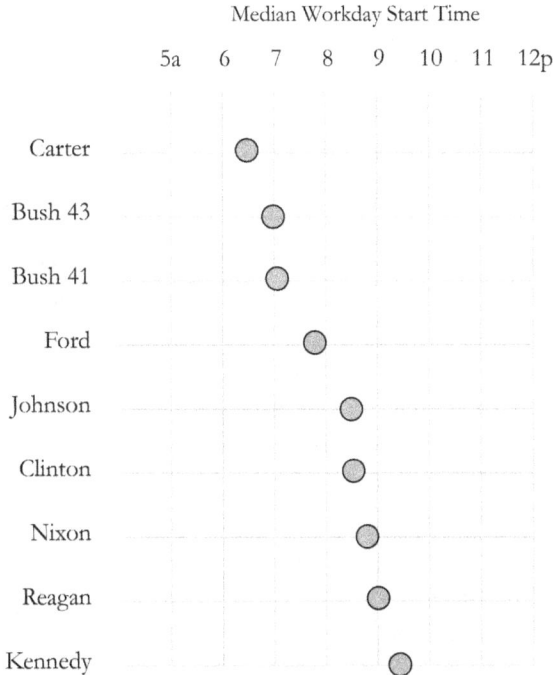

FIGURE 3.2 Median start times for presidential workdays (excluding travel), by president, 1961–2008.

Dependent variable: median start time of the president's first work activity during a representative sample of days each year, 1961–2008

presidents shape their own schedules. Indeed, having seen evidence that presidential starting times vary by president, let me now turn to their ending times.

PUNCHING OUT

President Obama sometimes called himself a "night guy," and by all accounts, he was. Having handed the president draft remarks for his Nobel Prize acceptance speech one evening, Jon Favreau was not particularly surprised when Obama returned with edits and ideas the following morning.

Then again, one must take staff-sourced reports with more than a grain of salt. Presidential aides impulsively cast their boss as a tireless workaholic. David Gergen, a Reagan communications aide, offered a master class: "At day's end, [Reagan] headed off for a workout and would plow through more papers in the evening in the upstairs residence. He made the presidency look easy in part by keeping a strict regimen." A different Reagan aide went even further: "After a couple weeks, a message came back down from Mrs. Reagan asking us not to send so much up in the evening because he would read it all."[13]

Auditing such claims is complicated, in no small part because the White House residence is designed to guard presidents' privacy. This is why the Daily Diary details when the president goes to the residence but not what he does once there. Indeed, unless the president makes a phone call or takes a scheduled meeting—activities that are memorialized in one of many automated logs and thus integrated into the diary—neither friend nor foe (let alone a prying academic) can tell if the president spent his evening revising a Nobel Prize acceptance speech or rewatching *The Sound of Music*.[14]

That said, there is good reason to suspect that solitary work in the residence constitutes a relatively small fraction of presidents' daily work. Presidents cannot get much done without help. It is the staff who know the issues; it is the staff who know the players; it is the staff who know the arguments. Moreover, because the staff must implement whatever decisions the president makes, staffers need to know what the president is doing—and vice versa.

What about the president's nightly briefing book? Elite interviews and archival research indicate that evening briefing books are usually prosaic—a way to prep the president for the next day's work.[15] If the president has a meeting, the briefing book specifies the purpose, the attendees, and the agenda. If the president has a speech, the briefing book gives the venue, the participants, and a draft of the remarks. If the president has a dinner, the briefing book includes a rundown of the evening, a profile of the guests, and a summary of the menu. Presidents do not typically "read" these materials in the normal way; rather, they skim to get a feel for what is on the horizon and, if necessary, flag items they wish to add or extend, edit or omit, clarify or amplify, and so on.

For my purposes, therefore, the end of the workday is the last recorded work activity in the Daily Diary. Although this excludes presidents' solitary work in the residence, it does capture the bulk of presidential work, including the most important moments. On this point, one respondent invoked a useful metaphor: "The president has a lot of energy. Our job is converting latent to kinetic." Adapting her line to my measures, I capture the kinetic portion of presidential work—those activities that occur with others or outside the confines of the president's private quarters.

Whereas sleep imposes something of a natural barrier to presidential start times, there is no comparable obstruction to working late. Take dinner. Whereas hunger can force many people to quit work, dinners at the White House are as much an opportunity to make an ally as to eat a meal. A president's dinner guests enjoy a surreal experience—one of those moments people tell their grandkids or, in the Washington tradition, write about in their memoirs. As stories go, it is hard to beat after-dinner cordials on the Truman balcony, pre-release movies in the White House theater, or late-night cigars on the Rose Garden patio.

Given the possibilities, it is no surprise that presidents' end times are more variable than their start times. Still, the details are telling. Figure 3.3 lays out the timing of presidents' final work activity on nontravel days.

The most conspicuous takeaway is how frequently workdays bleed into worknights. On average, a president ends work before 6 P.M. less than once a week. While the median end time is 9 to 10 P.M., nearly half of presidential days have at least one work activity coming after 10 P.M. And almost 1 in 3 days see the president's final work activity wrap up after 11 P.M.

Another noteworthy tidbit is that weekends do not provide much respite. The president's last work moment ends during the day's final hour for 29 percent of weekdays and weekends alike. Likewise, the median end time is between 9 and 10 P.M. on both weekdays and weekends. This does not mean that presidents' weekdays and weekends are indistinguishable—indeed, I will soon show that they are different in a myriad of ways—but it does mean that presidents rarely get a genuine day off.

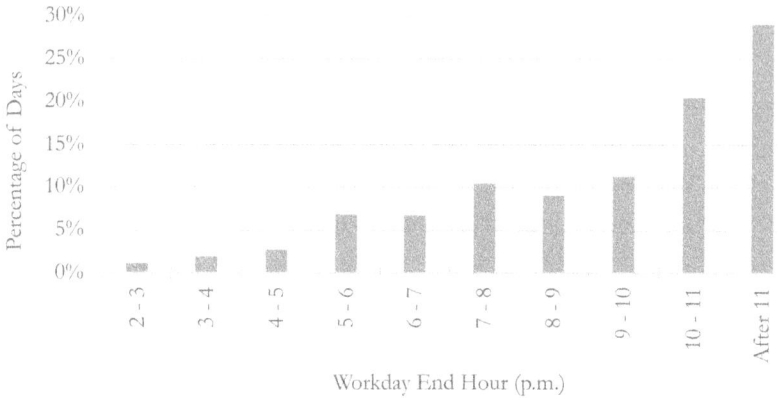

FIGURE 3.3 End times for presidential workdays (excluding travel), 1961–2008.

Dependent variable: end time of the president's last work activity during a representative sample of days each year, 1961–2008

Whenever presidents make time to get some exercise, go on a date, or catch a ballgame, their spokespeople hasten to note that the president is not really skipping work because the president is always at work. It is more than a convenient talking point. For the select few who ascend to the nation's highest office, every day is a workday, and workdays usually extend well into the evening, if not late into the night—weekends included.

Because the Oval Office never closes, the workday's limiting principle tends to be the president's limits. The workday does not end when the work is done; it ends when the president says "uncle."

Yet not all presidents are equally disposed to tap out. Some relish assembling late-night festivities with a revolving cast of lawmakers, diplomats, donors, celebrities, academics, aides, friends, and who knows who else. Others crave the opportunity to step off the incessant merry-go-round of early mornings, busy days, and late nights. The decision about when to call it quits says as much about a president's personality as his endurance.

Figure 3.4 displays each president's median end time, sorted from earliest to latest, which confirms that there is nothing like a regular "quitting time" in the modern presidency. Typical weekdays have

Median Workday End Time

5p   6   7   8   9   10   11   12a

Bush 43

Kennedy

Bush 41

Reagan

Nixon

Ford

Carter

Johnson

Clinton

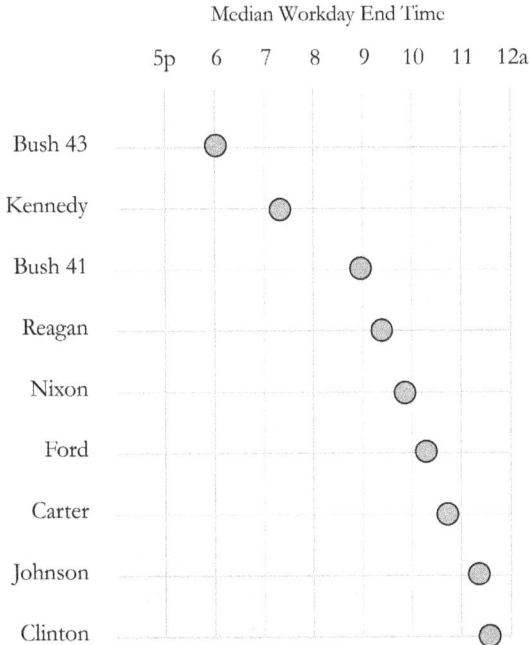

FIGURE 3.4 Median end times for presidential workdays (excluding travel),
by president, 1961–2008.

Dependent variable: median end time of the president's last work activity during a
representative sample of days each year, 1961–2008

ended as early as 5:40 P.M. (Bush 43 in 2005) and at late as 11:52 P.M.
(Clinton in 2000).

If Clinton and Bush 43 provide a study in contrasts, their example is
extreme but not unusual. Presidents differ, and the real lesson is that
each president fills a distinctive lane. Between the earlier finishers (e.g.,
Bush 43) and late finishers (e.g., Clinton) are presidents who run the
quitting-time gamut: Kennedy (7:25 P.M.); Bush 41 (9:00 P.M.); Reagan
(9:25 P.M.); Nixon (9:52 P.M.); Ford (10:20 P.M.); Carter (10:42 P.M.); and
Johnson (11:15 P.M.).

Having seen how presidents' end times differ, it is worth mentioning that little except for the presidents themselves appears to explain
the differences. There is no evident secular trend, no persistent partisan

divide, or any obvious circumstantial explanation (e.g., war or recession) underlying the general patterns. Indeed, this preliminary look into historical practices hints that the presidency's work shifts are calibrated to each president's work style.

That said, while timing and duration are surely related, they are not the same. It is possible that the early bird and night owl could work different hours but equivalent shifts. So even as details about when presidents work—when they start, when they stop—form the building blocks of how long presidents work, it is important to note that my theoretical variable of interest (i.e., stamina) is not "when" but "how long."

ON THE CLOCK

Having seen the variety in presidents' typical start and end times, my next scholarly step considers the duration between the two. To what extent do presidents' workday durations vary, and to what extent do presidents themselves explain how long the workday lasts?

As mentioned, the results to this point have been suggestive but not definitive. One cautionary note is that differences in median start and end times could obscure relative continuity in daily duration. A related caveat is that focusing on medians ignores variations, and it is possible that overall differences are less reliable than they appear on the surface. Another caveat is the perennial one: "correlation is not causation." In this case, the worry would be that president-specific differences are but a mirage formed by circumstances that merely correlate with different presidents.

By taking these possibilities seriously and tackling each empirically, I can clarify the nature of presidents' workday durations and, even more, the factors that help explain the ebbs and flows. On that journey, I start with a few basic facts about presidents' workday durations between 1961 and 2008.

- The overall *median* day stretched to 12 hours, 46 minutes.
- In all but four years (1962–1963, 1988, and 2007), the typical day's work extended beyond 10 hours.

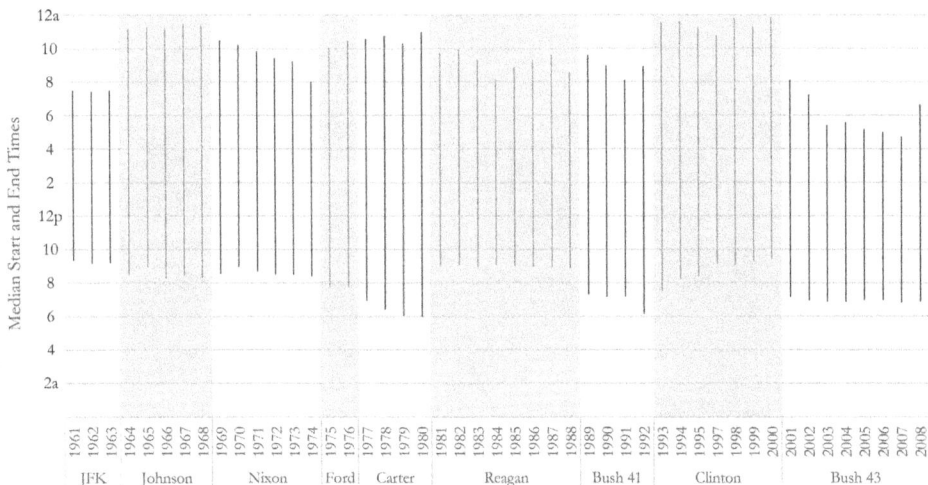

FIGURE 3.5 Median start and end times for presidential workdays,
by year, 1961–2008.

Dependent variable: median start and end time of the president's work activities during a
representative sample of days each year, 1961–2008

- In seven years (1977–1980, 1993–1994, and 1996), the typical day's work
  extended beyond 15 hours.
- In no year did the typical day see the president work less than
  9½ hours.

The presidency is a taxing job in many ways, and one of those ways
is the staggering hours it requires. It is for good reason that reporters
routinely consider presidential candidates' "fire in the belly" for doing
the job. The daily grind is a long grind.

Figure 3.5 combines each president's median start and end times
by year, 1961–2008. I have already reviewed the patterns in broad
strokes, but a few details deserve elaboration.

First, we again see that the modern presidency has nothing like
a set workday. Putting aside weekends/holidays and days when the
president traveled, a president's typical days are still anything but.
The 25th percentile day lasted 11 hours, 7 minutes; the 75th percentile was 15 hours, 3 minutes. Nobody suspected the presidency is a

FIGURE 3.6 Interquartile range of time between first and last work activity, by president.

9-to-5 job, but it is nonetheless useful to nail down just how long presidential workdays last.

If the range of workday durations is substantial, it is far from random. In fact, how long a president works is closely related to who is president. As Figure 3.6 shows, some presidents worked relatively shorter days (e.g., Kennedy, Reagan, and Bush 43); some presidents worked relatively longer days (e.g., Johnson, Carter, and Clinton); some presidents were in between (e.g., Nixon, Ford, and Bush 41). Again, every president puts in long days by conventional standards; however, some put in a long day by presidential standards.

Notably, these findings are robust to various ways of analyzing the data. For example, comparing successive presidents on either side of inauguration days (e.g., the final 6 months of one president versus the first 6 months of the next) also shows large president-specific differences. So too if we compare presidents at equivalent points in their terms (e.g., year 1 to year 1, year 2 to year 2, etc.).

Figure 3.7 demonstrates the idea. Focusing on presidents' workday durations during each president's third year (of their first term)—a relatively stable window after the honeymoon and before

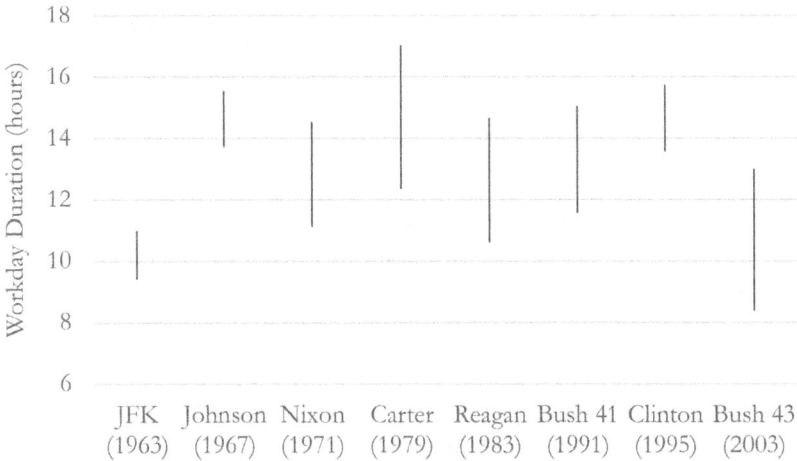

FIGURE 3.7 Interquartile range of time between first and last work activity in presidents' third year in office.

the reelection campaign—reaffirms how differently presidents worked. Here we see the interquartile range of presidential workday durations for each president at a comparable juncture of their respective tenures. What we see is that Clinton (in 1995) averaged almost 5 additional hours per day on the clock compared to Bush 43 (in 2003); Kennedy (in 1963) averaged 4 ½ fewer hours per day than Johnson (in 1967); and Nixon (in 1971) averaged 3 fewer hours per day than Carter (in 1979).

That speaks to a pattern that is less striking but no less important: each president exhibits relative consistency throughout their years as president. The basic pattern is that presidents tend to set *their* standard workday early on and then stick to it. Looking at yearly averages, the standard deviation across all years for all presidents is 107 minutes, which is considerably larger than the standard deviations within each presidency: Kennedy (3 min.); Johnson (56 min.); Nixon (102 min.); Ford (36 min.); Carter (20 min.); Reagan (34 min.); Bush 41 (50 min.); Clinton (71 min.); Bush 43 (54 min.). In other words, there is a lot of variability in how long presidents work, but most of that variation is between presidents, not between days or years.

There is a crucial exception to the general rule of intra-president consistency, one I examine in depth in chapter 5 but will foreshadow here as well. It is Nixon, specifically Nixon in 1974. As the Watergate scandal grew ever more dire, Nixon's work routines broke down. The manifestations were manifold, as I will show, but one part of it was that Nixon's workday shrank. From 1969 to 1973, Nixon's median day lasted almost 13 ½ hours per day. In 1974, it fell to 10 hours per day. So although stamina is generally a stable feature of a president's work behavior, there is some variability—and one outlier.

So far, then, the evidence indicates that (a) there is substantial variation in how long presidents work and (b) much of that variation appears centered on the president. This evidentiary combination squares nicely with my hypothesis: each president has limits, and the nature of a president's limits affects the nature of that president's work. Presidents often present as superheroes, but there is no mistaking that they are human, all too human.

TESTING DURATION

The descriptive results so far point to each president's primacy in setting his work schedule. For a more definitive test, however, I must consider how well workday durations map onto personal differences while also accounting for national conditions, political context, and the stochastic "noise" of daily events.

Inasmuch as national conditions drive presidents' schedules, two key "fundamentals" should structure presidents' days: prosperity and peace. I thus include measures of economic recessions (months within a recession as defined by the National Bureau of Economic Research) and military conflicts (U.S. military combat fatalities during each quarter, logged).[16] Since these two factors underlie so many dynamics in American politics, there is good reason to expect that a slow economy or an active war will induce presidents to work longer days.

For political circumstances, I add a suite of variables that reflect standard cycles of a presidential term. The first is the president's honeymoon year—the first 6 months of the inaugural year after winning a presidential election—when the president is learning the job and when policymaking options are best.[17] In addition, I include the president's reelection period (the last 6 months of a president's reelection year), term (first or second), and the lame duck period (days after a president loses reelection or from July to inauguration in his eighth year, plus Lyndon Johnson's final 6 months after he announced he would not run for reelection in 1968).

Finally, closer to ground, the model includes weekends and federal holidays, as well as days the president spent at least a portion of the day outside Washington, D.C. Accounting for off-days and travel days helps ensure that I am comparing presidents on comparable days.

In the interest of transparency, I first test these "presidency-centered" variables as model I before adding "president-centered" fixed effects as model II. Because the latter model is more theoretically interesting and statistically reliable, I focus my attention there except by way of comparison.

Table 3.1 relays the full results, but the bottom line is plain enough: the multiple regression results corroborate the descriptive ones that precede them. That is, both point to the fact that presidential workday durations are distinctive to each president, different from other presidents, and reliably so.

The first tell is that the R^2 for model I—the "presidency-centered" model that includes national conditions, political circumstances, and assorted control variables—is just 0.12, indicating context does not drive presidential workday duration. Contrast that to model II, which has all the same variables as model I but also includes president-specific fixed effects. With the presidents added, the R^2 moves up all the way to 0.94[18]

Digging deeper puts a finer point on it. For a standard day—a nontravel weekday during a period without recession or war, in the first term but not during the honeymoon, reelection campaign, or lame duck period—the model predicts that a generic president's day will last just over 13 ¼ hours. Thus if all I knew was that the president was working a typical day during a typical period (i.e., a weekday, without travel, during the first term, outside of the honeymoon, reelection, or lame duck periods), I would predict he would work a bit more than 13 hours.

TABLE 3.1 Ordinary least squares multiple regression, predictors of presidential workday duration

	COEFFICIENT (ROBUST-SE)	
	MODEL I	MODEL II
NBER[a] recession during month (1 = recession)	−20 (10)	9 (11)
Combat fatalities during quarter (logged)	1 (2)	1 (3)
Honeymoon year (first 6 months after first election)	6 (14)	13 (14)
Reelection year (last 6 months of reelection year)	−14 (33)	−23 (27)
Lame duck year (post-loss or last 6 months of second term)	61* (18)	9 (19)
Term (1 = second term)	−90* (13)	−58* (14)
Kennedy	—	577* (16)
Johnson	—	884* (23)
Nixon	—	758* (24)
Ford	—	856* (24)
Carter	—	903* (20)
Reagan	—	695* (18)
Bush 41	—	833* (13)
Clinton	—	924* (25)
Bush 43	—	711* (20)
Constant	796* (14)	
R^2	0.12	0.94
N	1,781	1,781

Note: Dependent variable: minutes between the president's first and last work activity during a representative sample of days each year, 1961–2008. The analyses exclude days that lack a Daily Diary. The models also control for weekends and federal holidays, as well as days the president spent at least some of the day outside Washington, D.C. Standard errors clustered by month.
*$p < 0.05$.
[a]NBER = National Bureau of Economic Research.

However, to make a prediction based on those parameters alone is to ignore the most relevant information—namely, who is president. Figure 3.8 illustrates the equivalent estimate but tailored to each president (ordered shortest to longest). Clearly, knowing who is president substantially alters (and greatly improves) the forecast

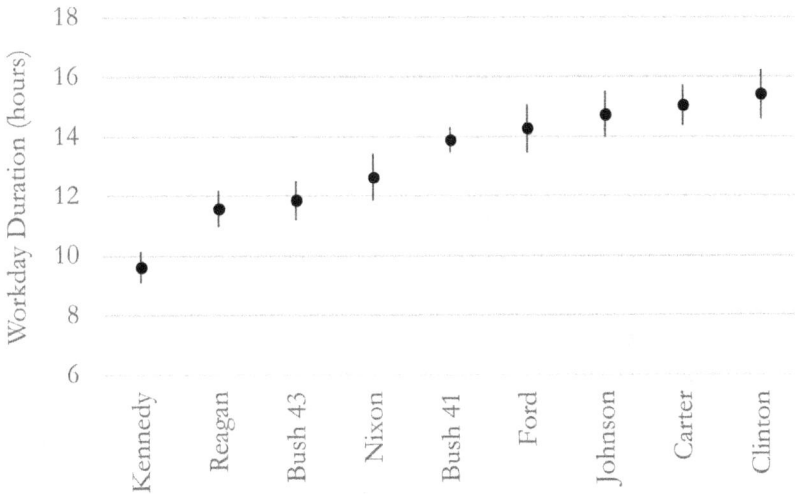

FIGURE 3.8 Predicted workday duration (hours), by president.

This is the predicted workday duration (± 2 standard errors) for each president on a typical day—a day not during a recession or war; not during the honeymoon, reelection campaign, or lame duck period; not during a weekend or national holiday; and not when the president was traveling outside Washington, D.C.

about how long that president will work. To know who is to know how long.

Take President Kennedy. Under the conditions previously described, Kennedy's predicted day would last 9 ½ hours. That is not just a full 3 ½ hours less than the "generic" prediction; it is also significantly below each of his actual successors. When it came to work stamina, Kennedy's level was distinctively low, significantly so.

Now consider President Clinton, the chief executive who loved work and loathed sleep. Replacing Kennedy with Clinton bumps the workday forecast by 153 percent—from 9 ½ hours (for Kennedy) to more than 15 hours (for Clinton). The "generic president" estimate is not wrong, necessarily, but it is most certainly lacking.

Importantly, one need not reach to the extremes to isolate presidential fingerprints. Actually, only Bush 41's predicted workday duration (13 hours, 54 minutes) is statistically indistinguishable from the generic prediction of 13 hours, 15 minutes. Kennedy, Reagan, Bush 43, and Nixon were significantly below the omnibus expectation; Ford, Johnson, Carter, and Clinton were significantly above.

To complete the thought, table 3.2 displays all presidential pairwise comparisons after controlling for the day's economic, security, and political context. Taken together, these tests confirm just how distinctive each president's work patterns have been over the last half century. Fully 25 of the 36 dyads have a statistically significant difference, and many of the comparisons that show no reliable difference are among presidents who pressed the upper bound of presidential stamina: Clinton, Carter, Johnson, and Ford.

Many details corroborate conventional wisdom. John Kennedy's workdays were significantly shorter than Lyndon Johnson's; Jimmy Carter's workdays were significantly longer than Ronald Reagan's; Bill Clinton's workdays were significantly longer than George W. Bush's.

TABLE 3.2 Pairwise comparisons for president fixed-effects coefficients in multiple regression, model II

	KENNEDY	JOHNSON	NIXON	FORD	CARTER	REAGAN	BUSH 41	CLINTON
Johnson	+							
Nixon	+	–						
Ford	+	n.s.	+					
Carter	+	n.s.	+	+				
Reagan	+	–	n.s.	–	–			
Bush 41	+	n.s.	+	n.s.	–	+		
Clinton	+	n.s.	+	n.s.	n.s.	+	+	
Bush 43	+	–	–	–	–	n.s.	–	–

Note: Table indicates pairwise comparisons (chi-squared, Wald test of equivalence) between president fixed-effects coefficients in table 3.1, model II. Specifically, it demonstrates the direction (+ meaning "greater than," – meaning "less than") and significance (p < .05) of the difference (n.s. means difference is not statistically significant) between the coefficient for the president in the row from that of the president on the column. For example, Richard Nixon's workday was significantly longer than for Kennedy and Bush 43; significantly shorter than for Johnson, Ford, Carter, Bush 41, and Clinton; and not significantly different from Ronald Reagan (all else being equal)

On the other hand, several findings cut against popular impressions. Jerry Ford, for example, is rarely remembered as a workaholic, yet in these results, he resides in the same class as Lyndon Johnson, George Bush 41, and Bill Clinton. While Gerald Ford did not get the chance to serve a full term, his window in the White House exemplified the old adage "The days are long, but the years are short."

Another unexpected result is that Richard Nixon's, Ronald Reagan's, and George W. Bush's workdays were statistically similar in terms of their duration, all else being equal. The model predicts that each would put in approximately 11 ½ to 12 ½ hours from the start of their first work activity to the end of the last, with the modest differences therein being statistically insignificant. So, although Nixon, Reagan, and Bush 43 were different in any number of ways, their work stamina was equivalent.

That finding leads to my final discovery: external forces have only a modest relationship with presidents' workday durations. Neither recessions nor wars reliably alter how long a president works. Nor do well-known cyclical features of presidential terms: the honeymoon, the reelection campaign, and the lame duck period. One contextual variable that does dependably forecast presidents' workdays is the second term, which trims about 1 hour off a president's predicted workday.[19] The other is "nonwork" days. After controlling for other factors, I find that Saturdays, Sundays, and holidays run about 2 ½ hours shorter than an analogous weekday.

Considering this rich set of systematic data on the overall duration of presidents' workdays, two lessons have stood out. The first is that there is substantial variability in how long presidents work. While all worked a long day by normal standards, the spreads ran from 9 ½ hours per day on one end to more than 15 hours on the other. For presidents, every day is a workday, most workdays are long days, and many workdays seem to last all day.

That first revelation punctuates the second: the ups and downs in workday durations are almost wholly explained by the presidents themselves. Presidents did not adopt *a* standard workday; rather, each president forged *his* standard workday. When it comes to presidential scheduling, the president dictates the terms—and times.

CONCLUSION

Thomas Jefferson described the presidency as a "splendid misery" in 1797, and the label still fits. The modern iteration still presents extraordinary highs and lows, often concurrently. The possibilities are limitless, the obligations are relentless, the clock never stops, the opposition rarely concedes, and the press seldom looks away.

As per usual, Richard Nixon brainstormed about how he could square the circle: "I have learned through the years that the most important asset a leader can have is the ability to concentrate on those subjects in which what he says or does can make the difference and to delegate to others all other subjects that really do not require his attention."[20]

Nixon's conclusion is interesting as far as it goes, but equally interesting is what it leaves out: the president could sleep less, skip breaks, forsake family, reject recreation, forgo exercise, and just work longer. I suspect that Nixon does not contemplate these possibilities because they appear nonsensical. From his perspective, he is running at full capacity, so to say "work longer" is akin to saying "grow taller." It is a theoretical possibility but not a practicable option.

As I see it, Nixon is basically right. Presidents do not call it a day because they are bored; they call it a day because they are spent. They can push to their limit, but they cannot push beyond their limit. Nixon's median workday lasted more than 12 hours. Could he have stretched it to 15? In theory, yes. In practice, no.

But looking at this topic president by president misses the bigger picture. The fact that each president works to his limit does not mean that all presidents have the same limit. While all presidents have worked long days on most days, some presidents worked *relatively* shorter days (e.g., Kennedy, Reagan, and Bush 43), others worked *relatively* longer days (e.g., Johnson, Carter, and Clinton), and others filled the range in between (e.g., Nixon, Ford, and Bush 41). Such peculiarities were apparent in the descriptive analyses and reliable in the statistical tests.

Mapping the foundation of presidents' work has thus shown that a typical day in the presidency has been determined more by the occupant than by the office or context. For start times, end times, and the duration between the two, modern presidents have tended to operate on their own schedule throughout their presidency, varied conditions and circumstances notwithstanding. Indeed, every run of the data returned the same result: the presidency does not impose its schedule on presidents; presidents impose their schedule on the presidency.

Now, having interrogated the presidents' workday duration, we turn to the obvious follow-up: What about composition? What do presidents do with the hours they have? Do all presidents end up following a similar routine (albeit at different paces), or does each president mold the work to fit his style? Such is my focus for the next chapter.

4

FILLING TIME

APPROACHING HIS FIRST TERM'S FINAL YEAR, President John F. Kennedy opted to kick-start his reelection campaign with a 2-day, five-city barnstorm across Texas. Day 1 included rallies in San Antonio and Houston before the president headed to Fort Worth for the night.

Then came day 2. Ahead of his scheduled itinerary, Kennedy briefly strolled outside his hotel—the aptly named "Texas Hotel"—for an impromptu address to onlookers corralled in a nearby parking lot: "There are no faint hearts in Fort Worth, and I appreciate your being here this morning. Mrs. Kennedy is organizing herself. It takes longer, but, of course, she looks better than we do when she does it."[1]

Kennedy headed inside and soon addressed the Fort Worth Chamber of Commerce about military preparedness, particularly Texas's crucial role therein. The presidential party then went to Carswell Air Force Base (in Fort Worth) for the brief 13-minute flight to Love Field (in Dallas).

Jack and Jackie deplaned toward an energetic audience straining to glimpse America's first couple. Amid the barrage of pictures, waves, and cheers, the president and first lady made their way to a customized 1961 Lincoln Continental four-door convertible for a deliberately slow-paced 10-mile drive into downtown Dallas.

As the presidential motorcade turned past the Texas School Book Depository at Dealey Plaza, three shots rang out. President Kennedy was struck by the latter two, once in the head, once in the neck. The presidential limousine raced to nearby Parkland Memorial Hospital, but there was nothing doctors could do. A priest administered last rites; the president was pronounced dead.

Walter Cronkite, CBS's news anchor, broke the terrible news: "From Dallas, Texas, the flash, apparently official: President Kennedy died at 1 P.M. Central Standard Time—2 o'clock Eastern Standard Time—some 38 minutes ago."[2] The news was as hard to believe as it would be impossible to forget. Americans reeled as much as they grieved.

Mere hours later—at 6:10 P.M. on November 22, 1963—Lyndon Johnson addressed the country for the first time as president of the United States. Standing on the Andrews Air Force Base tarmac, speaking in somber tones, he offered just fifty-eight words: "This is a sad time for all people. We have suffered a loss that cannot be weighed. For me, it is a deep personal tragedy. I know that the world shares the sorrow that Mrs. Kennedy and her family bear. I will do my best. That is all I can do. I ask for your help—and God's."[3]

"I will do my best." It was a modest promise—and a revealing insight. Lyndon Johnson did indeed throw himself into his work as president. His days were long; his schedule was packed.

Consider Tuesday, April 21, 1964. Johnson's workday began at 7:15 according to the Daily Diary: "awake—tea in bed—discussions with J.V. [Jack Valenti]." A while later, at 8:40, Johnson made his way to the president's dining room for breakfast with congressional leaders. At 9:30 he strode down the hall to the Oval Office, where he spent the next hour and a half making one call after another:

9:35	McGeorge Bundy (national security advisor)
9:41	Dean Rusk (secretary of state)
10:17	Robert McNamara (secretary of defense)
10:24	Larry O'Brien (assistant to the president)
10:25	Mrs. Anderson (Adam Yarmolinsky's nurse at Arlington Hospital)
10:55	Dorothy Nichols (personal secretary to the president)
11:00	McGeorge Bundy (national security advisor)

During that last call, McGeorge Bundy asked if he could add an unplanned visitor to the day's itinerary. Johnson responded plaintively at first—"If you find me a place to do it . . . I've got the damnedest schedule, I can't even see my wife"—but then quickly relented: "Well yea, if you want me to see him, go on, put him down there. That's alright."[4]

So it went. When Hurricane Betsy battered New Orleans on September 9, 1965, 140-mph winds destroyed homes and buildings. Subsequent flooding destroyed far more. Seventy-five people died.

An aide suggested that Johnson visit the stricken area, but the president balked because he had "a hell of a two days" already on the books. However, Johnson abruptly changed his mind—and schedule. Within 24 hours, the president was on the ground, surveying the damage, commiserating with victims, and speaking to reporters: "I have just completed an extensive tour of New Orleans and the surrounding area. I am saddened by the damage and the suffering that I have seen. . . . But I am determined that we can help these people in every way that human compassion and effective aid can serve them. I have ordered that all red tape be cut."[5]

Lyndon Johnson's example is entirely unique yet utterly familiar. As ever, the exact details change but the general pattern endures. No matter how much a president does, there is always something else; no matter how much a president plans, there is always something new. Everything is important, and there is no substitute for the president himself.

Drawn between infinite possibilities and finite hours, presidents must decide what to do. Which appearances should I make? Which calls should I take? Which speeches should I give? Which places should I visit? Which events should I host? Which meetings should I attend? And, of course, which assemblage of advisors, officials, or guests should join me at each? On the front lines, matters of leadership manifest as questions of time.

As I have told it, part of what makes this operational puzzle difficult to solve is that there are so many pieces. Another complication is that the picture is usually blurred, if not ever-changing. Ultimately, though, the real problem is that there is no "correct" solution. Scheduling is a process as much as a result, and the preferred time allocation depends as much on the president's judgment as on the particulars of the activities, the demands of the moment, and the context of the times.

This chapter affords a new, methodical look at how presidents fill their workdays. I investigate whether different presidents do indeed work differently in terms of the number of tasks they do (quantity), the number of tasks they do per hour (pacing), the sorts of tasks they do (thinking versus speaking), and the types of people they encounter along the way (breadth and depth).

THE DAILY DOCKET

Having reviewed details about the Daily Diary in previous chapters— as well as its history in appendix A and my sample in appendix B— I now get to the heart of the matter: the contents.

At the risk of repetition, I hasten to reiterate that what makes Daily Diaries so valuable for studying presidents' work is that they so carefully log what the president did. February 21, 1972, is illustrative. That was the day Nixon touched down in China, or as the diary put it, "The President and the First Lady flew by the 'Spirit of '76' Hung Chiao Airport, Shanghai to Capital Airport, Peking, PRC." It then lists Nixon's in-flight meetings:

10:00–10:11	Mr. Kissinger
10:05–10:07	Mr. Haldeman
11:05–11:25	Miss Woods
11:28–11:29	Miss Woods

The diary records the plane landing at 11:30 A.M. "China Time." "The President, the First Lady and members of the official U.S. party deplaned. For a list of members of the official U.S. party, see Appendix D. The Presidential party was greeted by Chou En-lai, Premier of the State Council of the PRC, and other PRC officials. For a list of the Chinese officials, see Appendix E."

This was the moment in which President Nixon and Premier En-lai famously shook hands before proceeding on the drive, during which En-lai told Nixon, "Your handshake came over the vastest ocean in the world—twenty-five years of no communication." [6]

Although Nixon's landing and greeting received worldwide attention, the day's most intriguing episode remained screened from public view: the moment when Chairman Mao invited President Nixon to his house for an unscheduled visit. Though the historic meeting was kept hidden at the time, it was dutifully logged in the day's presidential Daily Diary:

2:42　　　The President and Premier Chou motored from Taio Yu Tai to Chungnanhai, the residence of Mao Tse-tung, Chairman of the Politburo of the PRC.

2:50–3:55　The President met with Chairman Mao. Also in attendance were:
Premier Chou
Wang Hai-jung, Deputy Director of the Protocol Department of the Foreign Ministry
Mr. Kissinger
Tang Wen-sheng, Interpreter for the PRC

"Nixon to China" has become a metaphor as much as a moment. But it was a moment—actually, a week filled with moments: greetings, meetings, meals, motorcades, and calls—punctuated by various "made for television" events. Reporters eagerly covered the president's *public* activities; diarists judiciously documented the president's *public and private* activities.[7]

CONTENTS

Through Nixon's opening day in China, we observe several important details about the diaries' contents. First, entries are organized by "moments." Unlike a standard personal diary, which presents stylized reflections about the day's events, the presidential Daily Diary is a precise log of the president's activities—by the moment, to the minute.

Distinctive activities are memorialized as discrete moments. A meeting is a moment; a call is a moment; a flight is a moment; a motorcade is a moment; an interview is a moment; a speech is a moment; a movie is a moment; a ceremony is a moment. In essence, the diary tracks the president through the workday, logging each activity, starting with the first and ending with the last.

Logging the president's activities involves recording metadata about each activity. Each diary moment is detailed for the time it began, the time it ended, and who was present (people are listed by full name and title the first time they show up in a diary, then by honorific and last name every other time they appear).[8] Moments with phone calls indicate whether the call was "placed" or "received." Most moments include a brief descriptive title (e.g., "Breakfast with Congressional Leaders" or "Press Conference in the East Room").[9]

Another integral feature about the Daily Diaries' contents also bears repeating: diarists constructed each diary shortly after the fact to record the president's actual work activities, whether or not those activities were planned in advance, and whether or not those activities were disclosed to the public.[10] The diarists' charge was to document, faithfully and fully, work activities that the president personally executed and people with whom the president personally engaged. As one former director of the presidential libraries system told me: "The Daily Diary is an important historical record in its own right. . . . It is also important because it is a roadmap for everything else."[11]

A typical workday generates a 3- to 5-page diary. A light day with little work—for example, Christmas Day—will fill a page or two; a long and busy day will run much longer. The Daily Diary for September 11, 2001—the fateful day that terrorists hijacked and crashed commercial airliners in New York, Washington, and Pennsylvania—extends 23 pages (appendices included).

CODING

The sheer volume of Daily Diary records necessitated a regimented routine for turning diaries into data. In formulating this coding scheme, I strove for codes that captured each moment while also facilitating reliable comparisons across moments. Appendix C explains the specific coding choices and procedures that were implemented to those ends.

For the purposes of this chapter, the bottom line is that my research team and I tracked down every available diary for every day identified per the sampling design. Research assistants (RAs) scoured through each diary to identify every presidential "moment" that lasted 5 or more minutes. The coding protocol had RAs extract details about when each moment occurred, what the president was doing, and who else was present.

This project's most valuable research innovation was the coding scheme. Rather than strive to transcribe the diaries' every detail, our coding endeavored to systematize presidential activities into "categories" and presidential contacts into "types." This approach helped make the data analytically useful, but it had the added benefit of making the data collection more efficient, as I explain.

The activity categories had RAs flag whether the president was working in that moment (as opposed to being at leisure or doing something "unknown") and, if so, what the nature of that work was: the president was alone, in a meeting (in person or over the phone), giving a speech, holding a press conference, granting an interview, attending a ceremony, traveling, or doing something else (unknown). As will soon become apparent, this systematic coding allowed us to nail down what presidents have done during each day for nearly 2,000 days.

Similarly, to capture who was with the president, we coded whether different "types" of people were present during each moment. These types included various White House officials, Cabinet officials, lawmakers, or assorted outside actors (e.g., everyone from state officials to foreign officials, political candidates to members of the public). Again, appendix C explicates these points.

The upshot is that we turned a representative sample of Daily Diaries' contents into systematic codes that yielded a large dataset covering more than 1,700 days and 30,000 moments spread across forty-eight years and nine presidents. The breadth and depth of these data afford an unprecedented look at how presidents operate the presidency—day to day, month to month, year to year, and president to president.

TASKS AND TIME

This chapter began with Johnson showing how even a president with the "damnedest schedule" is tempted to add one more event, make one more call, grant one more meeting, shake one more hand, and take one more picture.

Eventually, though, every president hits a wall. When David Gergen joined the White House just a few months into Bill Clinton's presidency, he found that the president "was almost too tired to think straight." Having previously seen that different presidents work different hours, I now turn to how they fill whatever hours they put in.

GENERAL PATTERNS

For a first glimpse into how presidents fill their workdays, I begin with a simple dependent variable: the number of distinct work activities that presidents performed during each day. Figure 4.1 illustrates presidents' median weekday work activities during each year, 1961–2008.

To nobody's surprise, presidents are busy. Between 1961 and 2008, the presidents studied here executed 14 discrete work activities on a typical day (15 on weekdays, 6 on weekends). That presidents can

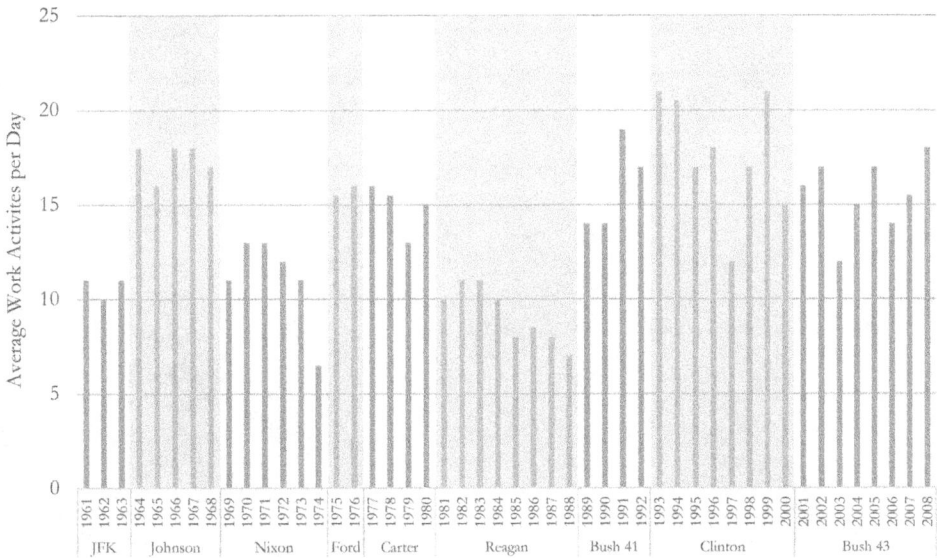

FIGURE 4.1 Median number of presidential workday activities, by year.

Dependent variables: For each "moment" of every in-sample Daily Diary,
research assistants coded what the president was doing, how long it lasted,
and whom he was with. The data here indicate the median number
of daily work activities the president performed that year.

maintain such a high pace over such a sustained period reflects White House staffers' ability to keep the president moving from this to that, here to there, tomorrow as today.

However, there is quite a bit of variability. It is not merely that some days are busier than others; some years are busier than others. At one extreme is Nixon in 1974, when the president managed just 6 to 7 daily tasks through his final calendar year in office.[12] At the other extreme is Clinton, who averaged 23 separate work activities per day through 1993.

Digging further, figure 4.2 shows presidents' median daily work activity against their median daily work duration, in hours, during

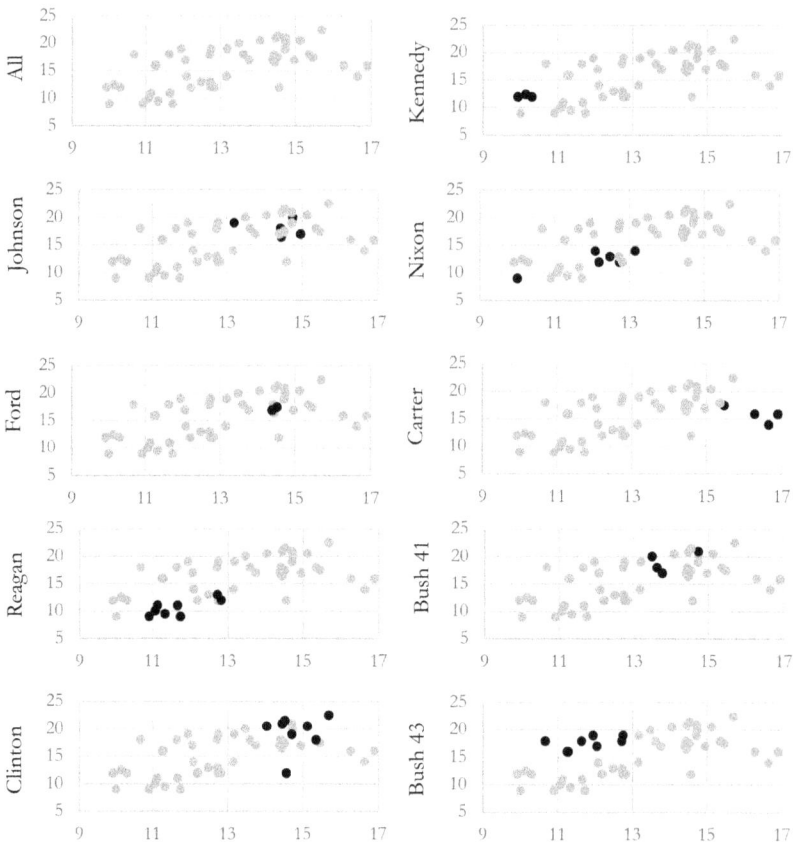

FIGURE 4.2 Yearly median number of workday activities by median number of workday hours.

each year of their presidency. Clearly, there is a strong, positive relationship between a president's workday duration and his workday activity. The correlation between hours and tasks is 0.51 across all days and 0.52 for median hours and activities across years. Working longer generally means doing more, and vice versa.

If stamina surfaces as one engine of activity, what about efficiency—activities per hour? Do some presidents move through their workload faster or slower than others? Revisiting figure 4.2 clarifies that although longer days are informative, they are not determinative.

Take George W. Bush, the only president who was below average in hours but above average in activites. Indeed, even as Bush 43's typical workday duration was relatively short (comparable to Ronald Reagan's), his activity level was relatively high (comparable to Gerald Ford's). By moving from one activity to the next so expeditiously, Bush 43 was able to chart a distinctive course: workdays that were relatively short but also relatively busy.

Another standout case in point is Jimmy Carter, though in the opposite direction. As we saw before, Carter worked extremely long days nearly every day. Now we can see that he did not proceed through those days at a particularly quick clip. Carter was at the very top of the duration scale but only slightly above average on the activity scale.

Notice, too, that whereas most presidents generally maintain a fairly steady pace—activities and hours alike—there are some interesting exceptions. There is the singular case of Nixon during Watergate, which I take up in the next chapter, but also Reagan through his second term. After four years during which Reagan's daily activity level hovered between 11 and 13 distinct work moments per day, his second-term work rate fell to 9 to 10 work events per day.

The bottom line is that the main variability in presidential activity levels occurs between presidents, not days or years. That is to say, the correlation between work hours and work activities does not appear because presidents spend some years working short, light days and other years logging long, full days. Instead, what figure 4.2 illustrates is that presidents mostly cluster in a specific region of the broader distribution. Reagan clustered toward the bottom, Nixon clustered toward the middle, Bush 41 clustered toward the top, and so on.

Again, this need not be the case. One could easily imagine a world in which presidential schedules are forged by circumstances, leaving little room for presidential discretion and less room for presidential differences. But that is not the evidence we observe. Instead, I find that how much a president squeezes into a workday is mostly related to the president himself. To know how much a president will do is to know who is president—and vice versa.

That said, the analyses to this point merely reflect simple averages and rudimentary comparisons. They do not capture the variability of presidential work patterns, nor do they systematically test alternative explanations, including mere chance. On that issue, I turn to a more rigorous examination.

TESTING ACTIVITY

To better investigate whether presidents' stamina and efficiency help explain their overall activity levels, I return to the multiple regression model from the previous chapter. Specifically, to examine whether such interpersonal differences predict daily work activity, I apply a statistical model that tests presidents' daily activity levels while controlling for national conditions, political context, and/or random chance. Having detailed these measures in the preceding chapter, I will only present a brief refresher here.

For national conditions, I include measures of economic recessions (i.e., months within a recession as defined by the National Bureau of Economic Research) and military conflicts (i.e., U.S. military combat fatalities during each quarter, logged).

To account for presidents' political circumstances, I include the president's honeymoon (i.e., the first 6 months of the inaugural year after winning a presidential election), reelection period (i.e., the last 6 months of a president's reelection year), term (i.e., first or second), and the lame duck period (i.e., days after a president loses reelection or from July to inauguration in his eighth year, plus Lyndon Johnson's final 6 months after he announced he would not run for reelection in 1968).

Finally, the model controls for weekends and federal holidays, as well as days the president spent at least a portion of the day outside

Washington, D.C. In this way, we get a better comparison of comparable workdays—that is, typical weekdays inside the White House.

Lastly, I estimate the relationship between presidents and presidential work with fixed effects for each president (model I). Then,
to partition stamina from efficiency, model II adds the day's work
duration as an independent variable. As such, model I tests whether
presidents' daily task levels were distinctive, controlling for national
conditions, political circumstances, and random chance; model II
clarifies whether any such differences were better captured by the
president's stamina (through the duration coefficient), efficiency
(through the fixed-effects coefficient), or some combination of both.

The results, detailed in table 4.1, make it clear that presidential
work patterns are not responsive to situational factors, at least not in
any fundamental way. Neither recessions nor wars, neither the honeymoon nor the lame duck period, and neither the reelection campaign
nor the second term reliably forecasts how many work activities a
president will pack into a day. On the presidential stage, changing the
set does not induce a president to add or delete scenes.

To be sure, the fact that prevailing conditions and underlying circumstances do not predict presidents' activity does not mean that
presidents' work is unpredictable. Far from it. The R^2 for model I is
0.86; for model II it is 0.88. Thus arrives the main result: presidents'
work activities are again best explained by the presidents themselves.
In fact, the details tell the story.

Looking at the presidential fixed effects in model I clarifies each
president's expected activity level under equivalent conditions. To
illustrate, let us set presidents into a first-term weekday in Washington, when the country is facing neither war nor recession, and
outside the honeymoon, reelection campaign, or lame duck period.
With their context thus standardized, we still find large, reliable differences by president. Kennedy and Reagan set the floor at 13 tasks
per day, while Johnson and Clinton set the ceiling at 22. The other
presidents filled the range in between: Nixon (15); Carter (17); Bush 43
(18); Ford and Bush 41 (19).

Given such stark differences in how many tasks presidents take on
(all else being equal), the theoretical question resurfaces: Do these
behavioral disparities reflect differences in stamina and/or efficiency?

TABLE 4.1 Ordinary least squares multiple regression, predictors of presidential workday activity level

	COEFFICIENT (ROBUST-SE)	
	MODEL I	MODEL II
NBER[a] recession during month (1 = recession)	0.8 (0.4)	0.7 (0.4)
Combat fatalities during quarter (logged)	0.0 (0.1)	0.0 (0.1)
Honeymoon year (first 6 months after first election)	1.0 (0.5)	0.9 (0.5)
Reelection year (last 6 months of reelection year)	0.9 (1.0)	1.2 (0.9)
Lame duck year (post-loss or last 6 months of second term)	0.0 (1.3)	−0.1 (1.2)
Term (1 = second term)	−1.0 (0.6)	−0.4 (0.5)
Duration of workday (hours)	—	0.6* (0.1)
Kennedy	13.4* (0.8)	6.8* (1.0)
Johnson	21.6* (1.1)	11.8* (1.5)
Nixon	15.1* (1.1)	6.6* (1.4)
Ford	19.1* (0.9)	9.6* (1.4)
Carter	17.1* (1.0)	7.1* (1.4)
Reagan	13.0* (1.0)	5.2* (1.3)
Bush 41	19.2* (0.8)	9.9* (1.1)
Clinton	21.6* (1.1)	11.4* (1.7)
Bush 43	18.4* (1.3)	10.4* (1.6)
R^2	0.86	0.88
N	1,781	1,781

Note: Dependent variable: total number of work activities the president executed during a representative sample of days each year, 1961–2008. The analyses exclude days that lack a Daily Diary. The models also include variables for weekends and federal holidays, as well as days the president spent at least some of the day outside Washington, D.C. Standard errors clustered by month.

[a]NBER = National Bureau of Economic Research.

*p < 0.05.

Model II attempts to disentangle the two. Regarding stamina, these results confirm that work hours are a modest but reliable predictor of presidential work activity (b = 0.6, SE = 0.1, p < 0.05). Controlling for conditions and circumstances, to go from a 10- to 15-hour workday is to handle an extra three work tasks—calls, meetings, travels, speeches, ceremonies, interviews, or the like.

But if stamina sets the base of each president's workday activities, efficiency adjusts how high the bar will rise. This is what we find via the presidential fixed-effects coefficients in model II, which detail each president's expected tasks *controlling for the length of his workdays.*

For an illustrative example, I contrast Kennedy and Johnson. While I have already shown that Kennedy worked substantially shorter days than Johnson, these results show that Kennedy also worked at a slower pace than Johnson. Indeed, if both presidents were forced into a 10-hour workday (holding all else equal), Kennedy would process 13 work activities while Johnson would complete 18.

This comparison is but an example of the general pattern: president-specific differences in work efficiency abound. Some presidents packed more work events into each hour (Johnson and Clinton); some presidents had fewer events per hour (Kennedy, Nixon, and Reagan); some presidents fell in between (Ford, Carter, and both Bushes).

Whereas all presidents encounter unlimited demands, we now know that presidents process that workload in distinctive ways. The number of discrete work tasks a president handles depends in part on how long his workday lasts (stamina) and in part on how much he packs into each hour (efficiency). In fact, when it comes to understanding the quantity of work activities that presidents perform day to day, year to year, a president's stamina and efficiency hold far more explanatory power than national conditions or political circumstances.

A TIME TO THINK, A TIME TO SPEAK

Having interrogated how many activities pack presidents' workdays, I turn to the logical follow-up: what those activities entail. Given my interests, how much time do presidents invest in thinking and speaking activities? Does time spent on one activity come at the expense of the other (or merely make for long, busy days)? And do presidential time allocations derive from national conditions, political circumstances, presidential particulars, or some combination of each?

Before jumping into answers, I hasten to note that appraising presidents' work composition is no easy chore. After all, a president's world is filled with one-offs—moments defined by exceptional settings, scripts, and casts. One day has Kennedy calling the defense secretary about missiles in Cuba; another has Clinton praying for the bombing victims at the Federal Building in Oklahoma City; a third sees Nixon ushering Elvis into the Oval Office; a fourth finds Reagan face to face with Gorbachev in Reykjavik.

Luckily for my purposes, the distinct details are less important than the general form. My theory does not predict specific moments per se; rather, it speaks to the overall allocations of time across general classes of work—namely, speaking and thinking. My coding scheme (introduced previously and detailed further in appendix C) allowed me to measure how much time the president spent on thinking and speaking activities.

MEASURING TIME

Theoretically, I conceptualized *thinking time* as the time that presidents allocate to the business of governance, particularly decision-making as the nation's chief executive. To operationalize "thinking time" required identifying those moments that the president was working alone (within the workday) or engaged with government officials—excluding speeches, press conferences, interviews, travel, ceremonies, fundraising or campaigning, public or press relations, or a reception or party.[13]

Having isolated moments in which the president was primarily "thinking," I then summed how long those moments lasted. The result is my thinking time variable: the total number of minutes the president spent engaged in "thinking" activities during each day. During the typical weekday, presidents averaged a little more than 5 hours of thinking time.

The flip side of the thinking time is *speaking time*. We identified speaking time as those moments when the president was engaged in any of a myriad public-facing activities: speeches, press conferences, interviews, travel, ceremonies, or moments when the president was otherwise focused on fundraising or campaigning, public or press relations, or a reception or party.

As with the thinking measure, knowing which moments the president engaged in speaking activities allowed me to compute the total time those moments lasted. The corresponding speaking time variable thus indicates the total number of minutes the president spent engaged in speaking activities during each day. The median weekday included 1 hour and 47 minutes of speaking time.

Hewing to my theoretical model, these coding rules treat thinking and speaking as mutually exclusive activities. Thus any given moment can count as thinking time or speaking time (or neither), but not both. An economic briefing in the Cabinet Room may immediately precede an economic speech in the Rose Garden, but I code the former as thinking time, the latter as speaking time. By my lights, these reveal two distinct phenomena—conceptually and, in turn, operationally.

GENERAL PATTERNS

Figure 4.3 illustrates the distribution of presidents' weekday thinking and speaking time. Among the stimulating findings is the fact that the president's typical day includes far more time thinking than speaking. More than 75 percent of weekdays had more thinking time than speaking time; the presidents' modal weekday included 5 to 6 hours of thinking time and 0 to 1 hour of speaking time.

Beyond the central tendencies, it is also interesting that speaking and thinking patterns follow distinct distributions. Whereas thinking time fits something of a normal distribution (centered around 5 to 6 hours), speaking time approximates something like a Poisson distribution—a low mean but long right skew. So whereas presidents' days almost always include a substantial amount of thinking time (3 to 9 hours), speaking activities usually get a more modest allocation (under 2 hours), though they sometimes eat up a substantial portion of the day (3 to 6 hours). Rarely do speaking activities take up most of a president's day (more than 6 hours).

These results hold several important lessons. First, covering presidential work vis-à-vis a president's public activities (as in most news coverage) gives a distorted view of presidential work. The reality is that most of a president's day occurs behind the scenes. This is true for the vast majority of days and every president.

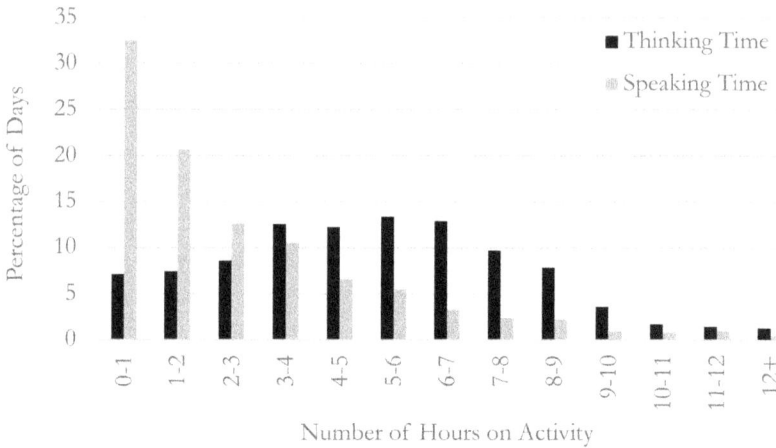

FIGURE 4.3 Distribution of workday speaking and thinking time (in hours).

Dependent variables: For each "moment" detailed in the Daily Diary, research assistants coded what the president was doing and how long the activity lasted. Activities were sorted into "thinking" or "speaking" (or neither) categories, and the figure here reflects the total time spent on each. Appendix C details the coding rules and results.

The other point, not as obvious in the graph as in the data, is that scheduling choices across activity classes demand trade-offs. For weekdays, the correlation between minutes spent thinking and minutes spent speaking is −0.31. Somewhere along the line, the price of adding a public event is the cost of attending a policy meeting.

To investigate president-specific imprints more directly, figure 4.4 plots each president's median weekday breakdown of time speaking and thinking. If presidents are more or less generic and their workdays more or less comparable, we would expect every president to cluster around the bull's-eye. If, however, different presidents build distinctive workdays, we would expect their time plots to scatter. Scattered they are.

At one extreme—the low extreme—is Ronald Reagan. Compared to the other presidents studied here, Reagan's days tended to be relatively porous, light on speaking time *and* light on thinking time. Reagan spent about 1.5 hours per day engaged in speaking activities plus another 4.0 hours engaged in thinking activities.[14] Like Reagan,

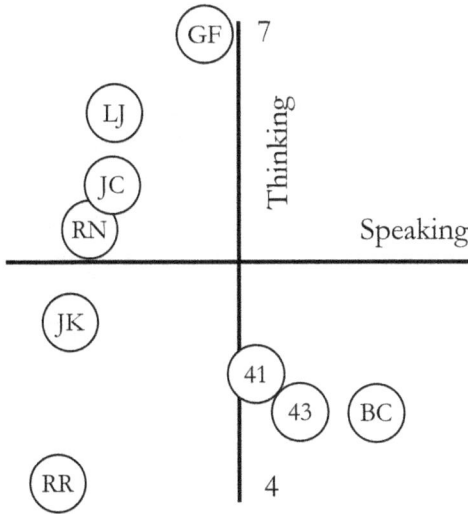

FIGURE 4.4 Median workday speaking and thinking time (in hours),
by president.

Kennedy also scored low on speaking time; however, he fell near the
middle of the pack regarding thinking time, which accentuates how
sparse Reagan's schedule was by comparison.

Several other presidents maintained workloads akin to Kennedy's—
that is, relatively light on speaking time but relatively heavy on thinking time. This group averaged fewer than 2 hours per day on speaking
activities while assuming a relatively heavy thinking time load. Nixon
and Carter averaged about 6 hours of thinking time; for Johnson it
was about 6.5 hours; and Ford tipped the scale at 7 daily hours spent
on thinking activities.

On the other side of the board are presidents whose days were relatively long on speaking time but relatively short on thinking time.
Here fell Clinton and the two Bushes, 41 and 43. Though each still
averaged more time thinking than speaking, the breakdowns were
closer than their predecessors. So even though there is no straightforward secular trend overall, it is at least suggestive that the three
presidents who tilted most heavily toward speaking time vis-à-vis
thinking time were this study's most recent presidents.

Before proceeding to a more exacting analysis, it is worth mentioning that most presidents' work patterns pair well with popular impressions. For example, it is no surprise that Lyndon Johnson and Richard Nixon preferred to spend time in meetings rather than in public. Likewise, that Clinton blurred the divide between governing and campaigning is very on brand.

Other findings, however, cut against the grain, none more than the case of Jerry Ford. These results show that he was far from the amicable dunce that comics and critics often portrayed; they patently refute the notion that Ford spent more time golfing than working. Ford's workdays were not the longest, but they were the fullest.

TESTING THINKING AND SPEAKING

To check whether president-specific practices are as distinctive as they appear, I reapply the previous statistical model to these new dependent variables: thinking time and speaking time. As before, the goal is to clarify what drives presidents' work by accounting for those factors that plausibly underly its rhythms.

Table 4.2 details the multiple regression results for predictor variables of presidents' daily time spent on thinking and speaking activities. Importantly, I include each dependent variable as an independent variable for the other to test whether time spent on one activity class affects time spent on the other (as per my theoretical model). In fact, because thinking time and speaking time are so intertwined, I will toggle between the two models to appraise their collective insights.

Here, as before, most "context" variables shed little light on how presidents do their job. For thinking, the only variables reliably correlated with presidential thinking time are military fatalities ($b = 9$, SE = 3, $p < 0.05$) and a president's second term ($b = -20$, SE = 9, $p < 0.05$). The former indicates that the change from 0 to 400 military casualties during a quarter extends the president's day by almost an hour through that period. The latter result—that second terms correlated with shorter days—is more suspect given that it is mostly driven by Nixon's collapse and Reagan's slowdown, which are surely important but hardly structural.

TABLE 4.2 Ordinary least squares multiple regression, predictors
of daily thinking and speaking time (in minutes)

	COEFFICIENT (ROBUST-SE)	
	THINKING	SPEAKING
NBER[a] recession during month (1 = recession)	9 (7)	13 (10)
Combat fatalities during quarter (logged)	9* (3)	2 (2)
Honeymoon year (first 6 months after first election)	3 (13)	21 (15)
Reelection year (last 6 months of reelection year)	8 (13)	37* (15)
Lame duck year (post-loss or last 6 months of second term)	−9 (23)	−2 (20)
Term (1 = second term)	−20* (9)	18 (14)
Duration of workday (hours)	14* (1)	14* (1)
Speaking time (hours)	−15* (3)	—
Thinking time (hours)	—	−12* (2)
Kennedy	194* (18)	−24 (13)
Johnson	195* (27)	−35 (21)
Nixon	189* (24)	−53* (18)
Ford	249* (26)	20 (25)
Carter	171* (25)	−56* (17)
Reagan	130* (12)	−63* (13)
Bush 41	175* (14)	−10 (18)
Clinton	197* (15)	61* (27)
Bush 43	173* (19)	35 (21)
R^2	0.80	0.64
N	1,781	1,781

Note: Dependent variable: minutes the president spent on "thinking" and "speaking"
activities during each day for a representative sample of days each year, 1961–2008.
The analyses exclude days that lack a Daily Diary. The models also include variables for
weekends and federal holidays, as well as days the president spent at least some of the
day outside Washington, D.C. Standard errors clustered by month.
[a] NBER = National Bureau of Economic Research.
* $p < 0.05$.

What is more, the speaking time results indicate that the only situational factor that moves the speaking time needle is a presidential reelection campaign. Into the home stretch of their reelection campaign, presidents spend an extra 37 minutes per day on public-facing activities—ceremonies, speeches, interviews, and press conferences.

Beyond that, there is little to no evidence that presidential time investing in public relations ebbs or flows based on national conditions or political circumstances.

That gets to the more interesting and informative results—those linked to each president. First, I find that longer days are not just longer days; they also help the president spend more time doing work. An extra hour on the workday clock corresponds to an extra 14 minutes of thinking time and an extra 14 minutes of speaking time. In other words, a president's stamina helps sustain longer days, and those extra hours enable presidents to invest more time doing work.

But there is a critical wrinkle: there are only so many minutes a president can work, and a minute spent on one activity reduces the time available for others. Indeed, these results show that every extra hour spent on speaking activities costs the president 15 minutes of thinking time; every extra hour spent on thinking activities costs the president 12 minutes of speaking time. Put differently, time spent in ceremonies and speeches comes at the expense of time for meetings and readings. Presidents can extend the workday to create more time for work, but they can only use each minute once.

Having controlled for their circumstances, the presidential fixed-effects coefficients indicate each president's relative investment in thinking or speaking given the length of his workdays and the amount of time he spent doing the other activity. To facilitate interpretation, I situate each president into an equivalent day: a weekday during the first term, when the country is not facing recession or war, when the president is in Washington, D.C., and when not inside the honeymoon, reelection campaign, or lame duck periods. Moreover, I assume that each president is set to a 12-hour workday.

When it comes to time spent on thinking activities (assuming the president allocates 2 hours for speaking activities), these results show that most presidents put in 5 to 5 ½ hours of thinking work. Indeed, this is the predicted range for Kennedy, Johnson, Nixon, Carter, Bush 41, Clinton, and Bush 43. There are, however, two relative outliers, one low and one high. While Reagan sets the predicted thinking time floor at 4 ½ hours, Ford sets the predicted thinking time ceiling at 6 ¾ hours.

For speaking time (assuming the president allocates 5 hours for thinking activities), the model is less predictive overall and vis-à-vis each president. Only half of the presidents have results that are reliably different from the generic baseline based on broader conditions, workday duration, and thinking time. Nixon, Carter, and Reagan all fall significantly below the typical speaking time (by about an hour), whereas Clinton comes in significantly above (by about an hour).

Adopting a more holistic perspective, these results highlight how presidential time allocations correlate with how long each president works and also how he splits time between thinking and speaking. Figure 4.5 maps these lessons by plotting an "average" president's predicted thinking time across different scenarios. As it shows, extending the workday increases the time we would expect a president to spend doing thinking work; however, the exact level of thinking time drops as the level of speaking time increases.

To bring the point home, consider a president who logs a 10-hour workday one day and a 15-hour workday the next. If he allocates 2 hours per day for speaking activities, his predicted thinking time will be 4 hours, 46 minutes for the first day and 5 hours, 54 minutes for the second. If, however, the president ends up getting pulled into 4 hours of speaking work on any given day, his expected thinking time will be cut by a little more than 30 minutes. Thus a longer day can cover the thinking time deficit that extra speaking time imposes,

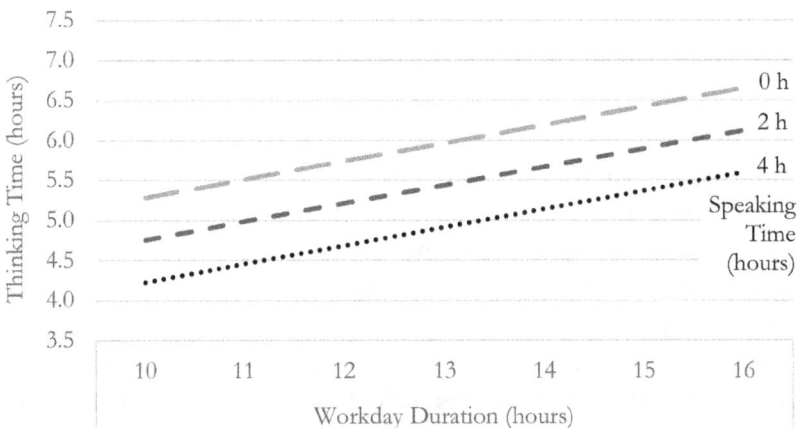

FIGURE 4.5 Predicted presidential thinking time (in hours),
by workday duration and speaking time.

but that is the point: each president can only do so much, and each president's limit forces trade-offs about what gets cut.

Then again, central tendencies show the big picture but sometimes overlook essential details. So it is with presidents. Reagan was significantly below average on both thinking and speaking time; Ford was significantly above average on thinking time; and whereas Nixon and Carter fell significantly short on speaking time, Clinton ran significantly long. Indeed, this is a recurring result: presidents routinely break whatever mold one tries to fit.

GRANTING AUDIENCE

For most people, the chance to meet a president presents a once-in-a-lifetime opportunity. As soon as it is scheduled, people start planning what they will wear and rehearsing what they will say. Everyone knows the moment will pass quickly, and nobody wants to miss their shot.

But if this is how practically everyone experiences (and imagines) a presidential encounter—that is, from the nonpresidential perspective—the real action is at the other side of the table. When everybody wants an audience with the president, the real question is not how it is received; it is how is granted.

This aspect of presidential scheduling—the "people" portion—can be easy to overlook. The challenge of sequencing the president's day is readily apparent; the challenge of choreographing who should join him along the way is more subtle. Yet people are as much a part of a president's schedule as time, and weaving the two is itself a full-time job. Gerald Ford saw this issue firsthand: "Every cabinet officer wants to see the President as often as possible, and [so do] other top people as well. The net result is there aren't that many hours in a day with all the other obligations that you have to handle on a daily basis."[15]

In the introduction and chapter 1, I reviewed how the modern presidency evolved to help presidents work more efficiently and effectively. To that end, I highlighted how the White House policy councils—the National Security Council (NSC), National Economic Council (NEC), and Domestic Policy Council (DPC)—were erected to streamline presidential deliberations by winnowing the people and information a president needs to see.

But if institutional edicts can guide access to the president, they do not render presidential discretion moot. Far from it. When push comes to shove, protocols yield to presidents, and, as a matter of fact, I expect that push rarely comes to shove precisely because aides purposefully tailor the president's schedule to fit the president's stamina, priorities and conditions, and efficiency.[16]

MEASURING PEOPLE

Before testing access to the president, it is useful to elaborate about what I expect—and do not. Actually, it is best to start with the latter point.

First, I do not have any firm view about the precise people or groups a president will meet on any given day. In my framing, an event with firefighters is equivalent to an event with teachers is equivalent to an event with Super Bowl champions. Likewise, a meeting with the director of the NSC is comparable to a meeting with the deputy director of the NSC. For my interest, the broader patterns are more important than the individual pieces.

Moreover, my model of presidential operations speaks to a president's workload, not the size of his audience. In terms of time, meeting a constituency's sole designated representative is no more or less burdensome than greeting all its members. That does not mean that all contacts are equivalent, but it does underscore an essential reality: work activities are not weighted by how many people are included.

Finally, my theorizing is indifferent to particulars like time, place, or method. By my lights, a presidential contact is a presidential contact whether it occurs in or out of Washington, D.C., in the Oval Office or the Rose Garden, in person or over the phone. Again, the relevant consideration is the president's limited bandwidth, not his location or chosen medium.

These conceptual moorings thus guided my methodological approach. Rather than catalog every person the president encountered, I sought to characterize the overall population—the forest rather the trees. To that end, I developed two measures of presidential contacts: their breadth and depth. Appendix C gives a full rendering, but I offer a synopsis here as well.

Breadth counts how many different types of people presidents encounter; *depth* counts how many contacts (of all types) presidents encounter. A president who scores high on breadth is one who meets many different types of people; a president who scores high on depth is one who meets many different types of people many different times.

My key task, therefore, was divining what "types" of people to code. Through an iterative process of trial and error, I ultimately honed a taxonomy detailing 21 people types, as listed in figure 4.6.

White House Officials
- Vice President
- Chief of Staff
- Domestic/Economic
- National Security
- Communications

Cabinet Officials
- State Department
- Defense Department
- Treasury Department
- Justice Department
- Central Intelligence Agency

Members of Congress
- Senate Democratic Leaders
- Senate Republican Leaders
- Other Senators
- House Democratic Leaders
- House Republican Leaders
- Other Representatives

Others
- Press
- Foreign Government
- State/Local Government
- Nongovernment Organization
- Private Individual

FIGURE 4.6 "People types" for coding presidential contacts.

No finite classification scheme will capture every presidential exchange, and mine certainly does not. But even though I miss contacts—for example, with family, secretaries, drivers, butlers, and outer cabinet officials—this coding does net the vast majority of presidential encounters, including the most important.

As before, RAs proceeded through each 5+ minute moment in every sampled Daily Dairy. For this portion of the coding, the RA looked at every person listed to see what "type" applied (if any). When one fit, the RA would check that box, thus indicating that that type of person was present at that moment. Summing all contacts across every moment for each day thus provided the two key variables: how many types of people the president encountered each day (breadth), as well as how many times he encountered them (depth).

GENERAL PATTERNS

To nobody's surprise, meetings and greetings are staples of presidential work. Most contacts are meticulously planned, though many arise on short notice, and some occur as mere happenstance. Even if presidents only see a small fraction of those hoping to be seen, in absolute terms, the number of people presidents encounter during any given day, week, month, or year is staggering.

Figure 4.7 adds some empirical meat to these intuitive bones by plotting the distribution of presidential contacts. The rows detail the "people types" already defined; the shading indicates how often each president encountered each people type during workdays of a typical month (i.e., 20 workdays).

Many patterns are consistent across all presidents, starting with presidential staffers' centrality in every president's orbit. Virtually all White House staffer types coded here saw their respective president more than once per workday, and several subsets encountered the president 3 to 4 times per day. There are variations between staffers and across presidents (discussed in following text), but the general trend is robust: nobody sees a president as often as that president's staff.

If presidents are flocked by their aides, they are far from trapped in a bubble. Presidents routinely meet many types of people, many

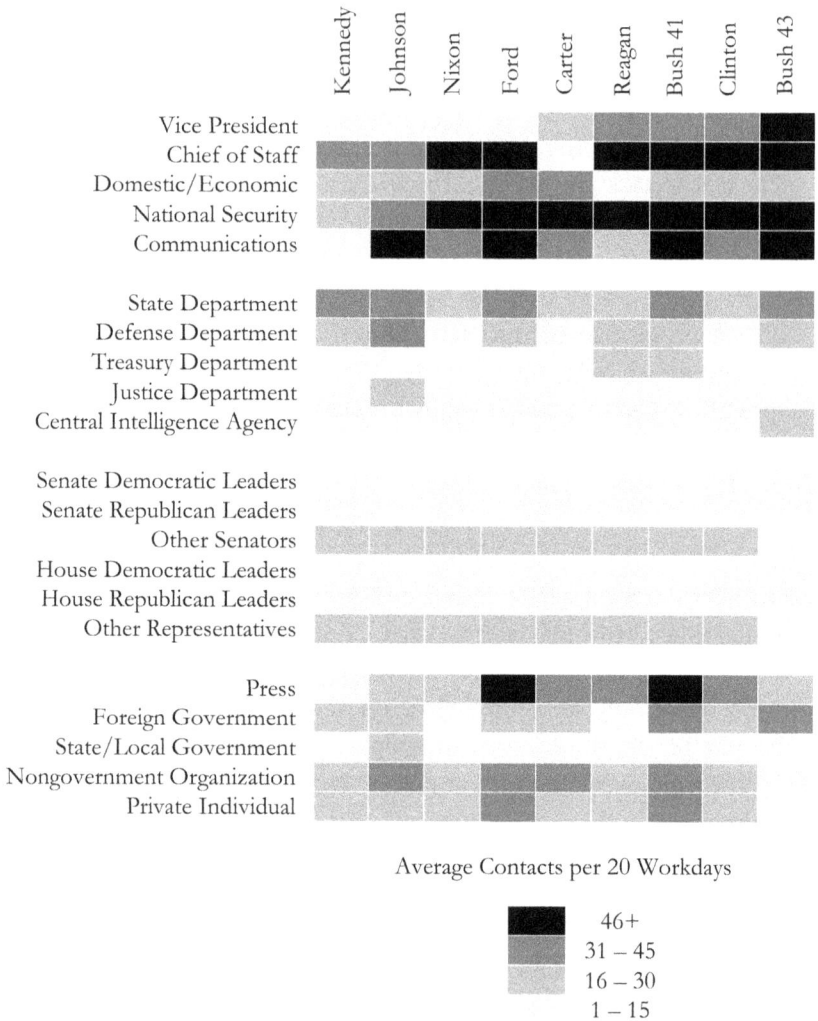

FIGURE 4.7 Frequency of presidential contacts with various people types, by president.

times a day. Cabinet officials had an audience with the president, especially officials from the departments of state and defense, roughly 1 to 2 times per day, which squares with another result in these data—namely, that presidents often engage in personal diplomacy with foreign officials.

Public demands on presidential time also manifest in the types of people presidents see. Returning to figure 4.7, presidents often met private individuals and nongovernment officials (usually a couple of times per week, with some variation president to president), state and local government officials (typically 2 to 3 times per week), and members of the press (from every other day for Kennedy to 3 times a day for Ford). Again, the particulars vary across presidents, but the basic contact pattern clearly extends beyond each president.

On that score, Capitol Hill contacts are particularly consistent. Encounters with congressional leaders were steady (roughly ranging from monthly to weekly) regardless of who was president. And while presidents connected with congressional leaders more than with any other lawmakers, the sheer numbers of non-leaders meant someone among the legislative masses was more likely to encounter the president on any given day. President George W. Bush had a little less direct contact with lawmakers than his predecessors, but even his is a modest difference.

But if there are mostly similarities across presidents, there are also a myriad of president-specific distinctions. To varying degrees, especially outside the realm of congressional contacts, presidents differed in whom they met and how often. Kennedy, for instance, met with the press less often than most other presidents; Johnson met with the Department of Defense more often than most other presidents; Nixon met with the CIA less often than anyone else. The list goes on.

Panning back from the minutiae, however, improves the resolution. In terms of breadth—how many people types presidents see on a typical day—the overall median weekday score is 9. That is to say, for the 21 types of people we coded, a president's typical day engaged more than 40 percent. There is less interpersonal variation here than in other aspects of presidential operations, but less variation is different from no variation. Nixon defines the low end (8), while Reagan and Bush 41 set the high end (11), which means that the latter two had 38 percent broader contact during a typical day.

The differences between presidents for depth—that is, how many distinct contacts presidents had with all people types—are more noteworthy. They range from Kennedy's and Nixon's relatively low levels (16) up to the two Bushes, whose median abundance scores were, respectively, 37 and 32, with other presidents in between: Carter (21), Reagan and Clinton (22), Johnson (23), and Ford (26).

The line to the Oval Office is always long, and it includes an eclectic mix. The follow-up question, of course, is: Who (or what) sets the invitation list?

TESTING BREADTH AND DEPTH

To what extent do presidential contacts reflect who is president? Does a president's stamina or efficiency allow him to see more types of people and/or more often, or does access to the president reflect national conditions, political circumstances, or the ups and downs of daily life in the modern White House? Seeking clarity, I use the multiple regression model introduced previously.

Before turning to the results, however, it is worth recapping the two dependent variables I use to characterize the nature of presidential contacts. The first, *breadth*, indicates how many different types of people presidents encountered on any given day (per the "types" already delineated). The second, *depth*, indicates how many total encounters presidents had with those people (regardless of type). In essence, these measures indicate how wide a net the president cast and how many people it caught.

For each dependent variable—breadth and depth—I run the statistical model twice, once without workday duration included (model I), and then again while accounting for how long the president's workday lasted (model II). See table 4.3. As before, this approach helps partition how much any president-specific differences reflect differences in stamina (through the duration coefficient), differences in efficiency (through the president-specific coefficient), or a combination of both.

I begin with the breadth models. Here we find that how many types of people presidents see is more correlated with context than other aspects of presidential scheduling. In broad strokes, presidents see one extra people type per day during the honeymoon ($b = 1.0$, SE = 0.3, p < 0.05) and one fewer people type per day during their reelection ($b = -0.7$, SE = 0.2, p < 0.05) or lame duck periods ($b = -1.2$, SE = 0.4, p < 0.05). Such deviations move off an estimated baseline of

TABLE 4.3 Ordinary least squares multiple regression, predictors of presidential contact breadth and depth

	COEFFICIENT (ROBUST-SE)			
	BREADTH		DEPTH	
	MODEL I	MODEL II	MODEL I	MODEL II
NBER[a] recession during month (1 = recession)	0.1 (0.2)	0.1 (0.2)	0.4 (0.7)	0.3 (0.6)
Combat fatalities during quarter (logged)	0.1 (0.1)	0.1 (0.1)	0.5 (0.3)	0.5* (0.2)
Honeymoon year (first 6 months after first election)	1.1* (0.2)	1.0* (0.3)	4.2* (1.4)	4.0* (1.5)
Reelection year (last 6 months of reelection year)	−0.8* (0.2)	−0.7* (0.2)	0.1 (1.1)	0.5 (1.0)
Lame duck year (post-loss or last 6 months of second term)	−1.2* (0.4)	−1.2* (0.4)	−4.2 (2.2)	−4.3 (2.1)
Term (1 = second term)	−0.6* (0.3)	−0.3 (0.3)	0.1 (0.7)	1.2 (0.7)
Duration of workday (hours)	—	0.3* (0.03)	—	1.1* (0.1)
Kennedy	8.7* (0.4)	5.7* (0.5)	16.1* (1.2)	5.6* (1.3)
Johnson	10.0* (0.4)	5.5* (0.6)	22.7* (2.0)	6.5* (2.0)
Nixon	8.8* (0.7)	5.0* (0.8)	18.9* (2.4)	5.1 (2.3)
Ford	10.8* (0.5)	6.4* (0.6)	27.2* (1.5)	11.6* (1.8)
Carter	10.1* (0.5)	5.6* (0.6)	23.8* (2.1)	7.3* (2.1)
Reagan	10.4* (0.3)	7.1* (0.5)	23.3* (1.2)	10.7* (1.7)
Bush 41	11.3* (0.5)	7.1* (0.6)	33.7* (2.0)	18.5* (2.3)
Clinton	10.0* (0.4)	5.4* (0.5)	24.2* (1.4)	7.3* (2.2)
Bush 43	9.4* (0.6)	5.8* (0.7)	29.3* (2.5)	16.3* (2.8)
R²	0.85	0.86	0.76	0.78
N	1,781	1,781	1,781	1,781

Note: Dependent variables: Breadth indicates how many types of people the president encountered each day. Depth indicates how many times he encountered all types of people each day. The analyses exclude days that lack a Daily Diary. The models also include variables for weekends and federal holidays, as well as days the president spent at least some of the day outside Washington, D.C. Standard errors clustered by month.
[a] NBER = National Bureau of Economic Research.
*$p < 0.05$.

10 people types for an average president on a typical 12-hour workday (i.e., not during a recession or war, honeymoon, reelection campaign, or lame duck period, and during the first term).

Here again, how long a president works is positively correlated with how much he does. The relationship is fairly modest—presidents roughly see 1 more people type per extra 3 hours worked—but hardly trivial given the duration variations noted in previous chapters. Indeed, 3-hour variations in presidents' workday duration are commonplace. The more telling result is how the context coefficients do not change much when workday duration is added to the model, whereas the president-specific fixed effects do attenuate in response. This fact underscores that stamina acts as a presidential trait rather than a circumstantial force.

Indeed, controlling for their context and workday duration, we see that some presidents opened the presidency's doors wider than others. All else being equal, Nixon saw the fewest types of people, though he was in the same ballpark as several others (i.e., Clinton, Johnson, and Carter), statistically speaking. Kennedy and Bush 43 were set firmly in the middle, higher than Nixon but lower than Ford, Reagan, and Bush 41. The high-end batch is interesting because Reagan saw more people types per hour than usual but worked shorter days than most, while Bush 41 saw more types of people per hour *and* worked longer days than most.

That gets to depth—the overall number of people types presidents see each day. On this score, there is more variety in general, more by president in particular.

First, the president's context does inform overall contacts. Military fatalities ($b = 0.5$, SE $= 0.2$, $p < 0.05$) and the first 6 months of a president's first term ($b = 4.0$, SE $= 1.5$, $p < 0.05$) both predict more presidential contacts. A president's lame duck period falls just short of the conventional threshold for statistical significance, but it is still instructive that presidents generally encounter fewer people as their time in office comes to a close. The other context variables—recession; reelection; term—do not correlate with how many people types presidents encounter during a day, all else being equal.

But if context sets the backdrop, stamina moves the plot. As with other dimensions of presidential scheduling, how long presidents work predicts how many people presidents engage with. Between models I and II, the context coefficients remain consistent; the president-specific coefficients do not. Stamina thus emerges as an important variable, one distinctive to each president and one that helps explain how many people a president can (and will) encounter.

The final calibration to how presidents encounter various people is through their efficiency. Fixing each president to a 12-hour workday (say, a first-term weekday with no recession or war and outside the reelection or lame duck windows) underscores how differently presidents churn through their daily contacts. For it is on equivalent days under equivalent circumstances that it is clear how differently presidents engage with various types of people.

At the extremes are Nixon (low) and Bush 41 (high). Whereas we would predict Nixon's typical day to include 18 contacts with assorted people types, Bush 41 would have 32—a 78 percent increase. Again, this difference applies to a typical day—but that means it is more or less repeated for each of the 1,041 weekdays that constitute a presidential term.

Though Nixon and Bush 41 set the limits, neither is an outlier. Other presidents expected daily depth scores fill the spectrum: Kennedy (19); Johnson, Carter, and Clinton (20); Reagan (24); Ford (25); Bush 43 (29). Presidential contacts thus reflect a president's context at some level, but mostly they say something about who is president. Indeed, differences in presidents' stamina and efficiency do not just define the presidents; they also regulate the flow of people who will fill their time.

CONCLUSION

In 1943, Norman Rockwell visited the White House. His meeting with Roosevelt was unforgettable, of course, but it was the waiting room that fascinated the artist. Soon afterwards, Rockwell memorialized that setting with several paintings collectively entitled, "So You Want to See the President." The series depicts various people—soldiers, senators, reporters, and so on—in the West Wing lobby, in the moment before *their* moment with the president.

This chapter endeavored to capture the other end of the encounter. More to the point, having established that different presidents work different hours, here I inspected how presidents fill those hours. What tasks do presidents do? How much time do presidents spend on each? Whom do presidents meet as they go?

Seeking answers, I built a large dataset, coded from presidents' Daily Diaries, that systematically captured the "moments" that filled their days for a representative sample of days from 1961 to 2008, John F. Kennedy to George W. Bush. For each day, I thus extracted a myriad of details: how many distinct work activities the president performed; how many minutes he spent on "thinking" and "speaking" activities; and how many types of people he encountered as he moved through his daily docket.

The descriptive results were fascinating; the inferential results were telling. On the first point, I discovered how differently presidents have operated their office. Although all presidents are busy in an absolute sense, some are busier than others. They handle different numbers of tasks, and they do so at different rates. And while all presidents spent more time doing "thinking" work than "speaking" work, the blend varied widely, mostly by president. Similarly, the best way to predict the breadth and depth of people granted access to the Oval Office is to identify who is behind the desk.

But if the details were revealing, the biggest insight is the broader lesson: it is impossible to understand how presidents operate the presidency without knowing who is doing the job. No president is generic, and the presidency does not make them so. To the contrary. At the operational level—on the ground, in the job, doing the work, day by day—presidents' priorities, stamina, and efficiency offer far more explanatory power than national conditions, political circumstances, or daily incidents.

This point raises an interesting question: while we instinctively imagine presidents trying to do as much as possible—optimize their efforts and maximize their impact—it is just as important to consider what happens if a president breaks down. In other words, if each president's capacity helps explain how they work under normal circumstances, what happens if a president's capacity wanes? Does the office steady a beleaguered occupant, or does a functioning presidency require a functioning president? The next chapter addresses this issue.

5

NIXON, MAN VERSUS MODEL

ON JUNE 17, 1972, WASHINGTON police arrested five men burgling the Democratic National Committee (DNC) headquarters in the Watergate complex. The evidence trail quickly led investigators to Nixon's campaign staff, then to Nixon's White House staff, and eventually to Nixon himself.

Knowing that "Watergate" was but one job in a larger criminal enterprise, President Nixon opted to conceal his culpability, to obstruct any investigation. Nevertheless, the administration's long "list of horribles"—illegal wiretaps, audits, bribes, burglaries, and beyond—proved impossible to contain.

By March 21, 1973, when White House counsel John Dean updated President Nixon about the unfolding scandal, the prognosis was dire: "We have a cancer within—close to the presidency, that's growing. It's growing daily. It's compounding. It grows geometrically now, because it compounds itself."[1]

Dean's cancer metaphor proved apt. The year following his diagnosis saw Watergate metastasize from a "third-rate burglary" into three articles of impeachment with an impending Senate trial and an all-but-certain conviction. Facing such calamitous prospects, on August 9, 1974, Richard Nixon announced his intention to resign: "I shall resign the Presidency effective at noon tomorrow. Vice President Ford will be sworn in as President at that hour in this office."

For all the scrutiny Watergate has received, one of the most interesting aspects has proven difficult to pin down: Did Watergate affect how Richard Nixon did his job? That is, did Nixon work differently as Watergate unfolded, or did his organizational model prop the president up even as the scandal grew stronger and drew closer?

The answers to these questions are interesting as presidential history, but they are also important as political science. Nixon purposefully institutionalized decision-making, bringing issues and officials to the president per a standard protocol rather than subject to haphazard events, chance encounters, daily headlines, or even the president's personal whim. If function followed form, then Nixon's organizational system ought to have steadied him through trying times.

In fact, tales of the president's wallowing, wandering, drinking, and mumbling hint that Nixon and his system broke down well before he resigned. By August 1973, Stewart Alsop worried that the president was "on the naked edge of a nervous breakdown."[2] By December, Admiral Elmo Zumwalt believed that Nixon was not "the haggard, palsied, drunken wreck" people claimed but "appeared to me to be incapable of carrying on a rational conversation."[3] After one meeting, Senator Barry Goldwater (R-AZ) wondered "whether I was witnessing a slow-motion collapse of Nixon's mental balance. Was the public pressure finally starting to tear the President apart?"[4]

Private whispers became public fodder when Bob Woodward and Carl Bernstein depicted a distraught Nixon roving the White House, whispering to his predecessors' portraits.[5] Such a portrayal gained credibility when Hunter S. Thompson described Nixon as "crazy with rage and booze and suicidal despair,"[6] and it gained corroboration when Alexander Haig, Nixon's final chief of staff, acknowledged that he did order White House physicians to hide the president's pills for fear he might kill himself.[7]

In this penultimate chapter, I delve into President Nixon's work habits throughout his presidency—inauguration to resignation—using systematic data and careful analyses. Specifically, after coding archival records that detail President Nixon's public events and behind-the-scenes contacts from January 20, 1969, to August 9, 1974,

I consider which portrayal—machinelike model or vanquished man—best explains Nixon's work patterns.

THE CANCER GROWS

The *Washington Post*'s lede paragraph in its first story about the Watergate break-in signaled that this was not a typical crime story: "Five men, one of whom said he is a former employee of the Central Intelligence Agency, were arrested at 2:30 A.M. yesterday in what authorities described as an elaborate plot to bug the offices of the Democratic National Committee here."

In fact, there was more to the story—a lot more. The two years between the Watergate break-in (June 1972) and Nixon's resignation (August 1974) were a political and criminal whirlwind that played out in the papers, through the courts, on Capitol Hill, and inside the White House.

Accounts disentangling the twisted strands of "Watergate" are vast in number and rich in detail. Many of these works remain canonical volumes of a historic moment.[8] For my purposes, however, the separate morsels are less important than the general trajectory. Here I briefly give an annotated timeline of the Watergate scandal, focusing on those junctures that most directly implicated Nixon and his work habits.

JUNE 1972

The break-in at the DNC headquarters in the Watergate complex occurs on June 17, 1972. The next day, the White House press secretary, Ron Ziegler, dismisses the episode as a "third-rate burglary." A few days later, President Nixon denies any involvement.

JULY–SEPTEMBER (Q3), 1972

In August, Nixon again denies any culpability, this time citing an internal review by John Dean as exonerating. In September the five burglars plus Howard Hunt and G. Gordon Liddy are indicted for their roles in the Watergate break-in.

OCTOBER–DECEMBER (Q4), 1972

In October, the *Washington Post* reports that a $25,000 check given to the Nixon campaign was deposited into one Watergate burglar's bank account. Subsequent stories detail extensive "dirty tricks" targeting Edmund Muskie (the Democratic candidate) and funded by Nixon's campaign and allies.

JANUARY–MARCH (Q1), 1973

Four Watergate conspirators plead guilty; two others are convicted. The presiding judge, John Sirica, pressures the defendants to reveal details about any other collaborators who planned, organized, or supported their activities. On March 21, Dean tells Nixon that the Watergate scandal is a "cancer . . . that's growing." Two days later Judge Sirica reads Watergate burglar James McCord's letter acknowledging a broader conspiracy.

APRIL–JUNE (Q2), 1973

White House chief of staff H. R. Haldeman and domestic affairs advisor John Ehrlichman resign for their part in the Watergate conspiracy, as does Attorney General Richard Kleindienst. Alexander Haig takes over as White House chief of staff.

John Dean, the White House counsel who initially led the cover-up, begins cooperating with Watergate prosecutors. On April 30, Nixon restates his innocence in a primetime address. In May, the Senate Select Committee begins nationally televised hearings about Watergate.

JULY–SEPTEMBER (Q3), 1973

Alexander Butterfield, Nixon's former appointments secretary, reveals that the White House has an extensive, covert taping operation. On July 18, Nixon orders the taping system disassembled and refuses to release any tapes to lawmakers or special prosecutors.

OCTOBER–DECEMBER (Q4), 1973

On October 10, Vice President Spiro Agnew is indicted for bribery and tax evasion. He resigns. A few days later, Nixon nominates Congressman Gerald Ford (R-MI) for the post.

October 20 is the "Saturday Night Massacre," the day when Attorney General Richardson and Deputy Attorney General William Ruckelshaus resigned in protest rather than follow Nixon's desire and fire Special Prosecutor Archibald Cox. Robert Bork, now serving as acting attorney general, fires Cox.

The White House tells Judge Sirica that the June 20, 1972, recording of a conversation between Nixon and Haldeman has an unexplained 18½-minute gap.

On December 6, 1973, Gerald Ford is sworn in as the nation's 40th vice president.

JANUARY–MARCH (Q1), 1974

Several top aides—including former Attorney General John Mitchell, Chief of Staff H. R. Haldeman, and Senior Advisor John Ehrlichman—are indicted for crimes related to Watergate. The grand jury cites Nixon as an "unindicted co-conspirator."

APRIL–JUNE (Q2), 1974

At the end of April, the White House releases 1,000+ pages of curated tape transcripts. In May the House Judiciary Committee begins impeachment proceedings.

JULY–AUGUST (Q3), 1974

The Supreme Court unanimously orders Nixon to release some tape recordings. At the end of July, the House Judiciary Committee passes three articles of impeachment against Nixon: obstruction of justice; misuse of power; and contempt of Congress.

On August 5, Nixon releases the "smoking gun" transcripts, which reveal his direct role in the cover-up. A few days later, on August 7, a group of Republicans, led by Senator Barry Goldwater (R-AZ), meet with Nixon privately to confirm that his impeachment and conviction are all but certain.

On August 9, 1974, Richard Nixon resigns as 37th president of the United States.

MAN VERSUS MODEL

President Nixon was not felled by a swift, devastating blow; rather, he was steadily pummeled by one damning disclosure after another. The Watergate break-in was a specific incident on a summer night in 1972; the "Watergate" scandal was an intricate, multifaceted set of political and criminal events that played out over more than two years.

Most research about Nixon regarding Watergate has tracked Senator Howard Baker's (R-TN) famous two-part question: "What did the president know, and when did he know it?" The yield has been impressive. Sifting through an extensive evidentiary record, researchers have been able to reconstruct a detailed timeline of Nixon's role in the Watergate break-in and cover-up. With considerable precision and gripping details, we now know what the president knew and when the president knew it.

My interests take a different tack. Instead of investigating Nixon's role in Watergate, I want to know how Nixon performed his normal work—the vital tasks that only a president can do and that cannot be deferred to a convenient time—before and throughout Watergate. Did Nixon's institutional structure and protocols keep him plodding through the unremitting inbox of presidential work, or did Nixon (and his model) break down, as Beltway rumors suggest?

NIXON AS MODEL

One possibility is that Nixon's institutionalized system kept him on track him even as the strains of Watergate grew ever more daunting. As foreshadowed, I call this the "model" hypothesis. Following the logic traced in chapter 1, the idea is that presidents do not serve as distinctive individual people so much as generic institutional actors. Their workflow derives from institutions and incentives, not personality, character, emotions, or stress.

The fact that Nixon liked working within a robust organizational structure comports nicely with the "model" framework. For unlike his immediate predecessors, Kennedy and Johnson, Nixon was loathe to be involved in every issue, at every stage. If anything, Nixon demanded that his staff sort issues, vet information, and curate deliberations, bringing him only those elements that required his attention.[9] Nixon wanted to be the key player in his system, not the only player, never mind the whole system.

Because Nixon's organizational machine was well oiled long before Watergate, to the extent that Nixon's workflow was institutionally derived, its prevailing processes should have ballasted him in turbulent times. Indeed, the structures that shaped Nixon's workdays before the Watergate break-in should have helped him maintain the structure of his schedule throughout the Watergate scandal.

NIXON AS MAN

An alternative possibility is one I have proposed: Nixon's organization and operation constitute two distinct systems that are designed to complement each other and normally do, but they need not in theory and may not in practice. As I see it, if the president breaks down, the operation breaks down; if the operation breaks down, the organization breaks down. I label this the "man" hypothesis.

To the extent that Nixon did in fact crack under the weight of Watergate, his diminished capacity should manifest itself in shorter workdays and fewer work activities, especially those related to "thinking." And because the presidency's organization and presidents' operation are endogenous systems, if Nixon was "nearly incapacitated," as David Gergen once put it, I expect that the institutional presidency will adapt to the president's decline, not countermand it.

That last point deserves some elaboration. To the extent that the presidency tailors itself to the president rather than the other way around, it follows that issues that would otherwise go to the president will get redirected elsewhere or stalled outright. Though the standard model would appear to be "working" in some sense, it is crucial not to confuse *working around* the president with *working for* the president. An absent president is a broken presidency—operationally and organizationally.

Nixon's workflow thus offers a critical test of rival hypotheses—man versus model, individual versus institutional, president versus presidency. Using Nixon's case, we can investigate if and how personal distress can affect a president's work.

MEASURING WORK

Assuming that Watergate rendered Nixon some combination of distracted, disinterested, or depressed, did those strains result in shorter hours and less activity, especially "thinking" activities? Reapplying research strategies that are now familiar, I measured Nixon's daily work patterns by coding the Daily Diary and Public Papers of the Presidents.

As before, I gauged Nixon's *thinking activities* by counting his 5+ minute contacts—face to face or by phone—with the following top government officials: chief of staff; national security advisor; White House counsel; White House press secretary; treasury secretary; defense secretary; secretary of state; speaker of the House; House minority leader; Senate majority leader; and Senate minority leader. Later in the chapter I focus on a smaller subset of Nixon's inner circle during his final years in office.

For Nixon's *speaking activities*, I summed each day's "oral addresses," "oral remarks," or "news conferences" per the *American Presidency Project*, an exhaustive database including the Public Papers of the Presidents.[10]

Combining the richness of the Daily Diaries and Public Papers of the Presidents with the precision of these measures offers a detailed look at Nixon's daily work patterns throughout his presidency—inauguration to resignation. With this evidence in hand, I can now turn from theory to practice—that is, from theorizing about Nixon's work behavior to analyzing data on that behavior.

FIRST-TERM EQUILIBRIUM

President Nixon entered the White House clear about the structure and process he wanted. He thus installed H. R. Haldeman as his White House chief of staff, charging him with converting vision into action. Haldeman did so with zeal, quickly building—and enforcing—what would become the modern presidency's standard organizational model.

POLICY CONTACTS

Because Nixon's vision was so sharp and Haldeman's implementation was so proficient, President Nixon's White House promptly settled into a regular routine. Perhaps it is no surprise, then, that Nixon's workflow was steady from the start. Figure 5.1 shows Nixon's average weekly policy contacts and public events through each quarter of his first term.

Refuting the popular image of Nixon alone in the White House, these data demonstrate that Nixon's first term included frequent contact with top government officials. The average was around 9 per day, 62 per week. There was one standout quarter in the spring of 1970 (when Nixon launched the U.S. military invasion of Cambodia), but that was a temporary blip. The general pattern shows that President Nixon had a very consistent level of policy contacts month to month, year to year, throughout the first four years of his presidency.

PUBLIC EVENTS

Compared to policy contacts, Nixon's public events were fewer in absolute numbers but more variable in relative terms. They increased near elections (midterm and presidential) but otherwise held steady. Nixon had the lightest public schedule in the first and fourth quarters of 1972 (approximately 2 per week) and the heaviest in his inaugural quarter as well as the fourth quarter of 1970 (6 to 7 events per week). The nature of presidential events being what they are, adding or subtracting an event here or there is no trifling matter—especially

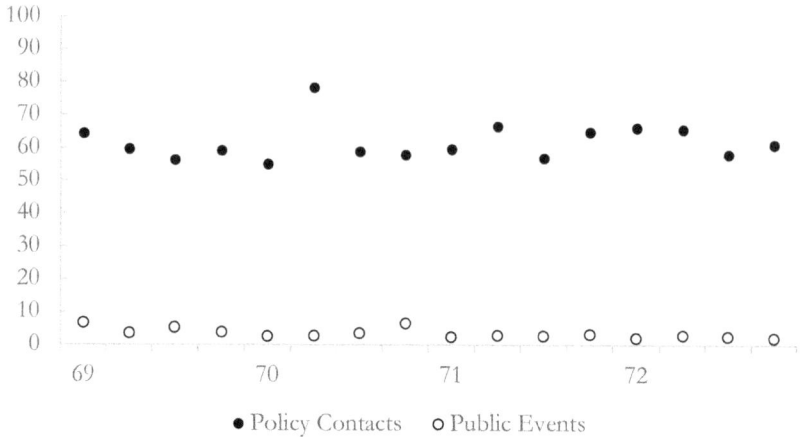

FIGURE 5.1 President Nixon's average policy contacts and public events per week, by quarter: first term.

Dependent variables: *Policy contacts* are the average 5+ minute contacts per week, in person or over the phone, between President Nixon and key officials through his first term: chief of staff; national security advisor; White House press secretary; White House counsel; treasury secretary; defense secretary; secretary of state; speaker of the House; House minority leader; Senate majority leader; and Senate minority leader.

Public events are President Nixon's weekly average of "oral addresses," "remarks," and "news conferences" (source: *The American Presidency Project*'s Public Papers of the Presidents, www.presidency.ucsb.edu).

for Nixon—but the general point remains: Nixon's participation in public events was consistent throughout his first term.

One thing worth mentioning is that there is no sign that Nixon's workflow was disrupted in the Watergate scandal's initial phases. For the first two quarters after break-in (1972, Q3 and Q4), Nixon's policy contact and public event levels were indistinguishable from the fourteen quarters that preceded them. In fact, as he wrapped up his first term, Nixon and his model appear undisturbed. The system kept plodding along, as did Nixon.

Suffice it to say, then, Nixon's first 1,461 days were not only busy—packed with policy meetings and various public events—but also steady. Nixon established his workflow early in his presidency and maintained it for the next four years. The consistency reflected in Nixon's work patterns is significant considering how much social, political, global, and economic tumult the nation experienced in the late 1960s and early 1970s. Clearly, the evidence of Nixon's first term corroborates the "model" perspective on Nixon's workflow.

SECOND-TERM PRESSURES

In his second inaugural address, Nixon articulated hopes for his second term but acknowledged that the work ahead would be difficult: "We are embarking here today on an era that presents challenges great as those any nation, or any generation, has ever faced." The president thus asked for Americans' prayers as he endeavored to meet the moment:

> As I stand in this place, so hallowed by history, I think of others who have stood here before me. I think of the dreams they had for America, and I think of how each recognized that he needed help far beyond himself in order to make those dreams come true.
>
> Today, I ask your prayers that in the years ahead I may have God's help in making decisions that are right for America, and I pray for your help so that together we may be worthy of our challenge.

Alas, Nixon's inaugural prayers failed to avert catastrophe. Just 10 days after Nixon commenced his second inauguration, James McCord and G. Gordon Liddy were convicted for their part in the Watergate break-in. As Nixon would soon learn, those verdicts were at once the end of the beginning and the beginning of the end.

That gets back to Nixon himself. Having observed the president's machine-like workflow through his first term, we see that figure 5.2 extends the time series into his second. The results are unremarkable at the start but stunning at the end.

POLICY CONTACTS

The main discovery in figure 5.2 is also the most dramatic: Nixon's contacts with top government officials fell markedly during his truncated

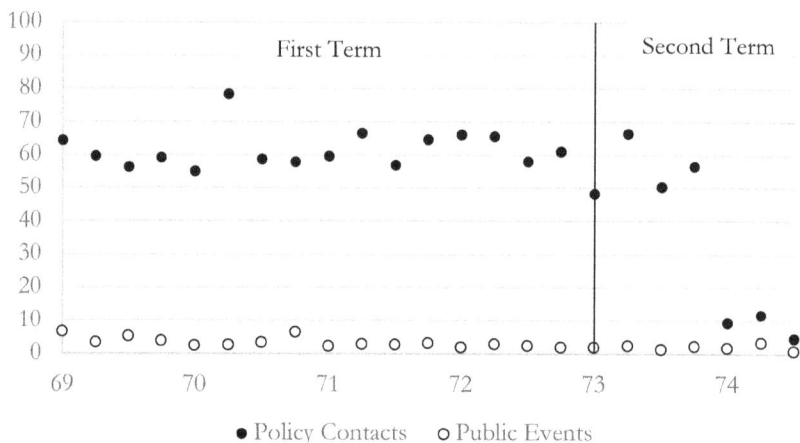

FIGURE 5.2 President Nixon's average policy contacts and public events per week, by quarter: first and second terms.

Dependent variables: *Policy contacts* are the average 5+ minute contacts per week, in person or over the phone, between President Nixon and key officials through his first term: chief of staff; national security advisor; White House press secretary; White House counsel; treasury secretary; defense secretary; secretary of state; speaker of the House; House minority leader; Senate majority leader; and Senate minority leader.

Public events are President Nixon's weekly average of "oral addresses," "remarks," and "news conferences" (source: *The American Presidency Project*'s Public Papers of the Presidents, www.presidency.ucsb.edu).

second term. After four years of averaging more than 60 contacts per week with top government officials, Nixon's average weekly contacts with those same officers tumbled to roughly 10 for his final 8 months as president. To put that in perspective, Nixon started his presidency averaging between 8 and 9 contacts per day with key officials; he ended his presidency averaging 1 or 2.

This finding is so astonishing as to be hard to believe. At least that was my initial reaction. To double-check, I contacted a few Nixon administration officials about this result.[11] These officials' recollections differed by degrees, but all agreed on several basic facts:

1. Nixon declined, psychologically and physically, as Watergate wore on.
2. Nixon's circle of advisors got smaller over time.

3. Nixon's "normal" work routines fell apart in the latter stages of his presidency.

Expert recollections are insightful on their own, but it is worth reiterating that such recollections do not stand alone. Indeed, this chapter began with several contemporaneous reports that Nixon had become some combination of distracted, drunk, disengaged, and depressed.

More recent historical research has mostly corroborated the rumors.[12] For example, Ray Locker's recent book, *Haig's Coup* (2019), draws on archival material to conclude that Nixon's final chief of staff, Alexander Haig, orchestrated Nixon's isolation—with Nixon's consent. On May 14, 1973, the tapes picked up Nixon telling Haig, "There are many things you do better than I do or just as well." Haig did not demur, let alone push back.

PUBLIC EVENTS

Considering the abrupt deterioration in Nixon's policy contacts during his second term, that his public events held firm is somewhat amazing. Figure 5.2 shows that Nixon's public-facing activities in his second term remained comparable to those in the first. There were ups and downs to Nixon's public schedule, but those variations were more or less within consistent bounds throughout his presidency. So unlike for Nixon's policy contacts, Nixon's second-term public event levels held steady. Beginning with 1973 Q1, Nixon's percentage of days with a public event through each quarter of his second term were as follows: 26 percent, 28 percent, 14 percent, 28 percent, 26 percent, 36 percent, and 23 percent.

To inspect this evidence further, I compared these results (using the Public Papers of the Presidents) to my research team's Daily Diary coding. Whereas the Public Papers measure indicates whether President Nixon had any oral addresses, remarks, or news conferences during each day, my research assistants coded public events in the Daily Diary as yes (1) or no (0): "Did President Nixon hold any event intended for a public audience" for that day?

Figure 5.3 displays the proportion of days with public events (by quarter) per each measure. The two sources mostly overlap.

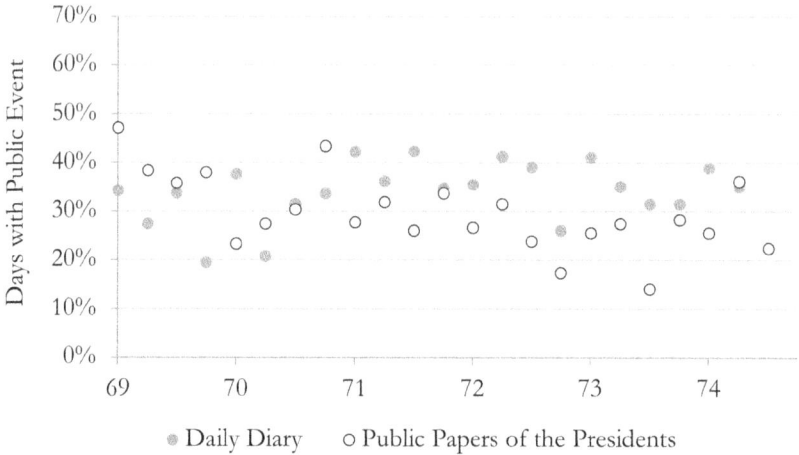

FIGURE 5.3 Proportion of President Nixon's days with public events by quarter: Daily Diary versus Public Papers of the Presidents.

Dependent variable: proportion of days when President Nixon held a public event during each quarter. The Daily Diary data were coded as "Did President Nixon hold any event intended for a public audience" during each day? The Public Papers of the Presidents data draw from the *American Presidency Project*'s (www.presidency.ucsb.edu) database and indicate whether President Nixon offered any oral addresses, remarks, or news conferences during each day.

The correlation between week and public events using the Public Papers of the Presidents measure is −0.09; the same correlation using the Daily Diary measure is 0.03. Digging deeper hints that the main difference between the two measures arises because research assistants coding the diary flagged ceremonial events and photo-ops even when President Nixon did not make a statement.[13] But that is minor. The real lesson is that both measures produce the same conclusion: Nixon's public activities did not decline during the Watergate scandal.

WHEN NIXON BROKE

If Nixon's work patterns suggest that he quit well before he resigned, several caveats prevent us from drawing firm conclusions, especially in the Nixon presidency's latter stages. One problem is that many

Nixon administration officials resigned along the way—some by choice, others by law. The starkness of Nixon's contact drop-off makes it unlikely that this is just an artifact of vanishing officials, but it is instructive to drill past the averages and into the details.

To get a better look into Nixon's work, I make two specific adjustments to the previous analyses. First, I go from observing Nixon's contacts across a myriad of top government offices to analyzing his contacts at three positions that were (a) the heart of Nixon's "inner circle" and (b) filled throughout Nixon's presidency. Specifically, I investigate Nixon's contacts, by phone or in person, with his chief of staff (H. R. Haldeman until April 30, 1973, and Alexander Haig thereafter), his national security advisor (Henry Kissinger), and his press secretary (Ron Ziegler). Plainly, this group was the center of the center, from beginning to end, thus obviating concerns that my policy contact measure is insufficiently tailored to Nixon's core group.

My other modification is to switch from quarterly to weekly analyses. By looking at these data week by week, I am better able to detect whether Nixon's work routine waned gradually or discretely. To facilitate such comparisons, I plot Nixon's weekly work patterns against time markers that highlight key moments in the Watergate scandal. If Nixon was felled by particular events (rather than diffuse pressure), these analyses will reveal this fact.

POLICY CONTACTS

Even without Watergate, Nixon's second term would have gotten off to a trying start. There was the troop withdrawal to wind down the Vietnam War. The inflation rate doubled, the Organization of the Petroleum Exporting Countries (OPEC) imposed an oil embargo, and the economy fell into recession. Vice President Spiro Agnew became mired in scandal before resigning his position and pleading "no contest" in an illegal financial scheme during his tenure as Maryland governor. Nixon, in turn, was induced to disclose his own taxes, which showed that the Nixons paid less than $1,000 in taxes in 1970 and 1971. Then, suddenly, Egyptian and Syrian forces launched a surprise offensive against Israel, an attack that immediately and unmistakably implicated the United States and the Soviet Union.

But, of course, there was no keeping Watergate at bay. To the contrary, 1973 was when the scandal grew increasingly ominous and deeply personal for Nixon. It accelerated when those closest to the break-in were convicted; it worsened when Haldeman and Ehrlichman resigned under the specter of impropriety; it escalated when Alexander Butterfield revealed that the White House had a secret taping system; and it intensified with the Saturday Night Massacre, the unexplained 18½-minute gap on a crucial tape, and the swearing-in of a new vice president—someone who was now available to assume the presidency at any moment.

This confluence of extraordinary policy demands and extraordinary political perils renders Nixon's second-term work patterns interesting anyway, but they are even more compelling given the reports that he suffered something of a personal breakdown along the way. On that path, figure 5.4 illustrates Nixon's weekly contacts with his closest advisors from the day of the Watergate break-in through the day of his own resignation.

Several details stand out; however, the less obvious one is that Nixon's contacts with his closest confidants held form deep into 1973. During that year, Nixon averaged 13 contacts per week with H. R. Haldeman while he served as chief of staff, and then 21 contacts per week with Alexander Haig when he held the job. Similarly, Kissinger averaged more than 8 contacts per week with Nixon, while Ziegler hovered around 14. In many ways, Nixon's relative stability amid the incredible stress of 1973 is remarkable.

Of course, the big story coming out of figure 5.4 is not Nixon's stability through 1973 but his collapse at the end. The plunge hits all three officials at exactly the same time, which turns out to be December 6, 1973, the day Gerald Ford was sworn in as vice president. In the 12 weeks before Ford became vice president, Nixon and Haig averaged 4 contacts per day; in the 12 weeks after Ford became vice president, they averaged 1 contact every 4 days. The splits for Kissinger drop from 1 or 2 per day to 1 every 2 days; for Ziegler they go from 4 per day to 1 per week.

Again, these specific details are but a microcosm of the big picture. Going back to the larger pool of officials but focusing on this critical period—the dozen weeks before and after Ford became

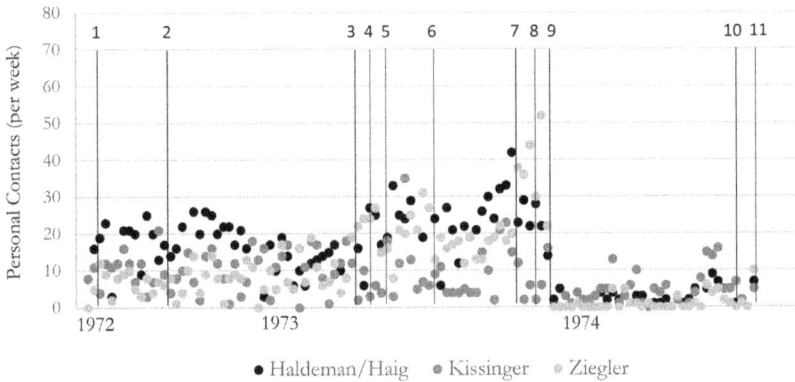

FIGURE 5.4 President Nixon's weekly contacts with top officials throughout the Watergate scandal.

Dependent variable: total number of 5+ minute contacts, in person or over the phone, between President Nixon and his chief of staff (H. R. Haldeman until 4/30/73 and Alexander Haig thereafter), national security advisor (Henry Kissinger), and press secretary (Ron Ziegler) during each week. Numbers across top of figure stand for the following events:

1. June 17, 1972. Break-in at DNC headquarters in the Watergate complex.

2. September 15, 1972. Five burglars plus Howard Hunt and G. Gordon Liddy are indicted for their part in the Watergate break-in.

3. April 6, 1973. White House counsel John Dean begins cooperating with federal prosecutors.

4. April 30, 1973. Assistants to the president, H. R. Haldeman and John Ehrlichman, resign. John Dean is fired. Alexander Haig takes over as chief of staff.

5. May 17, 1973. Senate Watergate Committee begins nationally televised hearings.

6. July 13, 1973. Alexander Butterfield reveals existence of the White House taping system.

7. October 20, 1973. "Saturday Night Massacre": President Nixon fires Watergate special prosecutor Archibald Cox. The attorney general and his deputy resign in protest.

8. November 17, 1973. White House attorneys disclose to Judge Sirica there was an 18½-minute "gap" on a subpoenaed tape.

9. December 6, 1973. Gerald Ford is sworn in as nation's 40th vice president. Alexander Haig testifies that "sinister forces" may explain the 18½-minute gap on a key subpoenaed White House tape.

10. July 24, 1974. Supreme Court, in *United States versus Nixon*, rules unanimously that President Nixon must turn over White House tapes to special prosecutor.

11. August 9, 1974. Richard Nixon resigns as 37th president of the United States.

vice president—indicates something akin to what chemists call a first-order phase transition. For in figure 5.4 we see that there was an abrupt shift at a precise moment that affected Nixon's contacts with White House staffers, Cabinet secretaries, and congressional leaders alike.

What is more, Nixon's isolation was not a passing phase—a fleeting escape or a temporary realignment. The pattern that began with Ford's promotion persisted until Nixon's resignation. Nixon's average monthly contacts with Kissinger for every month of his final year in office were as follows: January 3; February 6; March 5; April 4; May 1; June 13; July 4; August 4. These are almost inconceivable numbers. For the better part of a year, President Nixon was only occasionally speaking to the man who had been his most important advisor until then and who was now serving as the nation's national security advisor *and* secretary of state.

Supposing the diary's entries expose Nixon's reality, and I have every reason to believe they do, the conclusion is clear: on December 6, 1973, Nixon quit performing his work as before, and his organizational model proved unable to break his fall.

PUBLIC EVENTS

Nixon was often brooding in private, but he always wanted to project strength and poise in public. Fake it to make it if possible, and if not, fake it anyway. During his yellow pad brainstorming sessions, under the heading "Nixon the man," the president would urge himself to be the president he wanted others to see: "Above all don't let them break through and see what kind of man new RN is—Maintain mystery—don't be common"; "Need for joy, serenity, confidence, inspiration"; "Compassionate, Bold, New, Courageous"; "Zest for the job (not lonely but awesome)."[14]

Perhaps it is no surprise, then, that even as he veered toward isolation behind the scenes, Nixon maintained public appearances. Indeed, through the darkest days of the Watergate scandal, Nixon sought to project a "zest for the job" he was scarcely experiencing.

Figure 5.5 shows Nixon's public events each week from break-in to resignation. The bottom line is plain enough: the public events

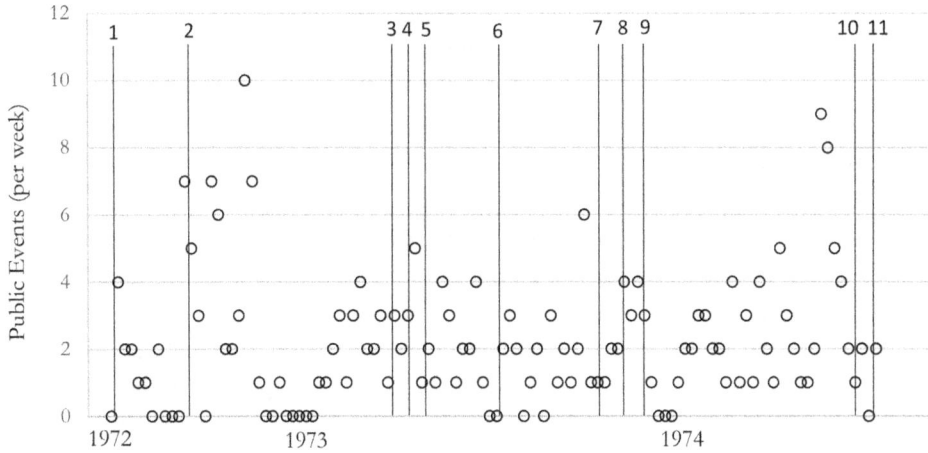

FIGURE 5.5 President Nixon's weekly public events throughout the Watergate scandal.

Dependent variable: total number of public events President Nixon held during each week, drawing from the *American Presidency Project*'s (www.presidency.ucsb.edu) database of oral addresses, remarks, and news conferences. Numbers across top of figure stand for the following events:

1. June 17, 1972. Break-in at DNC headquarters in the Watergate complex.

2. September 15, 1972. Five burglars plus Howard Hunt and G. Gordon Liddy are indicted for their part in the Watergate break-in.

3. April 6, 1973. White House counsel John Dean begins cooperating with federal prosecutors.

4. April 30, 1973. Assistants to the president, H. R. Haldeman and John Ehrlichman, resign. John Dean is fired. Alexander Haig takes over as chief of staff.

5. May 17, 1973. Senate Watergate Committee begins nationally televised hearings.

6. July 13, 1973. Alexander Butterfield reveals existence of the White House taping system.

7. October 20, 1973. "Saturday Night Massacre": President Nixon fires Watergate special prosecutor Archibald Cox. The attorney general and his deputy resign in protest.

8. November 17, 1973. White House attorneys disclose to Judge Sirica there was an 18½-minute "gap" on a subpoenaed tape.

9. December 6, 1973. Gerald Ford is sworn in as nation's 40th vice president. Alexander Haig testifies that "sinister forces" may explain the 18½-minute gap on a key subpoenaed White House tape.

10. July 24, 1974. Supreme Court, in *United States versus Nixon*, rules unanimously that President Nixon must turn over White House tapes to special prosecutor.

11. August 9, 1974. Richard Nixon resigns as 37th president of the United States.

data evidence no decline, let alone a breaking point. The correlation between week and public events during Nixon's second term is 0.03.[15]

Overall, President Nixon averaged 2 public events per week throughout this period. Tellingly, the averages before and after Gerald Ford was sworn in as vice president are no different. The pre-Ford average is 2.1 public events per week; the post-Ford average is 1.9. This means that at the very moment when Nixon disengaged from top government officials, including his closest advisors, his public calendar kept up its previous pace.

The variations are telling as well. While Nixon had between 0 and 4 public events in most weeks, there are two periods in which he routinely had more. The first came at the zenith of his reelection campaign, during the summer and fall of 1972. Looking through the transcripts, this is Nixon in full campaign mode, delivering speeches on the trail and making remarks from the White House.

The other public event surge is more intriguing because it occurs in the summer of 1974, just weeks before Nixon resigned. As it turns out, this public relations push corresponded with Nixon's final diplomatic travels—one nine-day, five-country visit to the Middle East (in June 1974), followed by a quick trip to the Soviet Union (from June 28 to July 1, 1974).[16] At various stops on his journey, Nixon made some combination of public "remarks," "toasts," and "exchanges."

In one of his last acts as president, Nixon bade farewell to his staff during the final morning of his presidency. It was an agonizing speech that included a notorious line: "always remember, others may hate you, but those who hate you don't win unless you hate them, and then you destroy yourself." In light of the evidence revealed through this chapter, it is interesting to note that Nixon did not deliver this personal message to his staff in private; rather, he had it broadcast live on national radio and television.

CONCLUSION

In the spring of 1971, Richard Nixon drafted a memo about presidential time management. At one point the president reflected: "The question about 'getting away from the Presidency' has never been one that particularly concerns me. I have no desire to get away from the burdens of the Presidency. As a matter of fact, when I feel most frustrated is when I am spending time doing something that I may really enjoy, but which I feel takes me away from what I really ought to be doing, to do the job of the Presidency adequately."[17]

He later elaborated on what he really "ought to be doing": "I enjoy the personal diplomacy aspects of the Presidency but I could well dispense with the ceremonial aspects . . . [unless] I can be convinced the ceremony is one that only I as President can perform and that it will help do the job in the long run."

Nixon's was not idle chatter, as I have already discussed at some length. With Nixon, work flowed from specialized advisors, systematized processes, and structured deliberations. The president's role was crucial but limited, aimed at giving Nixon those tasks "that only I as President can perform and that . . . will help do the job in the long run."

Having detailed the tenets of Nixon's model, the question turns to their practice. Did Nixon's operational behaviors track his organizational ideals?

This chapter examined Nixon's work patterns for the 2,027 days he served as the 37th president of the United States. Considering the reports that Nixon the man suffered something of a breakdown during the dark days of the Watergate scandal, I wanted to test whether Nixon's work showed evidence of a durable model or a broken man. Interestingly, I found evidence for both or, more precisely, one and then the other.

Through his first term, Nixon demonstrated machine-like consistency. He met with top officials in the White House, Cabinet, and Congress frequently and repeatedly. All the while Nixon maintained a healthy public docket for his first four years in office, punctuated by increases before elections, midterm and presidential. The ups and downs of international affairs and daily news did not shake Nixon off his routine. Nixon's first-term work reflected the model he espoused.

Then came Watergate. The scandal that came to define his presidency began in the summer of 1972, gained steam in 1973, and culminated in 1974. Salacious reports say that Watergate broke Nixon, leaving him drunk and depressed, unwilling or unable to perform his normal duties as president. Yet as well known as these rumors have become, there has been little to no systematic evidence on the point, until now.

A rigorous empirical investigation into Nixon's work behavior shows that Nixon quit doing his work well before resigning his office. Nixon's contacts with top government officials, which had been so steady during his first term and into his second, experienced a dramatic decline during the depths of Watergate. Actually, there was a specific day on which Nixon appeared to crack: December 6, 1973, the day Gerald R. Ford was sworn in as vice president.

Interestingly, the phase change that characterized Nixon's behind-the-scenes contacts did not extend into his public performances. Nixon continued his first-term pace of public events into his second term—including the 26 months between the Watergate break-in and the White House resignation. At the same time Nixon was withdrawing in private, he was persevering in public, attending a myriad of public events during trips to the Middle East and Soviet Union mere weeks before his presidency came to an untimely end.

These lessons help fill in the historical record on Richard Nixon, certainly, but they also fill in the political science literature about the modern presidency. For a standard assumption in presidency research is that presidents are purposeful, if not rational. This assumption usually makes sense, and it has helped researchers trace the (considerable) constraints on presidents' ability to get what they want.

But as we scrutinize what happens when presidents reach for the ceiling, it is important to recall how little we know about what happens when they fall to the floor—because they can, as Nixon did.

6

EVERYDAY LEADERSHIP

O RLANDO PATTERSON IS THE JOHN Cowles Professor of Sociology at Harvard University. He has published six academic books, dozens of scholarly articles, and scores of essays in nationally prominent outlets. Since 1991, Professor Patterson has been a member of the prestigious American Academy of Arts and Sciences.

Back in 1975, though, Dr. Patterson was not yet an eminent academic. Then he was a promising intellectual with stimulating ideas about race, culture, slavery, poverty, and other issues. In that context, Professor Patterson was surprised when President Gerald R. Ford invited him to the White House for a small, informal meeting about race and ethnicity in America.

Presidential invitations are hard to turn down. So on Saturday, September 27, 1975, from 12:04 to 2:35 P.M., Orlando Patterson joined Gerald Ford and eight other guests for a casual luncheon in the White House Solarium.[1] The roster included the following:

The president
F. David Matthews, secretary of health, education, and welfare
Donald H. Rumsfeld, White House chief of staff
Daniel P. Moynihan, permanent representative from the United States to the United Nations

Robert H. Bork, solicitor general, Department of Justice

Robert A. Goldwin, White House special consultant

Nathan Glazer, professor, Harvard University

John Higham, professor, Johns Hopkins University

Michael Novak, professor emeritus, Stanford University

Orlando Patterson, professor, Harvard University

Some thirty years later, Dr. Patterson reflected on the experience:

> The president's entry was refreshingly lacking in drama. There was no sudden hush, no ego filling up the room, not the slightest whiff of alpha male testosterone. He was a fine-looking man, in a Lake Wobegon sort of way. Casually dressed and relaxed in manner, he shook hands firmly. . . .
>
> As we talked over lunch it slowly dawned on me that the president's behavior was the most inspiring display of self-assured humility I had ever witnessed. Here he sat, the most powerful man in the world, eager to learn about his own society, even from a recent immigrant.
>
> He was a man at peace with himself. Uncomplicated but without a trace of shallowness; calm, dignified and quietly engaging, a person you would like to be your friend.[2]

It is always interesting to hear how guests react to meeting the president, but more instructive is discerning how those guests are selected in the first place. Per a *New York Times* profile about Dr. Robert Goldwin, the professor-turned-advisor who organized President Ford's "seminars," the prototypical session included four outside experts, four relevant insiders, plus the president and Dr. Goldwin. The outsider slots were filled in this manner: "Mr. Goldwin interviews every scholar he considers for an invitation. . . . His method for seeking diversity is to ask potential participants to name scholars in their field whose conclusions they reject but whose analyses they value."[3]

That President Ford chose to spend an autumn Saturday engaging academic minds about important social issues is revealing in many ways. Particularly telling is that he sought independent-minded experts and allocated considerable time to the encounter. Clearly, dipping into a scholarly dialectic was an enterprise the president found worthwhile.

Of course, that President Ford valued such experiences does not mean that their value is self-evident. Was an open-ended, 2-hour conversation about race and ethnicity a good use of Gerald Ford's time? Did it improve his decisions? Did it advance his agenda? Did it bolster his reputation? Did it increase his influence? Did it enhance his legacy?

Such questions relate to a fundamental one: Do presidents' different work styles produce different outcomes? Having examined the theory and practice of presidents' ways of working, I now consider the next scholarly step: assessing the effects.

As I have explained from the outset, presidential behaviors are notoriously difficult to study, and estimating their effects with much precision or reliability is even more so. The inferential problem is as it has always been: there are too many variables, too few presidents, and inexorable barriers to isolating each.

After briefly reviewing why prominent measures of presidential effectiveness mostly fall short, I conclude this book by pursuing a different path. Specifically, I endeavor to lay out the first principles of presidential work. The idea, a concept I call everyday leadership, is to make explicit how I believe presidents can harness each day to get the most out of themselves, the office, and their moment.

TODAY AND FOREVER

One prank the presidency plays on presidents is forcing them to live with their predecessors—the revered, the reviled, and the often forgotten. They linger in portraits, busts, plates, trinkets, pictures, ceremonies, decorations, and, most of all, memories. Their ubiquitous presence offers an unmistakable reminder: your work is today; your legacy is forever.

The link between today and forever is one that all presidents ponder, though some do so more than others, and some do so more explicitly than others. President Clinton often thought and talked

about his legacy. Sometimes the topic surfaced as a direct question—
"Where do I fit in?"—and other times it arrived with a preface: "So the
first thing I had to start with was, you know, we don't have a war, we
don't have a depression, we don't have a cold war."

A quick look at prominent data puts a finer point on it. Since
2000, C-SPAN has queried historians and "professional observers
of the presidency" about each president's "administrative skills."[4]
Figure 6.1 plots historians' ratings against various presidential behaviors: (a) median workday duration; (b) median workday activities;
(c) median workday thinking time; (d) median workday speaking
time; (e) median workday breadth of contacts; and (f) median workday
depth of contacts.

The analytic sextet includes many details but reveals just one
pattern: no relationship. That is to say, plotting presidents' contemporaneous workdays against historians' subsequent appraisals suggests each runs on separate tracks. The (non)correlation between
workday duration and perceived effectiveness is illustrative. Though
workday durations vary substantially and distinctively from president to president, those differences shed no light on how historians
later scored each president's administrative skill. Comparable "null
results" extend to presidents' thinking and speaking time, as well as
to the breadth and depth of their daily contacts.

Does this finding indicate that presidents' work practices are irrelevant? Surely not. Nobody, including myself, imagined that presidents'
daily work habits reveal themselves on a historical scale. Instead,
I theorized specific ways that presidents can work differently, with
the obvious implication that input differentials will have modest
but meaningful effects on presidents' proximate work output. Presidential operations are a discipline of precision, and discerning the
(direct and indirect) effects demands careful calibration.

For presidents, uncertainty about how short-term inputs affect
long-term outputs comes with the turf, and part of the job is estimating which methods will prove most effective. Actually, presidents
know as well as anyone that the future will depend on chance as
much as choice, and attribution of responsibility will be contested
anyway, so they might as well work in the manner they believe best.

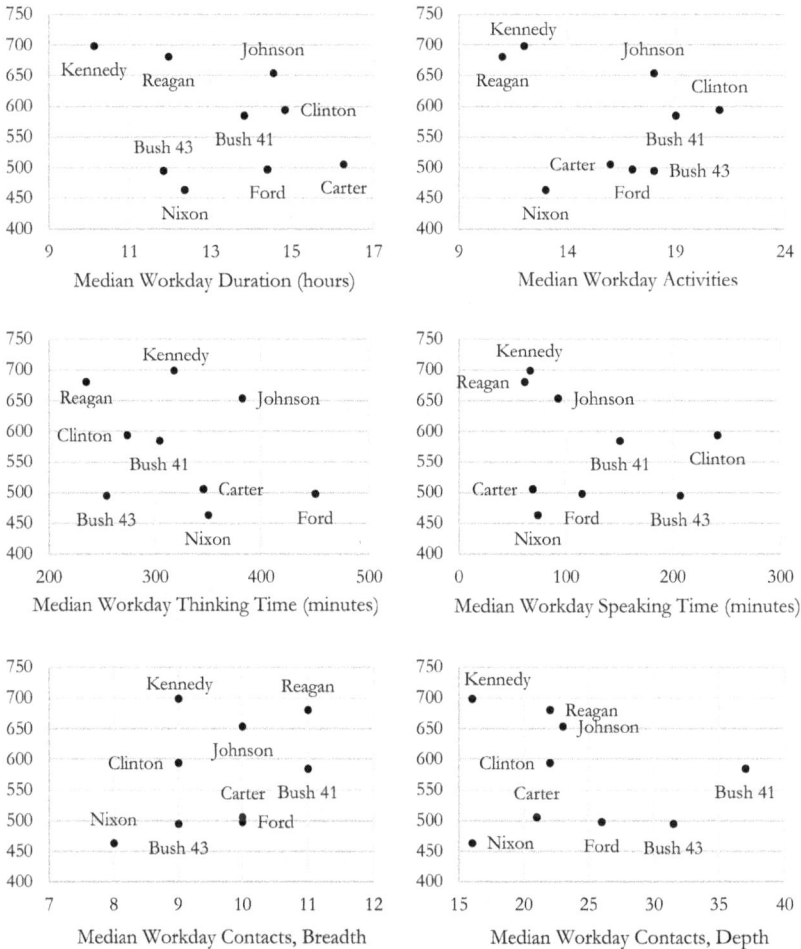

FIGURE 6.1 Presidents' "effectiveness" score by six measures of presidential work.

For political scientists, however, the lack of hard evidence linking presidential processes and products can be paralyzing. Establishing causal relationships is social science's raison d'être, so an inability to nail down how work inputs affect work outputs is fundamentally unsatisfying. Indeed, for those who believe that credible inferences require casual identification, presidency scholarship will usually fall short.

I see this issue somewhat differently. The presidency is, as it has been and always will be, an inherently difficult institution to study. First, there is the inexorable small-n problem (there are not many presidents to study). Second, presidents serve as one of one, meaning that there is no contemporaneous comparison group, let alone a true control group. And then there is the problem that neither presidents' work inputs nor their assorted work outputs are readily measured at high resolution, across multiple dimensions, or with consistency (over time and/or across presidents).

To clarify the point, take Christopher Berry and Anthony Fowler's ingenious method for detecting "leader effects" across myriad settings: among professional coaches, world leaders, city mayors, business executives, and so on.[5] As general and versatile as their method may be, it does not work for modern presidents. There are simply not enough presidents to compare, and because presidents (typically) serve sequential terms of fixed lengths, even if there were infinite presidents, it would still be impossible to isolate each president's uniqueness. And that is before getting to the other incurable issue: there is no straightforward measure for scoring presidential "outcomes" (e.g., there is nothing akin to coaches' wins and losses).

Again, inherent empirical limitations do not mean that presidents' work methods and work yields are unrelated, but it does mean that establishing causes for president-specific "leader effects" is more or less impossible as far as I can see.[6]

Absent compelling empirical estimates, then, what should guide presidents' daily work?

EVERYDAY LEADERSHIP

Occasionally circumstances demand that presidents take dramatic actions in defining moments. These are rare instances when a president has nowhere to turn and no time to waste. Such are the moments that define "heroic leadership."

But this book is not about how presidents handle extraordinary moments; it is about how they handle ordinary ones. What should the president do today, tomorrow, and, for that matter, nearly every day? In the following paragraphs I explicate a set of work principles that constitute "everyday leadership," a playbook that I believe can help presidents best leverage their most important resource: time.

KNOW THYSELF

Disturbed by the presidency's ever-growing burdens in the twentieth century, Woodrow Wilson glibly predicted, "Men of ordinary physique and discretion cannot be Presidents and live, if the strain be not somehow relieved. We shall be obliged always to be picking our chief magistrates from among wise and prudent athletes—a small class."

Although the presidency eventually offered presidents more help, the extra support did little to lighten the load. The job is what it is, it is the president's to do, and there is nothing to do but do one's best.

This gets to the first principle for everyday leadership: honest self-examination. A prerequisite to doing *your* best is knowing yourself.

It starts with physical stamina, understanding the president's basic needs: sleep, sustenance, exercise, family, and "down" time. This can be as banal as ascertaining the president's ideal sleep routine or determining whether the president works best after a full breakfast or a quick cup of coffee. Again, there is no universal correct answer. Each president (and team) must realize that optimizing the presidency requires optimizing the president.

In this vein, presidential staffers should plan based on the president's internal clock. They need to know when he is at his best—and worst. Does he perform best early in the morning or late at night? Before or after meals? In short bursts or deep dives? The challenge is less about how many hours a president can work than getting the timing and sequencing right.

Along these same lines, presidents ought not fetishize long hours or busy days per se. A president who is rested, focused, and motivated is far better than one who is tired, distracted, and irritated. If a president performs best when leisure activities are sprinkled into the day, he should acknowledge as much and resolve to strike the right balance.

As physically taxing as the presidency may be, it is even more draining mentally. Knowing how a president's mind works will help staffers put the president in a position to thrive. Does the president learn best in small or big groups, short or long meetings, back to back or spread throughout the day? The presidency is more a triathlon than a sprint or marathon, so strategic scheduling is essential for maintaining the president's pace through a whole term—or two.

One issue worth addressing is presidents' health, particularly times of poor health.[7] To the extent that a president becomes ill, never mind incapacitated, there is no true workaround. Only the president can be president, and any president who is unwilling or unable to work constitutes a dangerous link in the democratic chain. There is no remedy to the risks of an ailing president, which is why a prospective president's health is foundational to their fitness for the job.

In short, as aides estimate how best to invest a president's time, the first step is to contemplate the nature of the resource. This means knowing how many hours a president can productively work, but it also means thinking about the highest and best use of each hour. The presidency should not merely accommodate presidents; it should enhance them.

"THINKING" IS THE PRIORITY

After mapping the temporal landscape, the scheduling assignment becomes smartly filling each plot. This is the heart of presidential operations, the process by which a president's work takes shape.

As I see it, a president's most important work is "thinking" work—the activities that go into making informed decisions about the nation's business. This is so for several reasons, but foremost is that presidential "thinking" tasks tend to be ones that only the president can perform and otherwise end up at an impasse. By design and in practice, there are many tasks that cannot be handled until the president handles them.

Another reason that thinking work should take precedence is that thinking time tends to have higher yields. Plainly, presidential decisions help keep the federal government moving along. Moreover, just knowing that an issue is headed to the president spurs countless other officials to focus on that same issue. When some item lands on the president's schedule, throngs of government officials launch into developing analyses, options, arguments, and the like. What may be a half hour for the president is hundreds of hours across the executive branch.

But not all thinking time is equivalent. A savvy scheduler will balance the president's thinking time across a diverse portfolio of thinking work. Every president's inbox will inevitably attract an endless stream of "urgent" items. The president and his team have to process this workload in short order, which we might call "thinking for today." Contrary to Eisenhower's famous quip—"I have two kinds of problems: the urgent and the important. The urgent are not important, and the important are never urgent"—urgent work is often important work, and urgency can help secure a place on the president's calendar.

If only by substitution, less urgent thinking tasks can easily slip off the schedule. I sort them into "thinking for tomorrow" and "thinking for thinking's sake." By thinking for tomorrow, I mean the time a president spends working on issues that do not yet require an immediate decision but will in the foreseeable future. Here Eisenhower was right: one should find time for the important issues, and the more the president can invest time before a deadline arrives, the better prepared he will be to make decisions when the time comes.

Then there is thinking for thinking's sake. This is time for a president to consider significant questions that are not necessarily tied to a discrete action item. These questions could relate to long-term trends, emerging developments, new discoveries, or other weighty issues that have unmistakable but as yet undefined implications.

President Ford's seminar about race and ethnicity in America exemplifies this class of activity. A president can only benefit by thinking broadly and theoretically about major topics, contemplating unconventional issues, engaging controversial ideas, and considering heterodox proposals. That these sorts of open-ended thinking endeavors—reading, meeting, thinking, writing—are not tied to an imminent decision makes them easy to overlook on any given day, but that is precisely why they need priority status.

Nearly a century back, John Pell wrote that "it is easier [for presidents] to shake hands than to think."[8] He was right. Not only are speeches and ceremonies relatively easy to perform, but they also tend to induce smiles and applause. For presidents who reached the presidency through years of persistent campaigning, the public-facing parts of presidential work can be fun to do, and people seem to like it.

The daily business of executive management is rarely so affirming; however, my sense is that the biggest bang for a president's hourly buck comes when the president helps the federal government smartly process a large, complex, and consequential workload. This is why I say that presidential scheduling should prioritize thinking time. In practice, this means allocating more and better time slots to the president's thinking work and building the rest of the day around those pillars.

"SPEAKING" IS OVERRATED

Inside the White House, it is tempting to say that everything is important because everything is important. Yes, nominations are important. Yes, legislation is important. Yes, regulations are important. Yes, fundraising is important. Yes, speeches are important. Yes, diplomacy is important. Yes, travel is important. Yes, ceremonies are important. Yes, reelection is important. Yes, yes, yes.

Yes, but also no. As the saying goes, if everything is a priority, nothing is a priority. Presidents only have so much time to give, and one way or another, the scheduling book must balance. Having argued that thinking time is the priority, I hasten to note the corollary: speaking time is not.

Nowhere is the divide between pundits and political scientists greater than on the potency of the presidency's "bully pulpit." Whereas Washington insiders believe that presidents can wield their office to "lead" the public, academic research shows that presidents have a limited capacity to change public opinion via public appeals.

For one thing, Americans' politically relevant attitudes mostly derive from forces that are tough to change—such as partisan identification, economic growth, and national security.[9] Second, the types of people who follow politics closely enough to receive presidential messages are also the least likely to change their minds,[10] and people who get political news filtered through news or online sources generally receive a version that nudges them toward their own predisposition anyway.[11]

The same intuition explains presidents' limited leverage over their own reelection prospects, at least per microlevel tactics like ads, rallies, travel, ceremonies, and press conferences. Even as modern presidents have invested ever more time implementing a "permanent campaign," evidence shows that such campaigns mostly highlight the factors that really drive election returns: partisanship, peace, and prosperity.[12]

That presidents cannot drive national public opinion by messaging and campaigning does not mean that "going public" activities are irrelevant. Presidents surely exert influence in more modest ways—such as with an individual person, a specific community, or a particular organization. We also know that the presidency's unrivaled spotlight can help presidents steer the national conversation toward particular issues;[13] it can signal the president's intentions to lawmakers;[14] and it can signal the president's intentions to world leaders.[15] Also, the process of planning a presidential event can catalyze internal decision-making.[16]

When it comes to speaking time, therefore, my claim is not that it is wholly ineffectual. Instead, it is that people inside the White House often overestimate its value. Presidential speeches rarely persuade; presidential events quickly fade. Does that mean presidents should abandon public relations and campaign-style activities? Absolutely not, but the bar for slotting such "speaking" activities should be higher than most aides presume.

This thought leads back to a preceding point: schedulers should fit speaking work around thinking work. Vital speaking tasks should get time, but they should be timetabled in ways that privilege thinking tasks.

PROCESS IS PRODUCT

Establishing clear work priorities is an important step, but clarity alone does not guarantee that the president's schedule will reflect the president's preferences. A familiar warning from presidents and scholars who study them is that exigencies easily overrun aspirations. As noted, Richard Neustadt called it "the rule of first things first."

But it is not only events that conspire to steal the president's time. More often it is people. Some show up unannounced; others claim that the president wanted to see them; still more loiter in search of an opening. In interviews with more than a dozen White House staffers spread across a half-dozen presidencies, this was a familiar theme that led to a universal admonition: a disciplined schedule requires a disciplined scheduling process.

Before proceeding, I should acknowledge that my respondents' experience did not always match their guidance, nor did the scheduling process always function as planned. Nevertheless, I am convinced that a fair, clear, efficient process for allocating the president's time is a necessary (though not sufficient) condition for maintaining intentionality in time management. Here are some scheduling structures and methods that I concluded were "best practices."

First, every president needs a dedicated scheduler, someone responsible for managing the president's time, someone serving in an honest broker capacity. The scheduler must have the president's and chief of staff's confidence and must have senior staffers' trust. When a meeting request is delayed or denied, it helps everyone if the applicant reacts like one of my respondents: "I understood the president was dealing with issues more important than mine."

Because confidence is imperative, fairness and transparency are as well. Senior staffers need a mechanism for requesting time with the president, clarity about the criteria by which requests are adjudicated, and confidence that the verdicts rendered reveal the president's preferences.

One way to streamline requests is to limit who can submit them. In George W. Bush's administration, only senior staff could request time on the president's calendar. They could do so on behalf of others (e.g., they could recommend the president call a lawmaker or attend an event) or for themselves (e.g., the National Economic Council director might request a budget meeting). Proposals had a standardized format that included details about purpose, timing, location, attendees, and accommodations (meals, photos, press, and such).

With proposals rolling in, schedulers can pencil in open windows. As I explain in greater detail later, the goal is not to please everyone; it is to serve the president. It turns out that such judgments are not as difficult as they might seem. Schedulers (themselves and vis-à-vis the chief of staff) quickly develop a good feel for what the president needs and wants, so prioritizing among a pool of requests is not exactly easy, but it is not especially hard either.

If prioritizing tasks is fairly straightforward, knowing how best to sequence them is less obvious. Here staffers mentioned several tactics they found useful. One was to keep two windows open—approximately 45 minutes before lunch, and another 45 minutes in the afternoon. These windows let the president handle breaking news or an unexpected event, circle back to matters left over from previous days, or otherwise punch through urgent items. The more general point is that schedulers can plan for the unplanned by setting aside time for what I labeled "thinking for today."

With the remaining time, staffers can pencil in longer-term thinking activities as well as speaking activities they deem worthwhile. Again, this scheduling will depend on the president, the issues, and the moment, per the principles already detailed.

One final scheduling-as-process point deserves mention: it is helpful to hold a weekly "scheduling" briefing for senior staff (or deputies), including the chief of staff. At one level, staffers learn what the president will be working on; at another level, they can see (and discuss) how the schedule might be altered or improved. When top aides can comment on the draft schedule, they can better understand why the president's schedule looks as it does and, more importantly, have confidence that the chief of staff decided what to put in and what to leave out.

All that being said, it is important to reiterate that everything hinges on the president. If the president grants time through other, informal means, everyone will pursue those relentlessly. Likewise, if the president routinely eschews the planned schedule with impromptu adaptations, everyone will be less inclined to get on the schedule. So as much as it is true that "process is product," it is also true that the process depends on the president.

AGENDA DRIVES ATTENDANCE

The nature of the presidency—particularly the campaign gauntlet that candidates must run to get there—necessitates building a large, diverse coalition of supporters that includes voters and donors, staffers and volunteers, aides and advisors, and friends and family. President Clinton's political, professional, and personal network was so vast that its members were identified by a simple shorthand: FOBs, Friends of Bill.

Yet as expansive as a presidential candidate's network may be, it grows exponentially after a win. There are the staffers that presidents hire into the White House, the officials that they appoint around the executive branch, the legislators that they need in Congress, the leaders that they meet across the globe, the governors that they engage in each state, and the executives, activists, and citizens that they encounter throughout the country.

As mine is a study about operations rather than access, I do not have any firm views on the types of people presidents should meet on any given day, at any given moment. What I can say, however, is that presidents' schedules should be agenda-driven, not people-driven. Because time is the binding constraint on presidents' workdays, time is of the essence, and because decision-making is the crux of the president's job, people are generally a second-order consideration. More succinctly, agendas should usually drive attendance. Staffers need to decide *what* is the highest and best use of each presidential moment, and then they need to figure out *who* will enable the president to make the most of that moment.

To be sure, this principle is easier to articulate than to implement. Having accrued the debts all presidents accrue, it can be hard to refuse allies' requests for a moment with their president. How can a president decline to meet with a longtime colleague who joined the Cabinet, to campaign with a supportive senator locked in a close campaign, or to welcome a childhood friend who happens to be in town?

Though presidents certainly do not have to rebuff all such requests, they must know that every window granted for one activity is a window closed for another. A purpose-driven presidency requires lucidity about ends and means. By my light, purposeful goals should constitute the ends, and people who can help presidents achieve those goals should constitute the means.

WORKING TOWARD GREATNESS

This book began with a simple hunch: there is no obvious way for presidents to winnow an infinite workload into a finite workday. As I saw it, the fact that a president can go anywhere, do anything, and see anybody is as much a burden as an opportunity because no one president can go everywhere, do everything, and see everybody.

But becoming president of the United States is an incomparable opportunity. A president can only do as much as humanly possible, but when one is president, what is humanly possible can be historically important. Thus my final principle for presidential work is to plan for greatness.

More often than not, what we call leadership is but a catchall for daily work that weaves together vision, judgment, and discipline. This model of leadership, everyday leadership, does not make for great anecdotes in memoirs and biographies, but it is the kind of leadership that all presidents can achieve. Indeed, for those who ascend to the nation's highest office, the precepts of everyday leadership offer a blueprint for meeting Harry Truman's admirable standard:

> I have tried my best to give the Nation everything I had in me. There are a great many people—I expect a million in the country— who could have done the job better than I did it. But, I had the job, and I had to do it. And I always quote one epitaph which is on a tombstone in the cemetery at Tombstone, Ariz. It says, "Here lies Jack Williams, he done his damndest." I think that is the greatest epitaph that a man can have. When he gives everything that is in him to the job that he has before him, that's all you can ask of him. And that's what I have tried to do.[17]

Stating wants is easy. Working for results is hard. Because presidential leadership is less about wanting than working, respect accrues to those presidents who invest themselves in working hard and working smart. The president's day really is the president's day, and every president's charge should be to make the most of every day.

APPENDIX A

THE DAILY DIARY, 1961–2008

THREE DAYS AFTER LAUNCHING HIS presidential campaign, John Kennedy attended a small dinner party that included his wife Jackie, close friends Ben and Tony Bradlee, and James Cannon, then a reporter at *Newsweek*. When the conversation turned to Kennedy's political aspirations, Cannon asked if he could record the conversation. Kennedy agreed, and the first voice caught on tape was the future president's: "This is on? Can it get me from there?"

As it turned out, Kennedy liked to record his thoughts and actions. During his brief window in the White House, he amassed 265 hours of tape covering a mix of personal meetings, phone calls, and private reflections. Although Kennedy did not explain why he wanted a contemporaneous audio archive, his daughter Caroline recounted her understanding: "I was always told that my father installed secret Oval Office recording devices after the Bay of Pigs disaster so that he could have an accurate account of who said what, in case of any later disputes as to the exact nature of the conversations. And as an avid reader of history, and a Pulitzer Prize–winning author, he intended to draw upon this material in his memoirs."[1]

The last point is one many Kennedy researchers proffer as well. Tom Putnam (the John F. Kennedy Presidential Library and

Museum's fifth director) summarized the scholarly consensus: "We believe that the reason why he taped them was that he could later write a memoir."[2]

Beyond taping himself, Kennedy also urged careful recordkeeping among his aides. So began the Daily Diary, a centralized instrument for logging President Kennedy's work activities. Compiled by his personal secretary, Evelyn Lincoln, the Daily Diary was *the* mechanism for keeping track of the president's meetings, calls, travels, speeches, and other activities—in other words, his work. Using a standardized, streamlined format, Ms. Lincoln dutifully recorded what the president did, when, and with whom, more or less in real time. An example is shown in figure A.1.

To be sure, Kennedy's diaries have their shortcomings. There are some missing days and some missing data. The diary for November 22, 1963—the day Kennedy was assassinated—was never created, for example. Moreover, Ms. Lincoln's recordkeeping was squarely focused on President Kennedy's work as president. The Daily Diary, like its author, reveals no details about Kennedy's infidelities. More to the point, many of Kennedy's nonwork activities (e.g., bathroom breaks, family dinners, cat naps) and assorted informal, passing activities fell through the archival cracks.

After John Kennedy was killed and Lyndon Johnson became president, the Daily Diary continued apace, though responsibility for its construction transferred to Johnson's secretaries. Archivists at the Lyndon Johnson Presidential Library and Museum described how it worked: "The secretaries outside the Oval Office prepared President Johnson's Daily Diary. Juanita Roberts, the President's personal secretary, assigned the responsibility of preparing the Diary to secretaries in the office. A particular person would 'work' the Diary for a scheduled period. As visits and telephone calls occurred, the secretary 'working' the Diary would note them; occasionally the secretary missed noting a call or meeting. White House staff who worked closely with the President frequently entered the Oval Office without the visit being noted in the Diary."

The Johnson diaries are comparable to the Kennedy diaries in many ways. They track the president's activities, noting when each activity began and ended, where it occurred, and who else was present.

TUESDAY, OCTOBER 16, 1962

9:25 am	The President arrived in the office.
9:30 - 9:48 am	Commander and Mrs. Walter M. Schirra, Jr. Walter, III and Suzanne
9:50 - 9:54 am	Mr. Edward McDermott
10:00 - 10:26 am	(Congressman Ross Bass) OFF THE RECORD (Tennessee)
10:26 - 10:30 am	(Hon. C. Douglas Dillon) (Hon. Henry Fowler) (Hon. Myer Feldman)
10:33 - 11:15 am	The President met with the members of the Panel on Mental Retardation in the Fish Room.
11:15 - 11:46 am	Hon. Charles E. Bohlen U. S. Ambassador to France

11:50 - 12:57 pm	OFF THE RECORD MEETING RE CUBA
	    (The Vice President)
	    (Hon. Dean Rusk)
	    (General Maxwell Taylor)
	    (Hon. Roswell Gilpatric)
	    (Hon. Edwin Martin)

1:03 pm	The President departed the office and went to the Mansion.

1:00 pm	LUNCHEON at the White House in honor of His Royal
	Highness Hasan al-Rida al-Sanusi, Crown Prince of the
	United Kingdom of Libya:
	    The President
	    H. R. H. The Crown Prince of the United Kingdom of
	        Libya, Hasan al-Rida al-Sanusi
	    H. E. Waniis al-Qadhaafi
	        Minister of Foreign Affairs
	    H. E. The Ambassador of Libya
	        Dr. Mohieddine Fekini
	    H. E. Yunis Bilkhair
	        Minister of Defense
	    The Honorable Fathi al-Khoja
	        Master of Cermonies of the Royal Household

(continued)

FIGURE A.1 President Kennedy's Daily Diary for October 16, 1962
(first day of Cuban missile crisis).

Phone calls are labeled for whether they were "to" or "from" the nonpresidential participant (and whether they were "local" or "long distance"). And, most importantly, Johnson continued Kennedy's practice of treating the diary like a personal archive rather than a press release. An example is shown in figure A.2.

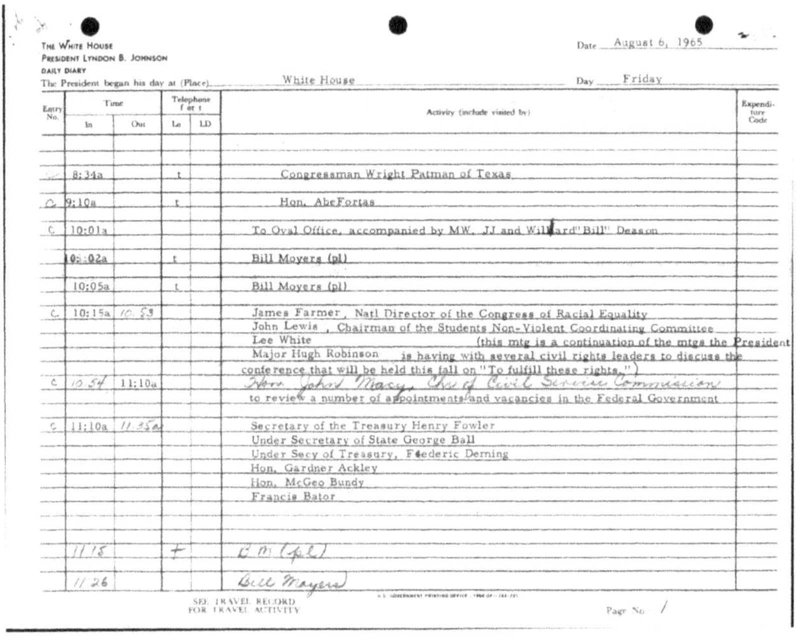

THE WHITE HOUSE
PRESIDENT LYNDON B. JOHNSON
DAILY DIARY

Date August 6, 1965

The President began his day at (Place) White House

Day Friday

Entry No.	Time In	Time Out	Telephone f or t Lo	Telephone f or t LD	Activity (include visited by)	Expenditure Code
	8:34a		t		Congressman Wright Patman of Texas	
C	9:10a		t		Hon. AbeFortas	
C	10:01a				To Oval Office, accompanied by MW, JJ and Willard"Bill" Deason	
	10:02a		t		Bill Moyers (pl)	
	10:05a		t		Bill Moyers (pl)	
C	10:15a	10:53			James Farmer, Natl Director of the Congress of Racial Equality John Lewis, Chairman of the Students Non-Violent Coordinating Committee Lee White (this mtg is a continuation of the mtgs the President Major Hugh Robinson is having with several civil rights leaders to discuss the conference that will be held this fall on "To fulfill these rights.")	
C	10:54	11:10a			Hon John Macy, Chm of Civil Service Commission to review a number of appointments and vacancies in the Federal Government	
C	11:10a	11:35a			Secretary of the Treasury Henry Fowler Under Secretary of State George Ball Under Secy of Treasury, Frederic Deming Hon. Gardner Ackley Hon. McGeo Bundy Francis Bator	
	11:15		t		B M (pl)	
	11:26				Bill Moyers	

SEE TRAVEL RECORD FOR TRAVEL ACTIVITY

Page No. 1

FIGURE A.2 President Johnson's Daily Diary for August 6, 1965 (signing day of the Voting Rights Act).

In other ways, though, the Johnson diaries are distinctive from their predecessors. The most obvious difference is also the most interesting. Whereas Kennedy's diaries were mechanical—typed details about when, where, what, who—Johnson's diaries often append secretaries' personal observations. These notes divulge details like the president's clothes, meals, asides, and other ephemera. Unlike other diaries in the time series, then, the Johnson diaries stand out for having entries that blend typed and handwritten entries.

The October 22, 1964, diary exemplifies the types of anecdotes that pepper Johnson's dairies. Having attended Herbert Hoover's funeral ("front row") and then consoled the Hoover family in a private anteroom, Johnson headed back to his hotel. There, the diary shows, he received various guests, including Robert Kennedy and James Farley. "In the entrance hall of the suite, the President shook hands with James (Jim) A. Farley and introduced Bobby Kennedy to him, saying

'You know Bobby . . . our next Senator from New York.' . . . The President noticed that Mr. Farley was not wearing an LBJ pin, so he gave him several."

Upon taking office, Nixon was immediately enamored with the Daily Diary. He saw its potential for building a legacy after his presidency, but he also quickly discovered its utility as a real-time database. One staffer from the Nixon years told me how the president would pass along queries like "People say we never meet Catholics. Can you find out how many Catholics I met with this month?" In fact, such requests were common enough that the Nixon diarists created a three-letter coding system for labeling the president's contacts—by race (e.g., BLK for African American), gender (e.g., WOM for woman), occupation (e.g., LAW for lawyer), and so on (e.g., REP for representative, SEN for senator).

As elsewhere, H. R. Haldeman was the one who institutionalized the Daily Diary's position within the White House's broader "staff system." Source materials like meeting agendas, call logs, and flight manifests were systematically routed to the staffers drafting each day's diary. Dwight Chapin and Alexander Butterfield, the aides who supervised the diary's construction, further adapted the existing diary format into a fully customized template. And because Nixon liked to study his diaries, his aides put a premium on getting them done promptly. The turnaround time between the lived day and the completed diary was quick—usually within a week. See figure A.3.

Compiling the Daily Diary proved demanding for those charged with keeping up. Looking to offload that burden, Nixon wrapped up his first year by asking the National Archives and Records Administration (NARA) to assume Daily Diary responsibilities. NARA accepted. The planning and transition took some time, but on June 14, 1971, the Daily Diary effort became a semi-autonomous unit within the Office of Presidential Papers and Archives (OPPA).

It was then that Susan (Davis) Yowell became NARA's first official diarist. Ms. Yowell told me, "They had been doing it already. I used their templates and got to work." Although Ms. Yowell was detailed to the White House (and working out of the Executive Office Building), she had no doubt about her role: "I considered myself a civil servant, not a White House employee. That was always how I felt."

THE WHITE HOUSE	PRESIDENT RICHARD NIXON'S DAILY DIARY

PRESIDENT RICHARD NIXON'S DAILY DIARY
(See Travel Record for Travel Activity)

PLACE DAY BEGAN	DATE (Mo., Day, Yr.)
THE WHITE HOUSE WASHINGTON, D.C.	JUNE 23, 1972
	TIME DAY
	8:10 a.m. FRIDAY

TIME		PHONE P—Placed R—Received		ACTIVITY
In	Out	Lo	LD	
8:10		P		The President telephoned Bryce N. Harlow, Chief of Public Relations for Procter and Gamble Corporation. The call was not completed.
8:38				The President went to the first floor Family Dining Room.
8:38	9:36			The President had breakfast with:
				House Minority Leader Gerald R. Ford (R-Michigan)
				House Majority Leader Hale Boggs (D-Louisiana)
				Maj. Gen. Alexander M. Haig, Jr., Deputy Assistant
				Richard K. Cook, Deputy Assistant
				Members of the press, in/out
				White House photographer, in/out
9:36				The President went to the Oval Office.
9:36	9:41			The President met with his Deputy Assistant, Alexander P. Butterfield.
				The President met with:
10:04	10:39			H. R. Haldeman, Assistant
10:33	10:39			Ronald L. Ziegler, Press Secretary
				The President met to discuss economic policy alternatives with:
10:39	12:15			George P. Shultz, Secretary of the Treasury
10:39	12:08			Caspar W. Weinberger, Director of the OMB
10:39	12:08			Herbert Stein, Chairman of the Council of Economic Advisers (CEA)
10:39	12:08			Ezra Solomon, member of the CEA
10:39	12:08			Marina v. N. Whitman, member of the CEA
10:39	12:08			John D. Ehrlichman, Assistant
10:39	12:15			Mr. Ziegler
10:50	12:08			Charles W. Colson, Special Counsel
11:06	12:08			Earl L. Butz, Secretary of Agriculture
11:06	12:15			Donald Rumsfeld, Counsellor
				Members of the press, in/out
				White House photographer, in/out
10:41		R		The President was telephoned by Mr. Haldeman. The call was not completed.
12:15	12:41			The President met with:
				Kermit Gordon, President of Brookings Institution and member of the Pay Board
				Secretary Shultz
				Mr. Rumsfeld
				White House photographer, in/out

FIGURE A.3 President Nixon's Daily Diary for June 23, 1972 (day of the "smoking gun" conversation).

As it turned out, Ms. Yowell was perfectly suited for her new position. She was organized, thorough, and tenacious. "I'm not a particularly shy person, and I was young and not in awe of the people there. Now I might be more cautious, but then I just called people up and asked my questions. . . . If I had to pester someone, I had no problem doing that." As Ms. Yowell saw it, she was hired to create a precise record of the president's activities, so that is what she did.

The bureaucracy being what it is, NARA sought to codify Ms. Yowell's practices for creating, distributing, and storing diaries. In early spring of 1972, NARA officials distributed an 18-page memo detailing "guidelines" for how to handle the Daily Diary.[3] The document is one part staff guidance, one part style guide. Here is but a small sample of its contents:

- Use a person's full name and title the first time it is entered in each diary. Include the middle initial. Check accuracy of names and titles in reliable sources. . . . Always *be consistent* [emphasis in original].
- When a meeting or phone call is less than one minute, avoid confusion on the typed diary by changing either the in or the out time so there will be a one-minute difference when it appears in the diary.
- All times should be entered according to the *local time* used where the President is on any given day [emphasis in original]. If there is a time change within the day, note this in the time column above the first entry given in that time zone.
- Initials of the writer, reviewer, and typist should appear on the last page of the diary. Example: CD/MF/MM

When I asked whether anyone ever asked Ms. Yowell to censor an entry or otherwise alter a diary, she said it never happened. "They liked having us for research. . . . Nixon was very organized. They were very interested in his time, not wasting his time. . . . [The diaries] were like the tapes; it never occurred to them that these things could be a problem."

That said, Ms. Yowell wanted to be clear that the diaries do have limitations: "If there is someone the President really wants to hide, there are ways they can do that. . . . The Diaries include practically all work-related events, but they are probably not great for the most personal or scandalous activities." In sum, "We worked very hard to get them as accurate as possible, and I think they are with a few exceptions [such as travel, vacations, and time in the residence]."

What about Watergate? Did White House aides want to stifle the diaries as the scandal grew more dire? According to Ms. Yowell, they did not. "The environment was much more intense. It was very stressful. There were lawyers around asking about the Daily Diaries. We started keeping them under lock-and-key." However, "nobody told us to stop doing our job and we just kept doing it. . . . By that point we had a routine down. We were pretty efficient, and we kept getting the records like always."

This brings up an interesting aside. On July 13, 1973, Alexander Butterfield revealed that the White House had a secret taping system. While Butterfield's disclosure is often cited as a watershed moment in the Watergate investigation, the reality is that the special prosecutor would have been overwhelmed trying to digest thousands of hours of nondescript tapes. However, Archibald Cox had discovered the Daily Diary, which provided the special prosecutor and his team with something like a table of contents, an easy-to-use means for deciding which tapes to pursue.[4]

Following Richard Nixon's resignation, Gerald Ford became president and his new administration abruptly shut down the Daily Diary. Ms. Yowell recalled, "It was a surprise." Her impression was that Gerald Ford had witnessed what a liability the diary had been and thus wanted to avoid the unnecessary risk.

A few months later, without explanation, Ms. Yowell learned that President Ford had changed his mind. He wanted to restart the diary exactly as it had been done before. Ms. Yowell returned to her office and "got started right away." To help, NARA allowed Ms. Yowell to hire a new assistant diarist, which led to Ellen (Jones) McCathran coming on board. The duo resuscitated the same format, materials, and process as before. And, to their great credit, they decided to go back and create diaries for the days that otherwise would have gone without one. Ms. Yowell explained, "It wasn't ever a question. We knew we had to do it . . . [but] it was a lot of work and was just awful to do."

The temporary shutdown notwithstanding, Ms. Yowell and Ms. McCathran both agreed that Ford and his staff were entirely supportive, collegial, and helpful. "We had total independence. We could talk to anyone and get whatever we wanted." Ford himself did not study the diaries like Nixon did, but his aides were just as responsive to the diarists' inquiries. What is more, the institutionalized protocols for directing source materials to the diarists' office were reinstituted without resistance.

From there things kept humming along, albeit with a longer gestation period for completing each diary, in no small part because the president was not eagerly awaiting it. The Ford Presidential Library's background summary gives the details: "The Diary staff pulled the information together into a single log of Presidential activities for each day and filled in gaps in the sources or resolved conflicts between them by querying staff members involved in the event. Because of delays in obtaining source materials and resolving problems, they generally completed each day's Diary about three to eight weeks after the day itself."

It was during this period that Congress sought to put presidential records on firmer statutory footing. The result was the Presidential Records Act (PRA) of 1978. Among its provisions was a requirement that presidents "adequately document" and maintain records of the president's "activities, deliberations, decisions, and policies." According to my research, this requirement did not change how the diarists approached their work, but it did bolster other staffers' belief that supporting diary personnel and protocols was a good way for the president to satisfy PRA requirements.

Enter Jimmy Carter. Carter did not just value the Daily Diary; he also personally met the diarists and studied their work. After seeing a few examples, Carter requested that completed diaries be included with his nightly briefing books. And he read them. "I remember that the President caught my spelling error. I had put 'fourty' and he corrected it to forty. . . . I never made that mistake again."

Channeling their boss, Carter's staffers frequently engaged the diarists (and diaries) as well. "They had a lot of questions." Jody Powell, Ham Jordan, Tim Kraft, and Phil Wise all used diaries for "analysis" about how Carter was spending his time. In fact, Ms. Yowell and Ms. McCathran again developed a specific coding system to summarize where Carter went, whom he met, and how he spent his time. They prepared several memos about the same.

During President Carter's reelection campaign, Ms. Yowell took a leave of absence from her diary work to volunteer for the Carter campaign. She was adamant: "My personal views had no effect on my work." Nevertheless, after Reagan won, his team asked for Ms. Yowell's resignation (part of a broader purge that affected approximately fifty employees). "It was tough when it happened, but it was good for me. I am a workaholic by nature. It wasn't my choice, but it let me focus on my family and new careers."

On January 20, 1981, Ms. McCathran took over as lead diarist.[5] She retained the protocols and practices Ms. Yowell (and she) had honed over the previous years. Starting each presidency with fourteen empty file cabinets lined up along the side wall—"just enough to hold two terms"—Ms. McCathran would methodically file supporting documents into folders arranged in chronological order. "I did not like piles of paper," she said.

Like Ms. Yowell, Ms. McCathran found my probes about censorship somewhat puzzling, if not misguided. As she saw it, White House staffers *needed* the diary to be complete, accurate, and reliable. In her words, "Most people focused on the present or the future . . . [and] things moved too fast for them to keep track of everything that was going on. I was the only one who was focused on the past. They relied on me because I could get them answers about the past." In short, "having the Diary was in their interest too."

One illustrative example occurred during George H. W. Bush's presidency. Because Bush liked to send his guests a picture from their visit along with a nice note, his personal secretaries often found themselves trying to find specific people among the hundreds of photographs taken each day. This was an area where the diaries (and diarist) proved invaluable. If Bush's secretaries gave her a name, Ms. McCathran could identify the day, time, location, activity, and company in which that person encountered the president. That the diary captured even intimate details like dinner guests and tennis partners ended up being valuable for everyone involved, from the secretaries and diarists to the guests and the president.

This sort of staffer reciprocity and collegiality was the norm according to the diarists, part of an esprit de corps among those who serve in the White House. Ms. McCathran was eager to help staffers do their jobs, and those same staffers were happy to help Ms. McCathran do hers. This was especially true for the career staff—ushers, phone operators, photographers, butlers, and residence staff—but it extended to political appointees as well. "You connect to key people— Oval Office operations, scheduling, secretaries, personal aides, Chief of Staff—and show you can be trusted and how helpful this information is now and for the president's legacy. . . . It doesn't take long. They get it."

So it was during the Reagan and Bush 41 administrations. While neither of these two chief executives was as interested in the diaries as Carter had been, Ms. McCathran reported that their staff were no less supportive or cooperative. "I had a good system going; everything I needed was routed to me as a standard practice. . . . When I had questions, I would call someone who would know."

That being said, I had noticed several gaps in the Reagan diary time series, including a sustained absence through Reagan's final months in office. I asked Ms. McCathran about this. Her response was that she fell too far behind and was unable to catch up.[6] In late 1988, in particular, Ms. McCathran remembered becoming overextended, which was problematic because the PRA (then in effect for the first time) dictated that anything still undone on inauguration day could not be completed because all the source materials were boxed up, hauled off, and stored away.

Happily for Ms. McCathran, President George H. W. Bush liked a tight schedule and long paper trail, which made diary construction less cumbersome. According to the Bush Library's holding description, "[The diaries] chronicle the daily activities of the President including meetings (with lists of attendees), social and speaking engagements, trips, telephone calls, meals, routine tasks, and recreational pursuits. . . . Except in rare instances, each Daily Diary entry provides a comprehensive list of presidential activities." Ms. McCathran affirmed that the Bush 41 administration was easy to work with, adding that this was the era when she started relying on computers, which made drafting more efficient, and editing even more so.

Not surprisingly, in some situations the recordkeeping was spottier. As with other presidents, the Reagan and Bush 41 diaries are less reliable when the president was traveling, especially when the travel was for leisure (rather than work). The Reagan Library cautions that "documentation for many days, especially those which President

Reagan spent at Camp David or Rancho del Cielo (his California ranch), remains sketchy." The Bush 41 Library includes an analogous caveat: "there are missing dates (sometimes covering as long as a month) in the series. They generally occur when President Bush is on vacation, most often in August and December."

That gets to the Clinton years. According to Ms. McCathran, President Clinton's eight years in office constituted the most stressful work environment of her career.

The strains started early. Ms. McCathran described how the transition felt chaotic, and she struggled to connect with the key people who would soon become her key sources. Then, once Clinton's team was up and running, a string of leaks and negative stories rendered staffers reticent to share information (and documents). Ms. McCathran said she eventually got what she sought, but doing so required far more effort and took far more time than in other administrations.

Clinton himself created other complications. The president routinely worked long hours, saw many people, and always ran late. The hours and people were not a problem per se, but the fact that Clinton deviated from his schedule meant that Ms. McCathran had to chase down mountains of details about what happened. "I could not use the schedule for much. People came and went; President Clinton was always running late. . . . This made my job harder than normal . . . and that created long backlogs."[7]

The backlogs grew so large that Ms. McCathran intermittently gave up on catching up. That is to say, at certain points Ms. McCathran would effectively declare bankruptcy—disregarding the backlog of source materials sitting in folders and focusing her efforts on diaries starting with the current date. This fact explains the data patterns in appendix B, which show substantial gaps in the Clinton diary time series (e.g., 1996)—ones unlike anything before or after his time in office.

Fortunately for my purposes, Ms. McCathran said that the completed diaries were usually well done; it was just that many went undone. Having examined the patterns more carefully, my impression is that the Clinton diaries miss more unstructured, unplanned activities than the diaries for other presidencies. So they are very reliable for things like National Security Council meetings or phone calls but likely miss a myriad of impromptu, in-person conversations. My best guess, then, is that my estimates for Clinton workdays are modestly biased downward and generally have larger confidence intervals.

If Bill Clinton complicated efforts to build Daily Diaries, George W. Bush was the opposite. Bush 43 liked a clear schedule, followed it to a T, and actively encouraged staffers to route all materials through the diarist's office. Moreover, because several top officials in the Bush 43 White House had worked in the Bush 41 White House, senior people already knew and trusted Ms. McCathran. More importantly, they already understood the value of having available the data that only the Daily Diary could provide.

Ms. McCathran was on vacation when the terrorist attacks occurred on September 11, 2001. She noted how everything felt so serious upon her return—heightened security and a prevailing sense of urgency. However, even though the presidency was a beehive of activity, the diarist's job did not really change. If anything, Ms. McCathran thought that the diary construction became even more efficient because the president's workdays became even more regimented. As for the 9/11 diary itself (see figure A.4), Ms. McCathran explained that she and her assistant spent more time drafting that one than any other. "There was no schedule we could use, but we knew it was important. We did more interviews for that one than any other I can remember."

In short, John Kennedy (via Evelyn Lincoln) may have spawned the Daily Diary for his own purposes, but the result has become an incomparable public good. The diaries give scholars of all stripes an extraordinary look into the daily work of the world's most powerful person. That it exists at all is remarkable; that it has endured is astonishing. In truth, presidential scholars could not ask for much more: consistent methods, applied by full-time professionals, driven by a commitment to accuracy, and over a time horizon that covers several decades, multiple presidencies, and defining moments of American history.

That gets back to the diarists, the public servants whose talents and commitments built such an incredible archive. Their labors did not bring them recognition, never mind fame or fortune, but they

THE DAILY DIARY OF PRESIDENT GEORGE W. BUSH

COLONY BEACH AND TENNIS RESORT
LONGBOAT KEY FLORIDA

September 11, 2001
6:00 AM TUESDAY

START	END	DESCRIPTION
		The President was an overnight guest at the Colony Beach and Tennis Resort, Longboat Key, Florida.
6:28 AM	6:35 AM	The President motored from the Colony Beach Resort to the Longboat Key Club, 301 Gulf of Mexico Drive.
6:40 AM *	7:20 AM *	The President went for a run.
7:23 AM	7:32 AM	The President motored from the Longboat Key Club to the Colony Beach Resort.
8:05 AM	* P	The President talked with his Assistant for National Security Affairs, Condoleezza D. Rice.
8:39 AM	8:54 AM	The President motored from the Colony Beach Resort to the Emma E. Booker Elementary School, 2350 Dr. Martin Luther King Way, Sarasota, Florida.
8:46 AM		NOTE: A hijacked passenger jet, American Airlines Flight 11, crashed into the World Trade Center North.
8:54 AM *		The President went to a holding area.
8:55 AM	8:56 AM R	The President talked with Ms. Rice who informed the President that a plane had crashed into the World Trade Center North.
8:59 AM *		The President went to classroom 301.
9:00 AM *	9:14 AM *	The President attended a reading program demonstration. He was accompanied by: Roderick R. Paige, Secretary of Education Frank T. Brogan, Lt. Governor (R-Florida) Gwen Rigell, Principal, Emma E. Booker Elementary School Kaye Daniels, Second Grade Teacher, Emma E. Booker Elementary School Edwina Oliver, Teacher of the Year, Emma E. Booker Elementary School Wilma Hamilton, Superintendent of Schools, Sarasota County School District

Page 1 of 24

(*) Indicates event time unconfirmed.   (P, R) Indicates phone call placed, received.   All times are POTUS local.

FIGURE A.4 President Bush 43's Daily Diary for September 11, 2001.

kept at it with diligence, professionalism, and integrity because they believed their work was valuable for presidents in the short term and would be valuable for researchers in the long term. These irreplaceable records are their inspired legacy.

APPENDIX B

SAMPLING DESIGN AND DETAIL

THE PERIOD FROM JANUARY 20, 1961, to January 20, 2009, includes forty-eight years and a riveting rundown of historic events: economic booms and busts, national tragedies and triumphs, military conflicts and diplomatic breakthroughs—and a steady stream of scandals, successes, errors, and achievements. First in line at this half century's forks in the road were nine presidents: John Kennedy, Lyndon Johnson, Richard Nixon, Gerald Ford, Jimmy Carter, Ronald Reagan, George H. W. Bush, Bill Clinton, and George W. Bush.

As detailed in appendix A, presidential diarists dutifully logged presidents' daily activities for the 17,532 days between President Kennedy's first day and President Bush 43's last. A handful of contemporaneous archivists worked diligently to record what the president did, when the president did it, and the people the president did it with.

Having discovered the Daily Diaries' existence and then conducted a preliminary investigation into their derivation, I had no doubt that the diaries presented a tremendous scholarly opportunity. The challenge was how to translate a vast archive into a feasible project.[1]

SAMPLE DESIGN

My conservative estimate is that there are more than 75,000 diary pages currently in the public domain, with tens of thousands more already archived but thus far unreleased.[2] To winnow this vast archive into a viable workload required sampling.[3] To that end, I fashioned a sampling strategy that would (1) produce a representative sample of days during each year and (2) facilitate valid comparisons across years (and presidents).

Befitting these dual aims, I selected a random sample, stratified by month (4 days per month), but organized by *day* rather than *date*. Thus, I did not include July 4 each year; rather, I included every "first Tuesday in July." In practice, I randomly selected a week (1–5, except for February, which was just 1–4) and then a day (M, T, W, etc.) four times for each month.

Figure B.1 details the resulting sample. My April sample, for example, includes the first Tuesday, second Wednesday, fourth Tuesday, and fifth Friday—not just for one year, but for every year. Applying this figure to every year from 1961 to 2008 thus unlocks all the days included in this study.

SAMPLE DETAILS

If identifying the days to study was the first step, securing the diaries to study took several more. Given my interests, I needed each Daily Diary and any corresponding appendices, but not the backup material (phone logs, flight manifests, movement logs, meeting agendas, and so on) from which diarists drew.

Each president's diaries are archived at each president's library. Some libraries have all their diaries (including appendices) online; some have the diary online, but not its appendices; some have paper files that are open to visitors but not online. For each in-sample day, we worked with archivists at each library—by email or phone where possible, in person when needed—to get a complete diary and its appendices.

The effort paid off. I am convinced that if an in-sample day had a corresponding diary, we got it—including its appendices. Of course,

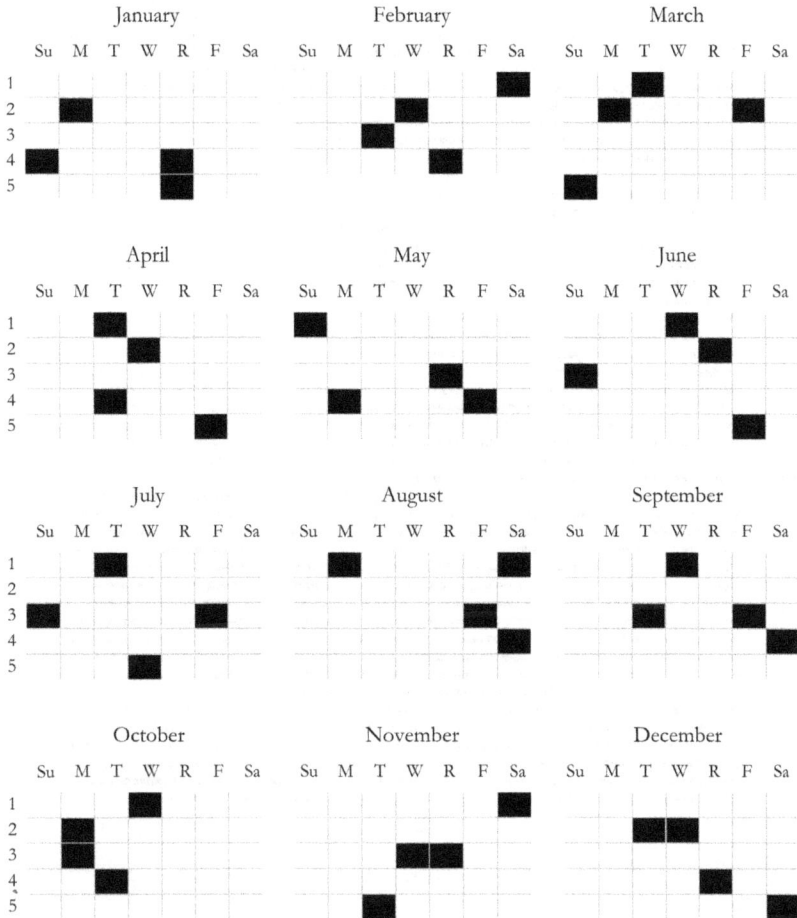

FIGURE B.1 Stratified (4 days per month) sampling frame and random sample.

Filled cells indicate the 4 days randomly sampled in each month (e.g., the second Monday in January; the fourth Thursday in December). However, not all sampled days apply to each year (e.g., for 1961, there is no fifth Thursday in January), so actual yearly samples are a little under 48 days per year

FIGURE B.2 Daily Diary availability for sampled days, by year.

Figure indicates the number of in-sample days by year, broken down by the number
with a Daily Diary available (black) or missing (grey)

that fact raises the obvious follow-up: What days did not have a corresponding diary?

Figure B.2 maps the sampling frame to the sample coded, which
uncovers several key points. First, the decision to sample by day
rather than date meant that some days in the sample frame did not

correspond to an actual day in a particular year. This occurred when there was no fifth day of a month during that year. For example, my sample includes every fifth Thursday in January, which does not exist in 1961 or 1962 (but does in 1963 and 1964). So although the theoretical sample is 48 days per year, the actual sample is a little less. In the figure, this actual sample maximum is indicated by the light grey line.

The next, more pressing point is about missing data—those days for which there is no diary.[4] As we can see, most years had little missing data. Eleven years had diaries for every day sampled; another seventeen years were only missing diaries for 1 or 2 of the 40+ days sampled.

There are two major exceptions—that is, years in which a substantial portion of our sampled days were not memorialized with a completed diary. These were focused on two presidencies: Clinton and, to a lesser degree, Reagan.

As noted in appendix A, the nature of Clinton's staffing and scheduling complicated the diarists' job. Those challenges are clearly in evidence. A fifth of the diaries in my 1993 and 2000 samples went undone, as did a third of those for 1999, more than half for 1994 and 1995, and nearly all for 1997. All told, there are completed diaries for just over half the days sampled during Clinton's time as president.

Reagan's archive has fewer gaps than Clinton's but certainly includes more missing data than is typical. One issue is that Reagan took real vacations, and his time at Rancho del Cielo was not as well documented. The other, more glaring issue is 1988, when the diarist was simply unable to complete many diaries through Reagan's final months in office.

Again, appendix A gives a fuller narrative of a diary's history, which helps contextualize these patterns. The bottom line, however, is that the sampling design mostly worked as intended. The overall diary-to-day "response rate" was 87 percent (1,781 diaries from 2,057 days). This would be a good harvest anyway, but it is better still because the missing data, while not random, did not result from manipulation or censorship. What is more, the days with diaries appear comparable to the days without diaries.

In short, by coupling a stratified random sampling method with a quasi-matching design, I sought to generate a representative sample of days within each year and facilitate comparisons across years and presidents. By all indications, it worked, bolstering our confidence that the differences observed in chapters 3 and 4 reflect real behavioral choices rather than differences in the mix of days sampled or coded.

APPENDIX C

CODING AND DATA

FTER PROCURING A REPRESENTATIVE SAMPLE of Daily Diaries from 1961 to 2008, Kennedy to Bush 43, the assignment turned to harnessing their contents. This was no simple chore, in part because there was so much material to process, but even more because presidents' days are anything but formulaic. Theirs is a world of one-offs—extraordinary people in unique settings during exceptional times.

My challenge, then, was to devise a coding regime that could (a) validly capture each moment and (b) reliably allow comparisons across moments. Happily, we were able to meet these specifications. Extending my discussion in chapter 4, this appendix explicates the coding protocols we adopted to illuminate the data they generated.

CODING

My first decision was to limit our coding to moments that lasted 5 or more minutes. This is a low bar, but it served to trim the coding without losing much content. For example, if the chief of staff (COS) pops in to let the president know that the National Security Council (NSC) is assembled in the next room, the 5+ minute threshold will ignore the COS announcement but count the NSC meeting. So while we did not code every recorded activity and contact, we did code the vast majority, including the most important.[1]

Thus was defined the corpus to code for this study: each 5+ minute moment, as logged in the Daily Diary, for every day in my sample. This turned out to be 37,781 moments, spread over 2,057 days (1,781 with diaries), spanning forty-eight years, covering nine presidencies.

The coding team was a large, rotating cast of undergraduate and graduate research assistants (RAs). The work was typically organized as an upper-division independent study course that extended 11 weeks per course. Our initial training regime included two 1.5-hour tutorials on the coding scheme and data entry, followed by a week of practice coding with a randomly selected partner, plus one more training week conducted independently, though each RA would then compare their codes with another RA who had unknowingly received the same assignment. RAs would proceed to the real coding assignments once their practice data proved reliable.

For the actual data collection, RAs and I worked via weekly assignments. RAs would get a randomly assigned set of diaries to code and then have a week to code them. They could email me whenever they hit a snag or had a question, and I often brought those issues to the whole group so we could collectively discuss how to handle such situations consistently. Students would upload their "deliverables" by specified due dates so I could check and clean them as we went. These files were ultimately merged, thereby producing the dataset utilized in chapters 3 and 4.

Because I defined key concepts and their corresponding measurement within the relevant chapters, the best way to explicate the underlying data is to walk through coding for a specific day, using a specific diary. To that end, I somewhat arbitrarily chose my birthday—August 19, 1975—for my illustrative case.

DATA

Gerald Ford was a busy president in general, and the summer of 1975 was no exception. After spending July 26–28 in West Germany,

Ford then spent a day (and night) in Poland before continuing through the rest of his international agenda in Finland (7/29–8/2), Romania (8/2–8/3), and Yugoslavia (8/3–8/4).

Ford spent the following week working from the White House. Then, on Sunday, August 10, the president and first lady flew to Arkansas for a "dedication ceremony of St. Edward Mercy Medical Center" before decamping to Veil, Colorado, for a "working vacation."

In Ford's case, "working vacation" was an apt description. Through the rest of August, Ford engaged in an extensive combination of calls, meals, meetings, greetings, photo-ops, briefings, and travel. Between August 10 and 30, Ford visited the following cities: Ft. Smith and Ft. Chaffee, Arizona; Grand Junction and Veil, Colorado; Des Moines, Iowa; Bloomington and Minneapolis, Minnesota; Chicago, Pekin, and Peoria, Illinois; Kalispell and Libby Dam, Montana; Milwaukee, Wisconsin; Portland, Maine; and Newport, Rhode Island.

August 19 fell in that time period. President Ford began his day at L'Hotel Sofitel in Bloomington, Minnesota, where he had stayed the previous night. Although the full day's Daily Diary spans 7 pages (plus another 25 pages of appendices), I need only the first and last pages of the basic diary, plus 1 page from its first appendix, to illuminate our coding means and ends.

Looking at the diary's first page (figure C.1), several coding elements are immediately discernible. First, because Ford was in Minnesota, we know he spent at least a portion of the day outside Washington, D.C. The second datum is the workday start time, which I define as the beginning of the president's first working moment. On this day it was 7:00 A.M., when the president's meeting with Dick Cheney and Mike Carmichael Jr. commenced.

As to the more general matter of identifying the "moments" to code, we followed the diarist's lead. Whatever diarists recorded as a distinct moment is what we coded as a distinct moment. If the diarist did not specify a moment's end time, RAs made a "reasonable infer- ence" based on the start time, nature of the activity, and context clues (e.g., the start time of the next moment).[2] In this case, we would need to fill in 5 moments' end times, as I did here (I identified these inferred times by enclosing them in dashed boxes). With the full complement of moments' start and end times, we coded all equivalently.

Scanned from the President's Daily Diary Collection (Box 77) at the Gerald R. Ford Presidential Library

THE WHITE HOUSE

THE DAILY DIARY OF PRESIDENT GERALD R. FORD

PLACE DAY BEGAN
L'HOTEL SOFITEL
BLOOMINGTON, MINNESOTA

DATE (Mo., Day, Yr.)
AUGUST 19, 1975
TIME   DAY
7:00 a.m. TUESDAY

Traveling

TIME In	TIME Out	PHONE P=Placed R=Rec'd	ACTIVITY	
7:00	8:00		The President was an overnight guest at the L'Hotel Sofitel, 5601 West 78th Street, Bloomington, Minnesota.	
7:30	8:00		The President met with: Richard B. Cheney, Deputy Assistant	COS
			O.C. "Mike" Carmichael, Jr., Treasurer of the Republican National Committee (RNC)	Political
8:00	8:02	P	The President talked with Congressman Bob Bergland (D-Minnesota). The purpose of the call was to express his condolences on the death of the Congressman's son, Jon, who died in an automobile accident on August 17th.	
8:00	8:05		The President and Mr. Cheney went to the Nice Room.	COS
8:05	9:25		The President hosted a breakfast meeting for media executives from Iowa, Minnesota, Missouri, Nebraska, North Dakota and South Dakota. For a list of attendees, see APPENDIX "A."	
8:15	8:19		The President greeted breakfast guests.	
8:20	9:00		The Presidential party had breakfast.	Multiple
9:10	9:20		The President addressed approximately 100 television and newspaper executives attending the regional media breakfast.	Multiple
9:25	9:25		The President went to the Le Cafe.	
9:25	9:55		The President attended a reception hosted by Mr. Carmichael for a group of Minnesota "Key Men" Republicans. For a list of attendees, see APPENDIX "B."	Multiple
9:55	10:00		The President went to his motorcade. Enroute, he was greeted by: Mayor Robert Benedict (Independent-Bloomington, Minnesota) Mayor Robert Bouden (D-Duluth, Minnesota) Senator Hubert H. Humphrey (D-Minnesota) Mayor Benedict presented the President with a key to the city of Bloomington and Mayor Bouden presented the President with a photograph and plaque.	State/ Local Senator – other

Start Time

Thinking

Speaking

Page 1 of 2 Page(s)

○ Policy Meeting
● Public Event

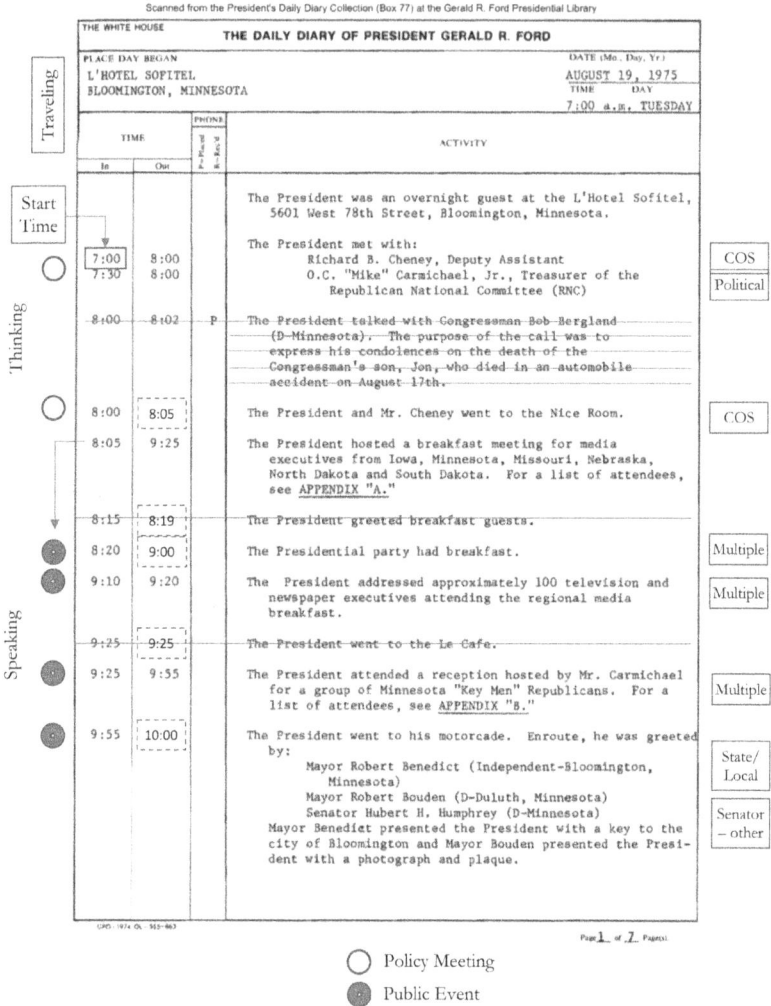

FIGURE C.1 President's Daily Diary for August 19, 1975 (first page).

This shows how the 5-minute coding threshold plays out in practice. Several fleeting moments would not make it into the dataset, such as President Ford's 2-minute call to Representative Bob Bergland regarding his son's recent death.

A different coding wrinkle is captured in Ford's 8:05 to 9:25 A.M. breakfast and speech. Notice how the diarist first identified overall event time (8:05–9:25) before subsequently delineating its constituent moments: breakfast (8:20–9:00 A.M.) and address (9:10–9:20 A.M.). In such situations, which are fairly common, we ignored the omnibus introduction and instead coded the itemized moments. While it did not make much difference this time, the broader point still holds: coding the disaggregated moments affords a more granular look into presidents' workdays.

Up to this point, then, we see that the diary's first page includes 6 distinct moments awaiting coding. For each, RAs would enter its start and end time, and then code details about what the president was doing as well as who else was present.

Regarding the "what" portion of the coding, RAs would adjudicate whether the president was (or was not) working during that moment. Our standard for determining work activities was whether the activity reflected the president's professional or personal interests. Breakfast with the family would be leisure; breakfast with approximately one hundred media executives would be work. On this page, then, all 6 codable moments are related to work.

Befitting my theoretical interest in how presidents allocate their time between speaking and thinking activities, my next task required partitioning moments into "speaking" and "thinking" activities. Conveniently, August 19, 1975, includes both.

Before delving further, I should reiterate that I use the term "speaking time" to capture a general class of public-facing behaviors— speeches, rallies, photo-ops, receptions, press conferences, ceremonies, and the like. This is why the breakfast with media executives is a public-facing event, even though it ostensibly precedes the explicit public "address." Likewise, the reception with "key" Republicans, hosted by the Republican National Committee (RNC) chair, is manifestly campaign-motivated. And, of course, the key-to-the-city presentation with Minnesota public officials is a canonical public relations play.

The "thinking" moments here were fewer and briefer, which makes sense given the day's agenda. Per my coding rules, there are two thinking moments on this page: Ford's initial meeting with Cheney and Carmichael, and then the moment when Ford and Cheney are together in the "Nice Room."

Having detailed how we did the "what" portion of the coding, I now turn to the "who" portion. As a reminder (see chapter 4), we coded people according to "types," as detailed in table C.1. In practice, RAs would go through the list and check off a box when one or more person of that type were present during each moment.

I illustrate with the day's first moment. Here RAs would check off the White House COS box and the White House communications box. Notably, because the national committees became an arm of presidential campaigns in the postwar era, we coded RNC or DNC officials (according to the president's party) as falling under White House "communications" (a category that also included officials who primarily fit into press secretary, communications, speechwriting, and political affairs offices, regardless of the specific title).

Cheney's case typifies this aspect of our coding protocol—namely, that we coded by type, not title. In August 1975, Donald Rumsfeld was the White House COS; Dick Cheney was the deputy COS. For my purposes, this was effectively a distinction without a difference. Both filled the same role, so the fact that it was Cheney rather than Rumsfeld did not change our coding: the White House COS "type" was present. This same logic held for Cabinet departments (e.g., a director of a Cabinet department agency was no different from its secretary), foreign governments (e.g., we coded a contact with a country's ambassador the same as contact with its leader), or other entities (e.g., a meeting with an automobile company official would count the same as a meeting with the CEO or another employee serving as the company's representative).

Figure C.2 displays the last of a 7-page appendix for the 8:05 A.M. breakfast event. The full appendix lists all the 97 media executives and 8 "White House staff" present (the appendix's first page notes that the asterisks indicate who sat at the president's table). For the coding, we defined the "press" type as employees of media organizations, which usually meant a reporter but applies here because publishers, editors, managers, and the like certainly fit the bill. So having checked the "press" box for the first name, there was nothing additional to code for the next 96. Then we would winnow the 8 staffers into their three basic types: communications, economics, and COS.

TABLE C.1 "People types" for coding presidential contacts

White House officials
- Vice president
- Chief of staff
- Domestic/economic
- National security
- Communications

Cabinet officials
- State Department
- Defense Department
- Treasury Department
- Justice Department
- Central Intelligence Agency

Members of Congress
- Senate Democratic leaders
- Senate Republican leaders
- Other senator
- House Democratic leaders
- House Republican leaders
- Other representatives

Others
- Press
- Foreign government official
- State/local government official
- Nongovernment organization official
- Private individual

Note: For each 5+ minute moment recorded in sampled days' Daily Diaries, the research assistant coded whether at least one person of that "type" was present with the president. From these raw data, I calculated how many types of people the president encountered (breadth) each day, as well as how many times he encountered them (depth).

APPENDIX "A" p. 12
8/19/75

Mr. J. Martin Wolman
Publisher
Wisconsin State Journal
Madison, Wisconsin

Press

✳ Mr. Howard B. Woods
Publisher and Editor
St. Louis Sentinel
St. Louis, Missouri

Mr. F. R. Woodward
Executive Vice President
Telegraph-Herald
Dubuque, Iowa

Mr. Lee E. Zanin
General Manager
WWTC Radio (all news)
Minneapolis, Minnesota

White House Staff

✳ Ronald H. Nessen, Press Secretary
Frank G. Zarb, Administrator of the Federal Energy Administration
William I. Greener, Deputy Press Secretary
Alan Greenspan, Chairman of the Council of Economic Advisers (CEA)
Margita E. White, Assistant Press Secretary
Richard B. Cheney, Deputy Assistant
John T. Calkins, Executive Assistant to Counsellor Robert T. Hartmann
John G. Carlson, Assistant Press Secretary

Commu-
nications

Economic

COS

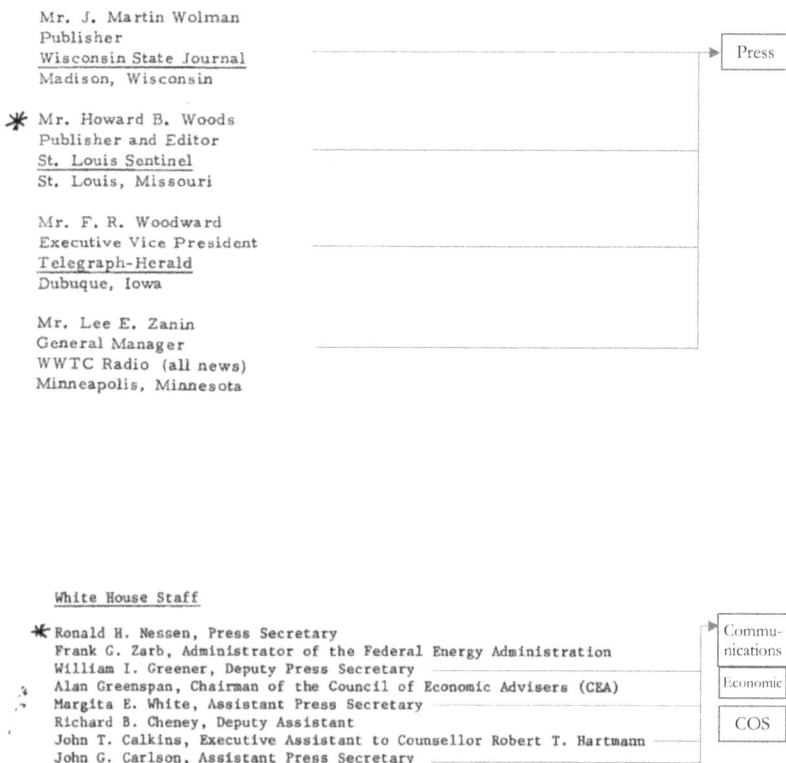

FIGURE C.2 President's Daily Diary for August 19, 1975 (appendix page).

No doubt, coding people by "type" has pluses and minuses. For this project, the pluses clearly outweighed the minuses. Winnowing from all people to specific types of people made coding events like the State of the Union address far more manageable, and again, knowing that the president met with members from both parties, both chambers, including leaders and backbenchers, is sufficient given my interests. As explained in chapter 4, the exact number of people at each moment is not especially enlightening because my relevant construct is presidential workload, not audience size.

Figure C.3 details the president's final activities per the diary's final page. I include it here to stress three final points. One emerges

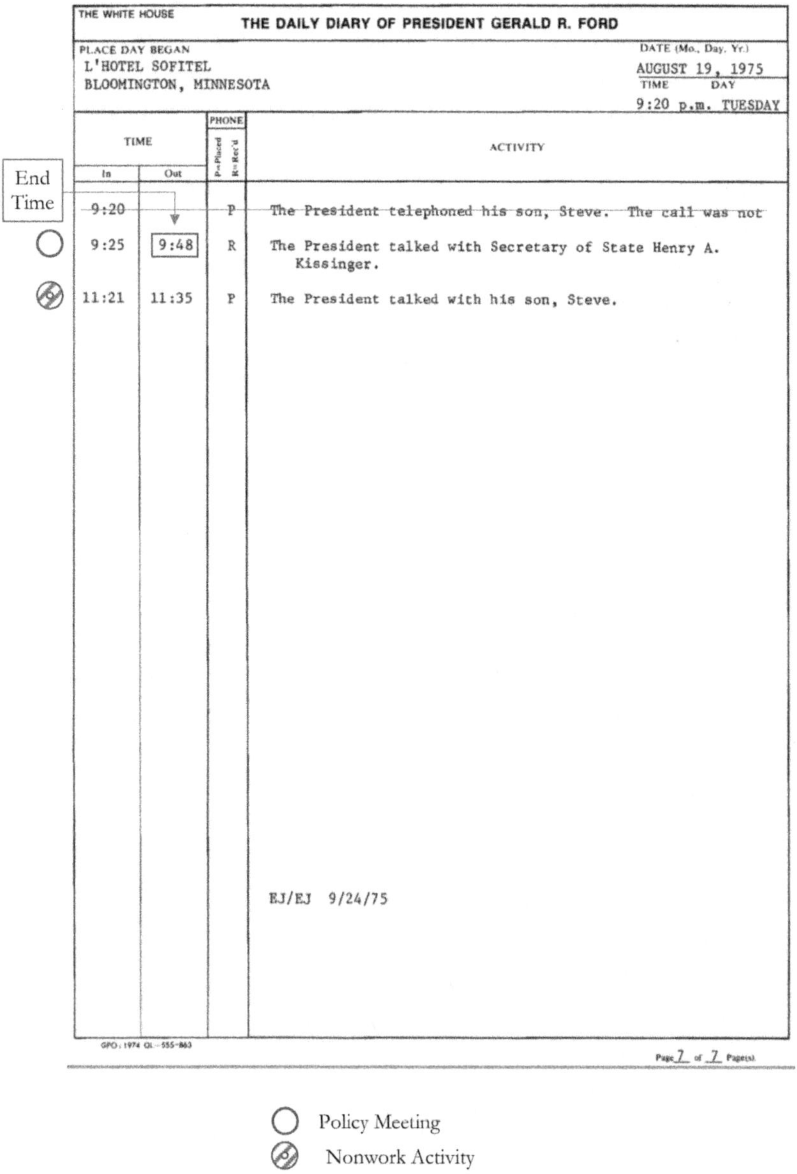

THE WHITE HOUSE

THE DAILY DIARY OF PRESIDENT GERALD R. FORD

PLACE DAY BEGAN
L'HOTEL SOFITEL
BLOOMINGTON, MINNESOTA

DATE (Mo., Day, Yr.)
AUGUST 19, 1975
TIME DAY
9:20 p.m. TUESDAY

TIME In	TIME Out	PHONE P=Placed R=Rec'd	ACTIVITY
~~9:20~~		~~P~~	~~The President telephoned his son, Steve. The call was not~~
9:25	9:48	R	The President talked with Secretary of State Henry A. Kissinger.
11:21	11:35	P	The President talked with his son, Steve.
			EJ/EJ 9/24/75

GPO : 1974 OL—555-863

Page 7 of 7 Page(s).

End Time
Policy Meeting
Nonwork Activity

FIGURE C.3 President's Daily Diary for August 19, 1975 (final page).

in the initial call President Ford placed to his son, Steve. Although the diarist failed to finish the last sentence, I know based on scores of comparable examples that the sentence should read, "The call was not completed." That was a common occurrence, and we treated uncompleted calls as if they did not exist or, in our parlance, as a nonmoment.

Of course, a few hours later the president tried to reach his son again, and this time they connected. The conversation lasted 14 minutes, from 11:21 to 11:35. While this does count as a moment in our coding scheme (because it lasted more than 5 minutes), it was not a work activity, and thus it would not get tallied in my measures of "speaking" or "thinking" time.

That gets to the final point: because the call with his son was not work, identifying when the president's workday ended required going back to his last work moment. That turned out to be a call from Henry Kissinger, the secretary of state, that lasted from 9:25 to 9:48 P.M. As we coded it, then, 9:48 P.M. closed the book on Ford's work for August 19, 1975—a mere 14 hours and 48 minutes after it began.

In these ways, per these rules, my research team and I were able to document how presidents work—where the president was, what he did, when he did it, and what types of people were with him.

NOTES

INTRODUCTION

1. Lyndon B. Johnson, "Annual Message to the Congress on the State of the Union," January 4, 1965, https://www.presidency.ucsb.edu/node/241819
2. Barack Obama, "Keynote: Qualtrics X4 Summit," March 6, 2019.
3. Edmund Morris, "Compassionate Conservatism," *New York Times*, August 17, 2005.
4. Tim Weiner, "Robert S. McNamara, Architect of a Futile War, Dies at 93," *New York Times*, July 6, 2009.
5. See Richard J. Ellis, *Founding the American Presidency* (New York: Rowman & Littlefield, 1999).
6. Theodore Roosevelt, *Theodore Roosevelt; an Autobiography* (New York: Macmillan, 1913), 357.
7. T. E. Cronin and W. R. Hochman, "Franklin D. Roosevelt and the American Presidency," *Presidential Studies Quarterly* 15, no. 2 (1985): 285. See also Matthew J. Dickinson, *Bitter Harvest: FDR, Presidential Power and the Growth of the Presidential Branch* (New York: Cambridge University Press, 1999).
8. Clinton Rossiter, *The American Presidency*, 2nd ed. (New York: Harcourt, Brace, 1960), 16.
9. Rossiter, *The American Presidency*, 16–39.
10. Dickinson, *Bitter Harvest*.
11. Kathryn Smith, *The Gatekeeper: Missy LeHand, FDR, and the Untold Story of the Partnership That Defined a Presidency* (New York: Atria, 2016).
12. U.S. President's Committee on Administrative Management, *Report of the President's Committee*, Washington, D.C., Government Printing Office, January 12, 1937: 5.

13. For a study that illuminates Franklin Roosevelt's managerial methods and the Executive Office of the President's origin story, see Dickinson, *Bitter Harvest*.

14. Stephen Hess and Jim Pfiffner carefully trace the presidency's transformation from "a small, personalized office to a set of centralized bureaucracies (with hundreds of people) in charge of the much larger bureaucracies (of millions of people) in the broader executive branch." S. Hess and J. P. Pfiffner, *Organizing the Presidency* (Washington, DC: Brookings Institution, 2002), 1.

15. Phillip G. Henderson, "Organizing the Presidency for Effective Leadership: Lessons from the Eisenhower Years," *Presidential Studies Quarterly* 17, no. 1 (1987): 43–69.

16. Letter, Dwight Eisenhower to Dillon Anderson, 1/22/68 [Post-Presidential Papers, 1968 Principal File, Box 36, "An"]

17. See Bradley H. Patterson, "Teams and Staff: Dwight Eisenhower's Innovations in the Structure and Operations of the Modern White House," *Presidential Studies Quarterly* 24, no. 2 (1994): 296; Fred I. Greenstein, *The Hidden-Hand Presidency: Eisenhower as Leader* (Baltimore, MD: Johns Hopkins University Press, 1994).

18. John F. Kennedy, "The Presidency in 1960," January 14, 1960.

19. Neustadt's memos to postwar presidents are as insightful as they are fascinating, and Charles O. Jones compiled them into a compelling volume. Charles O. Jones, *Preparing to Be President: The Memos of Richard E. Neustadt* (Washington, DC: AEI Press, 2000): 25.

20. Richard Tanner Johnson, *Managing the White House: An Intimate Study of the Presidency* (New York: Harper & Row, 1974).

21. Roger B. Porter, *Presidential Decision Making: The Economic Policy Board* (New York: Cambridge University Press, 1980).

22. M. Watson with S. Markman, *Chief of Staff: Lyndon Johnson and His Presidency* (New York: Thomas Dunne, 2004): 92.

23. C. E. Walcott and K. M. Hult, *Empowering the White House* (Lawrence: University Press of Kansas, 2004); C. E. Walcott and K. M. Hult, "White House Structure and Decision Making: Elaborating the Standard Model," *Presidential Studies Quarterly* 35, no. 2 (2005): 303–18.

24. Walcott and Hult, "White House Structure and Decision Making," 303.

25. For an exemplar, see Elizabeth Drew, "How Not to Run the White House," *New Republic*, February 14, 2018.

26. Mary McGrory, "Meet the Press More Often," *Washington Post*, November 9, 1993.

27. Robert H. Ferrell, ed., *Off the Record: The Private Papers of Harry S. Truman* (New York: Harper & Row, 1980), 256.

28. Ronald Reagan, "Remarks at a Meeting with Asian and Pacific-American Leaders," February 23, 1984. Online by Gerhard Peters and John T.

Woolley, *The American Presidency Project*: https://www.presidency.ucsb.edu/node/261667.

29. Richard Neustadt, *Presidential Power and the Modern Presidents* (New York: Free Press, 1990), 114.

30. Woodrow Wilson, *Cabinet Government in the United States* (Stamford, CT: Overbrook, 1947): 70.

31. See M. J. Dickinson and E. Neustadt, *Guardian of the Presidency: The Legacy of Richard E. Neustadt* (Washington, DC: Brookings Institution, 2007).

32. See Charles Cameron, *Veto Bargaining* (New York: Cambridge University Press, 2000); Brandice Canes-Wrone, "Game Theory and the Study of the American Presidency," in *The Oxford Handbook of the American Presidency*, ed. W. G. Howell and G. C. Edwards III, 30–50 (New York: Oxford University Press, 2009).

33. Terry M. Moe, "The Revolution in Presidential Studies," *Presidential Studies Quarterly* 39, no. 4 (2009): 704.

34. Moe, "The Revolution in Presidential Studies." See also several thoughtful rejoinders: Jeffrey E. Cohen, "Alternative Futures," *Presidential Studies Quarterly* 39, no. 4 (2009): 725–35; Matthew J. Dickinson, "We All Want a Revolution: Neustadt, New Institutionalism, and the Future of Presidency Research," *Presidential Studies Quarterly* 39, no. 4 (2009): 736–70; Lawrence R. Jacobs, "Building Reliable Theories of the Presidency," *Presidential Studies Quarterly* 39, no. 4 (2009): 771–80; Kenneth R. Mayer, "Thoughts on 'The Revolution in Presidential Studies,'" *Presidential Studies Quarterly* 39, no. 4 (2009): 781–85; Bert A. Rockman, "Off with the President's Head?," *Presidential Studies Quarterly* 39, no. 4 (2009): 786–94; Stephen Skowronek, "Mission Accomplished," *Presidential Studies Quarterly* 39, no. 4 (2009): 795–804.

35. W. G. Howell and T. M. Moe, *Relic: How Our Constitution Undermines Effective Government and Why We Need a More Powerful Presidency* (New York: Basic Books, 2016), 100. See also W. G. Howell and T. M. Moe, *Presidents, Populism, and the Crisis of American Democracy* (Chicago: University of Chicago Press, 2020). B. Dan Wood adds a critical wrinkle. Analyzing presidents' public statements, Wood finds that presidents present as standard partisans rather than national representatives, suggesting that they behave as "generic" partisans rather than generic presidents per se. B. Dan Wood, *The Myth of Presidential Representation* (New York: Cambridge University Press, 2009).

36. To be sure, there is a vast literature on decision-making and sense-making. For the presidency per se, several review chapters do heroic work to weave these threads together. See John P. Burke, "Organizational Structure and Presidential Decision Making," in *The Oxford Handbook of the American Presidency*, ed. W. G. Howell and G. C. Edwards III, 501–27 (New York: Oxford University Press, 2009); K. M. Hult and C. E. Walcott, "Influences on Presidential Decision Making," in *The Oxford Handbook of the American*

Presidency, 528–49; and Stephen G. Walker, "The Psychology of Presidential Decision-Making," in *The Oxford Handbook of the American Presidency*, 550–74.

37. Michael Lewis, "Obama's Way," *Vanity Fair*, September 11, 2012.
38. Neustadt, *Presidential Power*, 150.
39. Andy Card, "Leadership Lessons from Former White House Chief of Staff," interview with Nikita Bakhru, Nelson A. Rockefeller Center, October 26, 2016.
40. Chris Whipple, *The Presidents' Gatekeepers* (New York: Crown, 2017), 70.
41. Jimmy Carter, *White House Diary* (New York: Farrar, Straus and Giroux, 2010), 60.

1. TIME, PEOPLE, AND PROCESS

1. Garrett M. Graff, *Watergate: A New History* (New York: Simon & Schuster, 2022), 307–8.
2. Theodore C. Sorensen, *Decision-Making in the White House: The Olive Branch or the Arrows* (New York: Columbia University Press, 2005), 226.
3. Mo Fiorina explained it well: "Like all theoretical worlds, the one we posit is more or less unrealistic, an idealization of the empirical reality we hope to explain. But if we abstract appropriately and capture the most important features of the empirical situation, then we may expect to find that the theoretical processes present in the model world bear some correspondence to the behavior we observe in the empirical world." See Morris Fiorina, *Representatives, Roll Calls, and Constituencies* (New York: Lexington, 1974), 29.
4. There is an enormous literature on organizations, organizational behavior, executive management, and the like. I shall not attempt anything like a comprehensive review; rather, given my interests, I will highlight those threads that are most directly tied to the modern presidency.
5. Theodore C. Sorensen, *Counselor: A Life at the Edge of History* (New York: HarperCollins, 2008), 132.
6. Joe Heim, "Just Asking," *Washington Post*, December 5, 2014.
7. John Hart, *Presidential Branch: From Washington to Clinton* (New York: Chatham House, 1995); David E. Lewis, *Presidents and the Politics of Agency Design* (Stanford, CA: Stanford University Press, 2003); Bradley H. Patterson, *The White House Staff: Inside the West Wing and Beyond* (Washington, DC: Brookings Institution, 2000).
8. This is not to say that executive branch officials ignore presidential preferences. Andy Rudalevige shows that civil servants who draft effective orders are responsive to many institutional forces, including the president's wishes. See Andrew Rudalevige, *By Executive Order: Bureaucratic*

Management and the Limits of Presidential Power (Princeton, NJ: Princeton University Press, 2022).

9. Tevi Troy, *Fight House: Rivalries in the White House from Truman to Trump* (Washington, DC: Regnery History, 2020).

10. G. Allison and P. Zelikow, *Essence of Decision: Explaining the Cuban Missile Crisis*, 2nd ed. (New York: Pearson, 1999); Lucien S. Vandenbroucke, "The 'Confessions' of Allen Dulles: New Evidence on the Bay of Pigs," *Diplomatic History* 8, no. 4 (1984): 365–76.

11. Irving L. Janis, *Victims of Groupthink: A Psychological Study of Foreign-Policy Decisions and Fiascoes* (New York: Houghton Mifflin, 1972).

12. Janis, *Victims of Groupthink*, 9.

13. Kennedy's national security advisor, McGeorge Bundy, put more responsibility on Kennedy himself: "We do have a problem of management; centrally it is a problem of your use of time and your use of your staff. . . . Right now it is so hard to get to you with anything not urgent and immediate that about half the papers and reports you personally ask for are never shown to you because by the time you are available you clearly have lost interest in them." David Priess, *The President's Book of Secrets* (New York: Public Affairs, 2017), 19.

14. Matthew J. Dickinson, *Bitter Harvest: FDR, Presidential Power and the Growth of the Presidential Branch* (New York: Cambridge University Press, 1999); Hugh Heclo, *A Government of Strangers: Executive Politics in Washington* (Washington, DC: Brookings Institution, 1977); George A. Krause, "Organizational Complexity and Coordination Dilemmas in U.S. Executive Politics," *Presidential Studies Quarterly* 39, no. 1 (2009): 74–88; Richard Neustadt, *Presidential Power and the Modern Presidents* (New York: Free Press, 1990); Andrew Rudalevige, *Managing the President's Program: Presidential Leadership and Legislative Policy Formation* (Princeton, NJ: Princeton University Press, 2002); Rudalevige, *By Executive Order*; James Q. Wilson, *Bureaucracy: What Government Agencies Do and Why They Do It* (New York: Basic Books, 1989).

15. Robert Reich, *Locked in the Cabinet* (New York: Vintage, 1998).

16. To be sure, no matter how explicit the organization chart may be, the president can always reorder relative positioning—formally or practically, occasionally or routinely.

17. Alexander George used the term "managerial custodian," but I adopt Roger Porter's "honest broker" phrasing because it is more familiar in and out of Washington. Alexander L. George, *Presidential Decisionmaking in Foreign Policy: The Effective Use of Information and Advice* (Boulder, CO: Westview, 1980); Roger B. Porter, *Presidential Decision Making: The Economic Policy Board* (Cambridge: Cambridge University Press, 1980).

18. Research into the White House COS position is difficult, but several political scientists have provided important insights into the position's history,

structure, and roles. See D. B. Cohen and G. A. Krause, "Presidents, Chiefs of Staff, and the Structure of White House Organization," *Presidential Studies Quarterly* 30, no. 3 (2000): 421–42; D. B. Cohen, K. M. Hult, and C. E. Walcott, "White House Evolution and Institutionalization: The Office of Chief of Staff Since Reagan," *Presidential Studies Quarterly* 46, no. 1 (2016): 4–29; S. Kernell and S. L. Popkin, eds., *Chief of Staff: Twenty-Five Years of Managing the Presidency* (Los Angeles: University of California Press, 1986); Richard E. Neustadt, "Does the White House Need a Strong Chief of Staff?," in *The Managerial Presidency*, ed. James P. Pfiffner (Pacific Grove, CA: Brooks/Cole, 1991), 69–74.

19. John P. Burke, *Honest Broker? The National Security Advisor and Presidential Decision-Making* (College Station: Texas A&M University Press, 2009); I. H. Daalder and I. M. Destler, *In the Shadow of the Oval Office: Profiles of the National Security Advisers and the Presidents They Served—From JFK to George W. Bush* (New York: Simon & Schuster, 2009).

20. White House, *Memorandum on Renewing the National Security Council System* (Washington, DC: White House, 2021), https://www.whitehouse.gov/briefing-room/statements-releases/2021/02/04/memorandum-renewing-the-national-security-council-system/.

21. George was among several experts to theorize how presidents could routinize effective deliberation. Harold Wilensky similarly argued that "organizational intelligence" turns on informational quality as decision-makers need accurate, relevant, clear, timely, and diverse information. See Alexander George, "The Case for Multiple Advocacy in Making Foreign Policy," *American Political Science Review* 66, no. 3 (1972): 751–85, quote at 751; Harold Wilensky, *Organizational Intelligence* (New York: Basic Books, 1967), viii–ix.

22. Martha Joynt Kumar and Terry Sullivan's White House Transition Project has done heroic work to build "institutional memory" and then make various resources more reliable, more useful, and more accessible during presidential transitions (whitehousetransitionproject.org).

23. Abigail Abrams, "13 Pieces of Advice for the Trump Team from Obama's White House," *Time*, January 12, 2017.

24. Cohen and Krause, "Presidents, Chiefs of Staff, and White House Organizational Behavior," 424.

25. Andrew Rudalevige, "The Structure of Leadership: Presidents, Hierarchies, and Information Flow," Presidential *Studies Quarterly* 35, no. 2 (2005): 339.

26. Denis McDonough, "Views from the West Wing," *University of Notre Dame Going Global Forum*, October 4, 2017.

27. William G. Howell, *The Primacy of Power* (Princeton, NJ: Princeton University Press, 2013), 6.

28. All presidents promote policy deliberations, though earlier iterations tended to proceed with less formality and fewer specialists. Moreover, roles can evolve even when titles do not. National security advisors, for instance,

have extended the office's traditional "honest broker" role by also serving presidents as policy advisors and public advocates.

29. Charles E. Lindblom, "The Science of 'Muddling Through,'" *Public Administration Review* 19, no. 2 (1959): 79–88; M. D. Cohen, J. G. March, and J. P. Olsen, "A Garbage Can Model of Organizational Choice," *Administrative Science Quarterly* 17, no. 1 (1972): 1–25.

30. See Matthew N. Beckmann, *Pushing the Agenda* (New York: Cambridge University Press, 2010); Matthew J. Dickinson, "Bargaining, Uncertainty, and the Growth of the White House Staff, 1940–2000," in *Uncertainty in American Politics*, ed. Barry C. Burden, 27–47 (New York: Cambridge University Press, 2003); Rudalevige, "'Therefore, Get Wisdom,'" 177–87. Such consultations also reflect the fact that presidents believe intuitively what Elizabeth Saunders showed experimentally: if presidential aides publicize their opposition to the president's position, they undermine public support for the president and his agenda. Consultations have a way of reducing frustration throughout the process while also disarming complaints when the process concludes. Elizabeth N. Saunders, "Leaders, Advisers, and the Political Origins of Elite Support for War," *Journal of Conflict Resolution* 62, no. 10 (2018): 2118–49.

31. Abrams, "13 Pieces of Advice."

32. Sorensen 2005, xxxi.

33. The literature on problems with empty or multiple equilibria solution sets is foundational in many domains, which certainly speaks to presidents' work. To wit, president-level decision problems are those with multidimensional trade-offs in a nonlinear space, riddled by uncertainty, set to play out in multiple stages, and open to exogenous shocks, which requires nontrivial updating across the board. See Kenneth J. Arrow, *Social Choice and Individual Values* (New York: Wiley, 1951); Duncan Black, "On the Rationale of Group Decision-Making," *Journal of Political Economy* 56, no. 1 (1948): 23–34; J. H. Miller and S. Page, *Complex Adaptive Systems: An Introduction to Computational Models of Social Life* (Princeton, NJ: Princeton University Press, 2007).

34. H. W. J. Rittel and M. M. Webber, "Dilemmas in a General Theory of Planning," *Policy Sciences* 4, no. 2 (1975): 155.

35. The president's operational challenge is akin to the P = NP problem in computational complexity theory. NP-Complete problems are those in which it is possible to *check* if a proposed solution works but there is no known method to *find* a new solution—or to know if one can even be found.

36. Ronald Reagan, *The Reagan Diaries* (New York: HarperCollins), 43.

37. Neustadt, *Presidential Power*, 130.

38. To be sure, each dimension could be tagged with other labels (e.g., priorities and obligations, policy and politics, and so on). I chose "thinking" and "speaking" because they capture the key tension that presidents themselves often describe: balancing substantive work with public exigencies.

39. Ronald Reagan, *An American Life* (New York: Simon & Schuster, 1990), 393.

40. Henry A. Kissinger, *Years of Renewal* (New York: Simon & Shuster, 2000), 74.

41. M. D. Shear, K. Rogers, and A. Karni, "Beneath Joe Biden's Folksy Demeanor, a Short Fuse and an Obsession with Details," *New York Times*, October 28, 2021.

42. See John Helgerson, *Getting to Know the President: Intelligence Briefings of Presidential Candidates and Presidents-Elect*, 4th ed. (Independently Published, 2022); Priess, *The President's Book of Secrets*.

43. Helgerson, *Getting to Know the President*.

44. That presidents need to bargain within the executive branch is a recurring theme among presidency scholars, and Andrew Rudalevige masterfully shows how this is true even in the realm of executive orders. See Rudalevige, *By Executive Order*.

45. For example, a new president might not think to create a National Economic Council and Council of Economic Advisors if starting with a blank slate, but the slate is not blank, so presidents keep and fill both entities more or less like everyone else.

46. Lyndon B. Johnson, *The Vantage Point: Perspectives of the Presidency, 1963–1969* (New York: Holt, Rinehart and Winston, 1971), ix.

47. Neustadt, *Presidential Power*, 150.

2. JIMMY VERSUS RONNIE

1. Terrance Smith, "Social Call Symbolizes the Transition to the White House," *New York Times*, November 21, 1980.

2. Jimmy Carter, *Keeping Faith: Memoirs of a President* (Little Rock: University of Arkansas Press, 1995), 586.

3. When reporters hounded Reagan about the meeting, the president-elect remained coy, offering only that it was "a very complete briefing." Carter, *Keeping Faith*, 586.

4. Douglas Brinkley, *The Unfinished Presidency* (Hawthorn, VIC, Australia: Viking/Allen Lane, 1998), 17.

5. James P. Pfiffner, *The Strategic Presidency: Hitting the Ground Running*, 2nd ed. (Lawrence: University Press of Kansas, 1996), 6.

6. The canonical example is President Carter's insistence that requests to use the White House tennis court or pool should come to him personally, case by case, day by day. See "Tennis Court & Swimming Pool" (NAID 166114), in Hugh A. Carter Files, Records of the White House Office of Administration, Jimmy Carter Library, Atlanta, GA.

7. Brinkley, *The Unfinished Presidency*, 16.

8. Carter, *Keeping Faith*, 33.

9. Lou Cannon, *President Reagan: The Role of a Lifetime* (London: Simon & Schuster, 1992), 31.

10. The other transition from one first-term elected president to another during the half century studied here occurred when Clinton replaced Bush 41. The Bush 41/Clinton dyad, however, is not especially well suited for this project. This is in part because their interpersonal differences are not as stark as those between Carter and Reagan, but mostly because there were a series of major foreign policy events during Bush's term (e.g., the fall of the Soviet Union and the Gulf War) that were unlike anything Clinton faced.

11. Explaining why he waited until his second term to try a new approach with the Soviet Union, Reagan said, "My problem for the first few years was [that Soviet leaders] kept dying on me." Ronald Reagan, "Remarks and Question-and-Answer Session with Regional Editors and Broadcasters," September 16, 1985, https://www.presidency.ucsb.edu/node/260253.

12. Ronald Reagan Presidential Library and Museum, "Reagan's Daily Diary," https://www.reaganlibrary.gov/archives/reagans-daily-diary.

13. The exception, preliminary as it is, may be President Trump. A leaked diary reveals a 457-minute gap in the January 6, 2021, Daily Diary, which includes time during the Capitol insurrection.

14. National Archives and Records Administration, "Guidance on Presidential Records," https://www.archives.gov/files/presidential-records-guidance.pdf (accessed March 15, 2022).

15. While a president's innate stamina is not observable as such, workday duration serves as a good proxy. Indeed, actual hours worked maps onto my conception of stamina as workload capacity far better than, say, measures of president's health or fitness (e.g., age, weight, blood pressure, etc.), or even expert appraisals, which would surely signal presidents' reputations as workaholics but without the precision captured by workday duration.

16. G. Peters and J. T. Woolley, *The American Presidency Project* (www.presidency.ucsb.edu).

17. To maximize comparability between Carter and Reagan, I limit the analyses to nonholiday weekdays with Daily Diaries during each president's first term, which covers 1,868 days.

18. Furthermore, the fact that there is little to no relationship between official contacts and public events (b = −0.00, SE = 0.01, p = n.s.) comports with the idea that the presidency imposes some number of "first things first," but the president's stamina helps determine how much time is available for the rest.

19. Ronald Reagan, "Remarks at the Annual White House Correspondents Dinner," April 17, 1986.

20. Ronald Reagan's 1987 "Gridiron Dinner" speech was ostensibly off the record, but its contents were nevertheless widely reported. See Jacqueline Trescott and Victoria Dawson, "Reagan and the Gridiron's Good Sports," *Washington Post* (March 29, 1987).

3. MAKING TIME

1. William J. Clinton, "Remarks at the Inaugural Luncheon," January 20, 1993.
2. Caleb Daniloff, "A Running Conversation with John Podesta," *Runner's World*, May 1, 2014.
3. Richard L. Berke, "Bush Is Providing Corporate Model for White House," *New York Times*, March 11, 2001.
4. Sheryl G. Stolber, "Bush in the Background," *New York Times*, June 6, 2008.
5. Oliver Knox, "Inside President Obama's Secret Schedule," *Yahoo News*, July 7, 2014.
6. John Hart, "Neglected Aspects of the Study of the Presidency," *Annual Review of Political Science* 1, no. 1 (1998): 388.
7. Here again, the criterion for determining whether an activity included "work" was whether it was related to the president's professional or personal interests. One illustrative analogy our research group cited was the difference between an "office party" and a "party party." The former is work; the latter is fun.
8. As to what fills these hours—the number and nature of the president's activities—that is the subject of the next chapter.
9. Ariel Alexovich, "Clinton's National Security Ad," *New York Times*, February 29, 2008, https://archive.nytimes.com/thecaucus.blogs.nytimes.com/2008/02/29/clintons-national-security-ad/.
10. Tevi Troy, "Don't Worry, America: The 3 A.M. Phone Call Is a Myth," *Politico*, September 10, 2016.
11. More prosaically, most modern presidents have had a standing morning appointment for the CIA to deliver the presidential daily brief. This scheduling provides a logical time and place to bring breaking news to the president.
12. Consider the case of the Cuban missile crisis. When National Security Advisor McGeorge Bundy learned that the previous night's plane found evidence that the Soviet Union was newly erecting missile sites, Bundy's initial response was for the CIA to double-check the findings. After they confirmed the threat, Bundy still "decided that a quiet evening and a night of sleep were the best preparation [Kennedy] could have" to handle the difficulties ahead.
13. Independent research paints a different picture. Lou Cannon found the following: "After Reagan became president, White House officials would assiduously promote the fiction that Reagan read everything that was sent to him, but his closest aides knew better. Reagan read far more than outsiders realized, but he read what he wanted to read." Lou Cannon, *President Reagan: The Role of a Lifetime* (New York: PublicAffairs, 2008), 74.
14. Famously, on the eve of the 1983 G7 Summit, Chief of Staff James Baker learned that President Reagan had ignored his preparatory briefing book.

The president's excuse? "Well, Jim, *The Sound of Music* was on last night." See Cannon, *President Reagan*, 37.

15. The briefing book can also provide a catchall for materials that the president needs or requests. These might be forms that need the president's signature or news that piques the president's interest. President Obama, for instance, had staffers add a few letters sent to him by fellow Americans.

16. Replacing Real GDP growth with the National Bureau of Economic Research's measure, which indicates the months when the nation was in an economic recession, does not affect the results, substantively or statistically.

17. This definition of honeymoon puts Lyndon Johnson's honeymoon after his inauguration in 1965, not after he assumed office in 1963. Gerald Ford had no honeymoon. See also Paul Light, *The President's Agenda: Domestic Policy Choice from Kennedy to Clinton*, 3rd ed. (Baltimore, MD: Johns Hopkins University Press, 1999); Matthew N. Beckmann and J. Godfrey, "The Policy Opportunities in Presidential Honeymoons," *Political Research Quarterly* 60, no. 2 (2007): 250–62; L. J. Grossback, D. A. M. Peterson, and J. A. Stimson, *Mandate Politics* (New York: Cambridge University Press, 2012).

18. A model with only presidential fixed effects has an R2 of 0.88.

19. Adding an additional variable for Nixon post-Watergate attenuates the coefficient showing a second-term slowdown, but only a little, and not significantly.

20. Richard Nixon memo to H. R. Haldeman, "Memorandum for RMW from the President," Richard Nixon Library, March 31, 1971.

4. FILLING TIME

1. John Kennedy, "Remarks at a Rally in Fort Worth in Front of the Texas Hotel," November 22, 1963, https://www.presidency.ucsb.edu/node/236817.

2. "JFK Assassination: The Fateful Day in Dallas Unfolds," *CBS News*, November 22, 2013.

3. Lyndon Johnson, "Remarks upon Arrival at Andrews Air Force Base," November 22, 1963, https://www.presidency.ucsb.edu/node/238784.

4. Lyndon Johnson tape, "Phone Call Lyndon Johnson and McGeorge Bundy," conversation 3082, Lyndon B. Johnson Library, April 21, 1964.

5. Lyndon Johnson, "President Johnson's Remarks upon Departure of New Orleans to Washington, DC," September 10, 1965, http://www.lbjlibrary.net/collections/quick-facts/lyndon-baines-johnson-hurricane-betsy/lbj-new-orleans-hurricane-betsy.html.

6. Richard Reeves, *President Nixon: Alone in the White House* (New York: Simon & Schuster, 2002), 437.

7. At the end of a long day, having concluded the welcoming dinner hosted by the premier, President Nixon headed to his guest house for the night. Before reaching his room, however, the diary notes that Nixon stopped by a downstairs conference room, where, at 10:27, "The President signed S.J. Res. 197, an arbitration settlement procedure for the West Coast dock strike." At 10:30 "The President returned to his suite," thereby ending Nixon's first day in China.

8. Moments with many attendees typically are named in a lettered appendix (i.e., Appendix A, B, etc.) attached to the end of that day's basic diary.

9. Lyndon Johnson's diaries are a glorious exception. Compiled by personal secretaries who were often at the president's side during the events being logged, Johnson's diaries regularly added colorful asides. On October 24, 1964, the diary notes that the president had to "stop at the nearest drugstore to purchase a manicure set for him [Johnson]—his hands were in poor shape from much handshaking." On August 25, 1965, the diarist reports that Johnson wore his eyeglasses, "making him appear old and tired."

10. In interviews with the diarists, I learned that the lag between day and diary varied. During Carter's years, the diarists were eager to finish diary entries promptly—within a week—because the president liked to review them as soon as possible. A more typical lag time was between 1 and 2 weeks. Occasionally the diarists would get behind and so were forced to stay late and close the gap. A few times—especially one interval at the end of the Reagan administration and another, longer period during Clinton's second term—the diarists were overwhelmed and stopped trying to catch up. Appendices A and B develop these points in greater detail.

11. White House staffers gave a similar account in my interviews. For them, the diary was an essential resource, a way to identify people in a picture, the date of a meeting, the time of a call, and the like. When Ronald Reagan privately told Howard Baker that he barely knew Oliver North, the new chief of staff decided to check it out. As Baker explained, "After I left [that meeting]—you know, we keep detailed records of whoever sees the President, who goes in the Oval Office—[I] found out truly [that North had] only been in the Oval Office two or three times, and only once with the President alone, and then only for a very few minutes." This is why it has worked so well: archivists view the diary as invaluable for history; insiders view it as invaluable for themselves.

12. Setting aside Nixon's collapse after Watergate, the next-lowest work rate was during Reagan's second term, which averaged between 9 and 10 work activities per day.

13. We only coded moments that diarists recorded. Thus any time that is undocumented in the diary—such as downtime in the residence, quick snacks between meetings, or bathroom breaks before events—did not

get included as "thinking" or "speaking" time. In a future project, I will examine the nature of this "dark matter" that occurs within presidential workdays.

14. When President Trump's schedules leaked to the press, the extensive blocks of unspecified "executive time" became a euphemism for having time off the grid while on the clock. If nothing else, Reagan's example shows that the phenomenon existed well before the label.

15. Martha Joynt Kumar, "The White House as City Hall: A Tough Place to Organize," *Presidential Studies Quarterly* 31, no. 1 (2001): 44.

16. When schedulers err, presidents have no problem offering feedback to help them do better. Every former scheduling aide I interviewed could recall a time when the president indicated some combination of frustration, disappointment, or confusion about his schedule. Alyssa Mastromonaco, who led President Obama's scheduling team, recounted how the president signaled his irritation: "Uh, who thought this was a good idea?" A. Mastromonaco and L. Oyler, *Who Thought This Was a Good Idea? And Other Questions You Should Have Answers to When You Work in the White House* (New York: Grand Central, 2017), 8.

5. NIXON, MAN VERSUS MODEL

1. Richard Nixon Tapes, "Cancer on the Presidency with Richard Nixon and John Dean," Tape 886–008 A, March 21, 1973, Richard Nixon Library.

2. Stewart Alsop, "The President and His Enemies," *Washington Post*, September 1, 1973.

3. Elmo R. Zumwalt, *On Watch: A Memoir* (New York: Quadrangle, 1976), 479.

4. B. Goldwater with J. Casserly, *Goldwater* (New York: Doubleday, 1988), 270.

5. B. Woodward and C. Bernstein, *The Final Days* (New York: Simon & Schuster, 2005).

6. Hunter S. Thompson, "Fear and Loathing on the Campaign Trail '76," *Rolling Stone*, June 3, 1976.

7. This came after Nixon told Haig, "You fellows, in your business, you have a way of handling problems like this: somebody leaves a pistol in the drawer." See John A. Farrell, *Richard Nixon: The Life* (New York: Doubleday, 2017), 530.

8. Among these are C. Bernstein and B. Woodward, *All the President's Men* (New York: Warner, 1974); Woodward and Bernstein, *The Final Days*; Stanley Kutler, *The Wars of Watergate: The Last Crisis of Richard Nixon* (New York: Norton, 1992); Stanley Kutler, *Abuse of Power: The New Nixon Tapes* (New York: Free Press, 1997); G. Gordon Liddy, *Will: The Autobiography of G. Gordon Liddy* (New York: St. Martin Media, 1991); and John Dean, *Blind Ambition: The White House Years* (New York: Open Road Media, 2016).

9. After taking an angry call from a frustrated Secretary of State William Rogers, an exasperated Nixon sighed, "It would be god damn easy to run this office if you didn't have to deal with people." See Garrett M. Graff, *Watergate: A New History* (New York: Simon & Schuster, 2022), 3.

10. G. Peters and J. T. Woolley, *The American Presidency Project*, www.presidency .ucsb.edu.

11. Likewise, anxious that these patterns might reflect an archival artifact rather than real behavioral differences, I consulted Nixon Library archivists and interviewed the diarist who compiled the diaries throughout Nixon's presidency. All agreed that it was Richard Nixon, not the Daily Diary, that changed. One shared a useful perspective: Nixon could (and, in July 1973, did) deactivate the voice-recording system, but the Daily Diary was woven into the presidential paper flow, which had nonpresidential inputs and no presidential off-switch.

12. Farrell, *Richard Nixon*; Graff, *Watergate*; Ray Locker, *Haig's Coup* (Sterling, VA: Potomac Books, 2019).

13. These public event results bolster our confidence in the policy contact ones that preceded them. The fact that the diaries logged Nixon's public events, including ones not captured in the Public Papers of the Presidents, corroborates the view that the diaries accurately logged Nixon's behavior throughout his presidency.

14. Richard Reeves, *Richard Nixon: Alone in the White House* (New York: Simon & Schuster), 21.

15. By comparison, the correlation between week and policy contacts during Nixon's second term is −0.52.

16. Dubious about the timing given his troubles at home, critics labeled Nixon's hastily planned travels "impeachment diplomacy." Senator Henry Jackson (D-WA) gave voice to such suspicions: "It is more cosmetic and ceremonial than it will be substance." See Bernard Gwertzman, "The President's Mideast Gamble," *New York Times*, June 10, 1974.

17. Richard Nixon memo to H. R. Haldeman, "Memorandum for RMW from the President," Richard Nixon Library, March 31, 1971.

6. EVERYDAY LEADERSHIP

1. In recounting the experience, Patterson surmised that Ford had spent the morning golfing when, in fact, the president had been hard at work. Before heading to the Solarium for his "luncheon seminar," President Ford entered the Oval Office at 8:20, received a CIA briefing at 8:30, greeted a group of schoolchildren in the Rose Garden at 8:50, and then spent the next several hours in meetings: with his deputy chief of staff; with a delegation of Chinese scientists; with officials from France (and

the U.S. secretary of state); and with a group of economic, energy, and legislative affairs staffers.

2. Orlando Patterson, "A Meeting with Gerald Ford," *New York Times*, January 6, 2007.

3. Joseph Lelyveld, "Former Professor Holds Seminars for President and His Top Advisors," *New York Times*, October 6, 1975.

4. C-SPAN reports presidents' scores and rankings, along with details about the process by which they were produced (www.c-span.org/president survey2021).

5. The key empirical feature is multiple leaders (e.g., NFL coaches) who serve for different intervals, which enables comparisons about each one's relative performance, controlling for other factors. The test effectively pinpoints how likely (or unlikely) it is for individuals to have their record by chance alone. See C. R. Berry and A. Fowler, "Leadership or Luck? Randomization Inference for Leader Effects in Politics, Business, and Sports," *Science Advances* 7, no. 4 (2021).

6. No doubt, I would love it if new data sources and methods, combined with ever-evolving estimation strategies, would permit researchers to pin down both presidential inputs and their multifarious outputs, while also credibly accounting for confounding factors. Until then, presidency researchers should not shy away from informative methods that deviate from the experimental ideal.

7. In her incisive yet unsettling book about presidents' various illnesses, Rose McDermott analyzes how presidents' illnesses have afflicted their core functions at vital moments in ways that were mostly hidden at the time. See Rose McDermott, *Presidential Leadership, Illness, and Decision Making* (New York: Cambridge University Press, 2007). Obviously, this book raises the red flag higher.

8. John Pell, "Mr. Hoover's Hair-Shirt," *North American Review* 5, no. 8 (1930): 5.

9. James A. Stimson, *Tides of Consent* (New York: Cambridge University Press, 2004); John R. Zaller, *The Nature and Origins of Mass Opinion* (New York: Cambridge University Press, 1992).

10. William J. McGuire, "Attitudes and Attitude Change," in *The Handbook of Social Psychology*, ed. G. Lindzey and E. Aronson (Reading, MA: Addison-Wesley), 136–314; Zaller, *The Nature and Origins of Mass Opinion*.

11. S. Iyengar and K. S. Hahn, "Red Media, Blue Media: Evidence of Ideological Selectivity in Media Use," *Journal of Communication* 59, no. 1 (2009): 19–39; Matthew Levendusky, *How Partisan Media Polarize America* (Chicago: University of Chicago Press, 2013).

12. Brendan J. Doherty, *The Rise of the President's Permanent Campaign* (Lawrence: University Press of Kansas, 2012); Brendan J. Doherty, *Fundraiser in Chief: Presidents and the Politics of Campaign Cash* (Lawrence: University

Press of Kansas, 2023); Samuel Kernell, *Going Public: New Strategies of Presidential Leadership* (Washington, DC: CQ Press, 2006).

13. Brandice Canes-Wrone, *Who Leads Whom? Presidents, Policy, and the Public* (Chicago: University of Chicago Press, 2005).

14. Matthew N. Beckmann, *Pushing the Agenda: Presidential Leadership in U.S. Lawmaking, 1953–2004* (New York: Cambridge University Press, 2010); Charles C. Cameron, *Veto Bargaining* (New York: Cambridge University Press, 2000).

15. B. Dan Wood, *Presidential Saber Rattling: Causes and Consequences* (New York: Cambridge University Press, 2012).

16. Martha Joynt Kumar, *Managing the President's Message* (Baltimore, MD: Johns Hopkins University Press, 2007).

17. Harry Truman, "The President's News Conference," April 17, 1952, https://www.presidency.ucsb.edu/node/231717.

APPENDIX A: THE DAILY DIARY, 1961–2008

1. Caroline Kennedy, "Forward," in *Listening In: The Secret White House Recordings of John F. Kennedy*, ed. Ted Widmer (New York: Hyperion, 2012), 24.

2. John F. Kennedy. *The Secret Recordings of John F. Kennedy*. September 1962. WBUR Radio Station, Courtesy of the John F. Kennedy Presidential Library and Museum, https://www.wbur.org/radioboston/2013/01/01/jfk-tapes-redux

3. Susan Davis, March 9, 1972. Office of Presidential Papers and Archives (OPPA)—Daily Diary, Box 1, "Series I: Administrative Files, 1971–73." Richard Nixon Presidential Library and Museum.

4. The *New York Times* excerpted a briefing that the Watergate special prosecutor submitted to Judge Sirica that listed subpoenaed material (contrary to President Nixon's claims of executive privilege). The submission reads like a summary of Daily Diary entries—a rundown of dates, times, locations, and participants likely captured by the tape being subpoenaed—likely because it was.

5. Ms. McCathran lamented Ms. Yowell's firing. "We worked together, but we were friends as well." Nevertheless, the experience impressed upon Ms. McCathran the importance of hewing to her role as a civil servant. "My loyalty was to the office of the presidency."

6. Sometimes NARA would allow Ms. McCathran to hire an assistant diarist, but not always, and some assistants were more productive than others. The bigger issue, however, was more structural. One challenge was that diary work required security clearances, which took a long time to process. Another challenge was that NARA often resisted allocating a second full-time employee for work that had previously been done by one person. A final challenge was that assistants tended to have a short shelf life, in

part because the work was some combination of monotonous and relent-less, but even more because there were not really opportunities for promo-tion without moving to something else, somewhere else.

7. Additionally, Ms. McCathran was swept up by Ken Starr's investigation of President Clinton. The issue was that Monica Lewinsky did not appear in any Daily Diaries, and the special prosecutor wanted to know if Ms. McCathran (or other White House officials, including the president himself) had purposefully obscured evidence of Clinton and Lewinsky's relationship. Ms. McCathran testified about the nature of the diary and her role as a civil servant, and then she made it clear that she had not done anything to hide anyone, nor had anyone asked her to do so. In our inter-view, Ms. McCathran elaborated. She later realized that Lewinsky being an intern allowed her to access the West Wing without having to sign in, and Clinton propped open doors so she could slip into his office without getting on the schedule or going through the "Outer Oval Office"—the room adjacent to the Oval Office where virtually all presidential visitors enter (and get logged).

APPENDIX B: SAMPLING DESIGN AND DETAIL

1. I wildly underestimated how long it would take to get, code, clean, and analyze a representative sample of diaries. While the presidential libraries' archivists were unfailingly helpful at every turn, I nevertheless hit a multi-tude of snags throughout the data collection. Usually it was a minor glitch (e.g., a diary labeled as one date was actually the diary for another date); sometimes it was a major ordeal (e.g., the Bush 43 redactions were far more restrictive than anything I had seen before, so I submitted an appeal, which ultimately resolved in my favor but took *years* to complete).

2. By statute, the National Archives and Records Administration (NARA) starts taking Freedom of Information Act (FOIA) requests for presidential records five years after a president leaves office. President Obama's records opened on January 20, 2022, which is when I requested diaries for the days in my sample (and that request is still pending). FOIA requests for Presi-dent Trump's records will be possible starting on January 20, 2026.

3. At some point, optical character recognition (OCR) may be able to map all diary contents into usable data. I collaborated with three different software engineers to see if and how I might be able to do as much here. As far as we could tell, OCR is not yet a viable option. The amount of "cleaning" needed to turn any given diary page into a standardized format was extensive; to get thousands of pages into a standard format was not feasible.

4. Where there is no diary, archivists often insert some sort of substitute: usually that day's schedule or the source materials that would have helped

create the diary. To ensure maximum consistency, we only coded days on which there was a full, completed diary.

APPENDIX C: CODING AND DATA

1. To the extent this coding misses the significant moment that takes fewer than 5 minutes, there is good reason to suspect they are usually extensions of other, longer moments, which we did code.
2. Though far less common than missing end times, occasionally a diary does not detail a moment's start time. In such instances, we inferred when the moment began by applying the same process and standards used to fill end times – i.e., from context clues based on the activity itself and those surrounding it.

BIBLIOGRAPHY

Abrams, Abigail. "13 Pieces of Advice for the Trump Team from Obama's White House." *Time*, January 12, 2017.

Allison, G., and P. Zelikow. *Essence of Decision: Explaining the Cuban Missile Crisis.* 2nd ed. New York: Pearson, 1999.

Ambrose, Stephen E. *Nixon: Ruin and Recovery, 1973–1990.* New York: Simon & Schuster, 1991.

Arrow, Kenneth J. *Social Choice and Individual Values.* New York: Wiley, 1951.

Barber, James D. *The Presidential Character: Predicting Performance in the White House.* Englewood Cliffs, NJ: Prentice-Hall, 1972.

Baum, M. A., and S. Kernell. "Has Cable Ended the Golden Age of Presidential Television?" *American Political Science Review* 93, no. 1 (1999): 99–114.

Beckmann, Matthew N. "Did Nixon Quit Before He Resigned?" *Research and Politics* 4, no. 2 (2017): 1–7.

——. "A President's Decisions and the Presidential Difference." In *Leadership in American Politics*, ed. J. A. Jenkins and C. Volden, 65–87. Lawrence: University Press of Kansas, 2017.

——. *Pushing the Agenda: Presidential Leadership in U.S. Lawmaking, 1953–2004.* New York: Cambridge University Press, 2010.

Beckmann, Matthew N., and J. Godfrey. "The Policy Opportunities in Presidential Honeymoons." *Political Research Quarterly* 60, no. 2 (2007): 250–62.

Beckmann, Matthew N., and M. M. Kaminski. "Speaking, Thinking, and Being President." *Journal of Political Institutions and Political Economy* 4, no. 2 (2023): 159–82.

Bernstein, C., and B. Woodward. *All the President's Men.* New York: Warner, 1974.

Black, Duncan. "On the Rationale of Group Decision-Making." *Journal of Political Economy* 56, no. 1 (1948): 23–34.

Bobic, Igor. "Bill Clinton's Work Habits Took a Toll on His Staff, but Hillary Might Do Things Differently." *HuffPost*, May 21, 2014.

Bond, J. R., and R. Fleisher. *The President in the Legislative Arena*. Chicago: University of Chicago Press, 1990.

Bose, Meena. *Shaping and Signaling Presidential Policy: The National Security Decision Making of Eisenhower and Kennedy*. College Station: Texas A&M University Press, 1998.

Brinkley, Douglas. *The Unfinished Presidency*. Hawthorn, Australia: Viking/Allen Lane, 1998.

Burke, John P. *Honest Broker? The National Security Advisor and Presidential Decision-Making*. College Station: Texas A&M University Press, 2009.

——. "Organizational Structure and Presidential Decision Making." In *The Oxford Handbook of the American Presidency*, ed. W. G. Howell and G. C. Edwards III, 501–27. New York: Oxford University Press, 2009.

Burke, John P., and F. I. Greenstein. "Presidential Personality and National Security Leadership: A Comparative Analysis of Vietnam Decision-Making." *International Political Science Review* 10, no. 1 (1989): 73–92.

Burns, James MacGregor. *Presidential Government: The Crucible of Leadership*. Boston: Houghton Mifflin, 1965.

Cameron, Charles. *Veto Bargaining: Presidents and the Politics of Negative Power*. Cambridge: Cambridge University Press, 2000.

Cameron, C., and N. McCarty. "Models of Vetoes and Veto Bargaining." *Annual Review of Political Science* 7, no. 1 (2004): 409–35.

Canes-Wrone, Brandice. "Game Theory and the Study of the American Presidency." In *The Oxford Handbook of the American Presidency*, ed. W. G. Howell and G. C. Edwards III, 30–50. New York: Oxford University Press, 2009.

——. *Who Leads Whom? Presidents, Policy, and the Public*. Chicago: University of Chicago Press, 2005.

Cannon, Lou. *President Reagan: The Role of a Lifetime*. London: Simon & Schuster, 1992.

Card, Andrew, and Denis McDonough. "Views from the West Wing: How Global Trends Shape U.S. Foreign Policy." Forum, University of Notre Dame, Indiana, 2017.

Carter, Jimmy. *Keeping Faith: Memoirs of a President*. Little Rock: University of Arkansas Press, 1995.

——. *White House Diary*. New York: Farrar, Straus and Giroux, 2010.

Cohen, D. B., K. Hult, and C. Walcott. "White House Evolution and Institutionalization: The Office of Chief of Staff Since Reagan." *Presidential Studies Quarterly* 46, no. 1 (2016): 4–29.

Cohen, D. B., and G. A. Krause. "Presidents, Chiefs of Staff, and White House Organizational Behavior: Survey Evidence from the Reagan and Bush Administrations." *Presidential Studies Quarterly* 30, no. 3 (2000): 421–42.

Cohen, Jeffrey E. "Alternative Futures." *Presidential Studies Quarterly* 39, no. 4 (2009): 725–35.

——. *Going Local: Presidential Leadership in the Post-Broadcast Age.* New York: Cambridge University Press, 2010.

——. *The Presidency in the Era of 24-Hour News.* Princeton, NJ: Princeton University Press, 2008.

Cohen, M. D., J. G. March, and J. P. Olsen. "A Garbage Can Model of Organizational Choice." *Administrative Science Quarterly* 17, no. 1 (1972): 1–25.

Cook, Stephen. "The Complexity of Theorem-Proving Procedures." In *Proceedings of the Third Annual ACM Symposium on Theory of Computing*, 151–58. New York: Association for Computing Machinery, 1971.

Corwin, Edward S. *The President: Office and Powers, 1787–1957: History and Analysis of Practice and Opinion.* New York: New York University Press, 1957.

Cronin, T. E., and W. R. Hochman. "Franklin D. Roosevelt and the American Presidency." *Presidential Studies Quarterly* 15, no. 2 (1985): 277–86.

Daalder, I. H., and I. M. Destler. *In the Shadow of the Oval Office.* New York: Simon & Schuster, 2009.

Dean, John W. *Blind Ambition: The White House Years.* New York: Open Road Media, 2016.

Dickerson, John. *The Hardest Job in the World: The American Presidency.* New York: Random House, 2020.

Dickinson, Matthew J. "Bargaining, Uncertainty, and the Growth of the White House Staff, 1940–2000." In *Uncertainty in American Politics*, ed. Barry C. Burden, 27–47. New York: Cambridge University Press, 2003.

——. *Bitter Harvest: FDR, Presidential Power and the Growth of the Presidential Branch.* New York: Cambridge University Press, 1999.

——. "We All Want a Revolution: Neustadt, New Institutionalism, and the Future of Presidency Research." *Presidential Studies Quarterly* 39, no. 4 (2009): 736–70.

Dickinson, Matthew J., and M. J. Lebo. "Reexamining the Growth of the Institutional Presidency, 1940–2000." *Journal of Politics* 69, no. 1 (2007): 206–19.

Dickinson, Matthew J., and E. Neustadt. *Guardian of the Presidency: The Legacy of Richard E. Neustadt.* Washington, DC: Brookings Institution, 2007.

Doherty, Brendan J. *Fundraiser in Chief: Presidents and the Politics of Campaign Cash.* Lawrence: University Press of Kansas, 2023.

——. *The Rise of the President's Permanent Campaign.* Lawrence: University Press of Kansas, 2012.

Drew, Elizabeth. *Washington Journal.* New York: Random House, 1975.

Druckman, J. M., and L. R. Jacobs. *Who Governs? Presidents, Public Opinion, and Manipulation.* Chicago: University of Chicago Press, 2015.

Edwards, George C. *At the Margins: Presidential Leadership of Congress.* New Haven, CT: Yale University Press, 1989.

——. *On Deaf Ears: The Limits of the Bully Pulpit.* New Haven, CT: Yale University Press, 2003.

——. *The Strategic President: Persuasion and Opportunity in Presidential Leadership.* Princeton, NJ: Princeton University Press, 2009.

Edwards, George C., J. H. Kessel, and B A. Rockman, eds. *Researching the Presidency.* Pittsburgh, PA: University of Pittsburgh Press, 2009.

Eisinger, Robert M. *The Evolution of Presidential Polling.* New York: Cambridge University Press, 2003.

Farrell, John A. *Richard Nixon: The Life.* New York: Doubleday, 2017.

Galvin, Daniel J. *Presidential Party Building.* Princeton, NJ: Princeton University Press, 2009.

Gilmour, John B. *Strategic Disagreement: Stalemate in American Politics.* Pittsburgh, PA: University of Pittsburgh Press, 1995.

Goldwater, B. with J. Casserly. *Goldwater.* New York: Doubleday, 1988.

Graff, Garrett M. *Watergate: A New History.* New York: Simon & Schuster, 2022.

Greenstein, Fred I. *The Hidden-Hand Presidency: Eisenhower as Leader.* Baltimore, MD: Johns Hopkins University Press, 1994.

——. *The Presidential Difference: Leadership Style from FDR to Barack Obama.* 3rd ed. Princeton, NJ: Princeton University Press, 2009.

Grossback, L. J., D. A. M. Peterson, and J. A. Stimson. *Mandate Politics.* New York: Cambridge University Press, 2012.

Hagar, G., and T. Sullivan. "President-Centered and Presidency-Centered Explanations of Presidential Public Activity." *American Journal of Political Science* 38, no. 4 (1994): 1079–103.

Hamilton, James T. *All the News That's Fit to Sell: How the Market Transforms Information into News.* Princeton, NJ: Princeton University Press, 2004.

Haney, Patrick J. *Organizing for Foreign Policy Crises: Presidents, Advisers, and the Management of Decision Making.* Ann Arbor: University of Michigan Press, 1997.

Hart, John. "Neglected Aspects of the Study of the Presidency." *Annual Review of Political Science* 1, no. 1 (1998): 379–99.

——. *The Presidential Branch: From Washington to Clinton.* New York: Chatham House, 1995.

Heclo, Hugh. *A Government of Strangers: Executive Politics in Washington.* Washington, DC: Brookings Institution, 1977.

Heith, Diane J. *Polling to Govern: Public Opinion and Presidential Leadership.* Palo Alto, CA: Stanford University Press, 2003.

Helgerson, John. *Getting to Know the President: Intelligence Briefings of Presidential Candidates and Presidents-Elect.* 4th ed. Independently Published, 2022.

Henderson, Phillip G. "Organizing the Presidency for Effective Leadership: Lessons from the Eisenhower Years." *Presidential Studies Quarterly* 17, no. 1 (1987): 43–69.

Hermann, Margaret G. "Assessing Leadership Style: Trait Analysis." In *The Psychological Assessment of Political Leaders: With Profiles of Saddam Hussein and Bill Clinton,* ed. Jerrold M. Post, 178–212. Ann Arbor: University of Michigan Press, 2003.

Hess, S., and J. P. Pfiffner. *Organizing the Presidency*. Washington, DC: Brookings Institution, 2020.

Howell, William G. *Power Without Persuasion: The Politics of Direct Presidential Action*. Princeton, NJ: Princeton University Press, 2003.

——. *The Primacy of Power*. Princeton, NJ: Princeton University Press, 2013.

Howell, William G., and T. M. Moe. *Presidents, Populism, and the Crisis of American Democracy*. Chicago: University of Chicago Press, 2020.

——. *Relic: How Our Constitution Undermines Effective Government and Why We Need a More Powerful Presidency*. New York: Basic Books, 2016.

Hult, K. M., and C. E. Walcott. "Influences on Presidential Decision Making." In *The Oxford Handbook of the American Presidency*, ed. W. G. Howell and G. C. Edwards III, 528–49. New York: Oxford University Press, 2009.

Hunter, Majorie. "Ford Sworn as Vice President After House Approves, 387–35; He Vows Justice for All." *New York Times*, December 7, 1974.

Iyengar, S., and K. S. Hahn, "Red Media, Blue Media: Evidence of Ideological Selectivity in Media Use." *Journal of Communication* 59, no. 1 (2009): 19–39.

Jacobs, Lawrence R. "Building Reliable Theories of the Presidency." *Presidential Studies Quarterly* 39, no. 4 (2009): 771–80.

Janis, Irving L. *Victims of Groupthink: A Psychological Study of Foreign-Policy Decisions and Fiascoes*. New York: Houghton Mifflin, 1972.

Johnson, Richard Tanner. *Managing the White House: An Intimate Study of the Presidency*. New York: Harper & Row, 1974.

Jones, Charles O. *The Presidency in a Separated System*. Washington, DC: Brookings Institution, 1994.

Kennedy, John F. *The Secret Recordings of John F. Kennedy*. September 1962. WBUR Radio Station, Courtesy of the John F. Kennedy Presidential Library and Museum. https://www.wbur.org/radioboston/2013/01/01/jfk-tapes-redux

Kernell, Samuel. *Going Public: New Strategies of Presidential Leadership*. Washington, DC: CQ Press, 1993.

Kernell, Samuel, and S. L. Popkin. *Chief of Staff: Twenty-Five Years of Managing the Presidency*. Los Angeles: University of California Press, 1986.

Kissinger, Henry A. *Years of Renewal*. New York: Simon & Schuster, 2000.

——. *Years of Upheaval*. Boston: Little, Brown, 1979.

Kumar, Martha Joynt. *Managing the President's Message*. Baltimore, MD: Johns Hopkins University Press, 2007.

——. "The White House as City Hall: A Tough Place to Organize." *Presidential Studies Quarterly* 31, no. 1 (2001): 44–55.

Kutler, Stanley. *Abuse of Power: The New Nixon Tapes*. New York: Free Press, 1997.

——. *The Wars of Watergate: The Last Crisis of Richard Nixon*. New York: Norton, 1992.

Lee, Frances E. *Beyond Ideology: Politics, Principles, and Partisanship in the U.S. Senate*. Chicago: University of Chicago Press, 2009.

Levendusky, Matthew. *How Partisan Media Polarize America*. Chicago: University of Chicago Press, 2013.

Lewis, Alfred E. "5 Held in Plot to Bug Democrats' Office Here," *Washington Post*, June 18, 1972.

Lewis, Michael. "Obama's Way." *Vanity Fair*, September 11, 2012.

Light, Paul. *The President's Agenda: Domestic Policy Choice from Kennedy to Clinton*. 3rd ed. Baltimore, MD: Johns Hopkins University Press, 1999.

——. *Thickening Government: Federal Hierarchy and the Diffusion of Accountability*. Washington, DC: Brookings Institution, 1995.

Lindblom, Charles E. "The Science of 'Muddling Through.'" *Public Administration Review* 19, no. 2 (1959): 79–88.

Mastromonaco, A., and L. Oyler. *Who Thought This Was a Good Idea? And Other Questions You Should Have Answers to When You Work in the White House*. New York: Grand Central, 2017.

Mayer, Kenneth R. "Thoughts on 'The Revolution in Presidential Studies.'" *Presidential Studies Quarterly* 39, no. 4 (2009): 781–85.

Mayhew, David R. *Congress: The Electoral Connection*. New Haven, CT: Yale University Press, 1974.

Mayton, D. M. II, and M. Z. Brink. "Groupthink." In *The Encyclopedia of Peace Psychology*, ed. Daniel J. Christie. Oxford: Blackwell, 2011.

McDermott, Rose. *Presidential Leadership, Illness, and Decision Making*. New York: Cambridge University Press, 2007.

Meacham, Jon. *The Soul of America: The Battle for Our Better Angels*. New York: Random House, 2019.

Miller, J. H., and S. Page. *Complex Adaptive Systems: An Introduction to Computational Models of Social Life*. Princeton, NJ: Princeton University Press, 2007.

Moe, Terry M. "The Revolution in Presidential Studies." *Presidential Studies Quarterly* 39, no. 4 (2009): 701–24.

Morris, Edmund. *Dutch: A Memoir of Ronald Reagan*. New York: Random House, 1999.

Nathan, Richard P. *The Plot That Failed: Nixon and the Administrative Presidency*. New York: Wiley, 1975.

Neustadt, Richard E. "Does the White House Need a Strong Chief of Staff?" In *The Managerial Presidency*, ed. James P. Pfiffner, 69–74. Pacific Grove, CA: Brooks/Cole, 1991.

——. *Presidential Power and the Modern Presidents*. New York: Free Press, 1990.

Nixon, Richard. *RN: The Memoirs of Richard Nixon*. New York: Simon & Schuster, 1976.

Patterson, Bradley H. "Teams and Staff: Dwight Eisenhower's Innovations in the Structure and Operations of the Modern White House." *Presidential Studies Quarterly* 24, no. 2 (1994): 277–98.

——. *The White House Staff: Inside the West Wing and Beyond*. Washington, DC: Brookings Institution, 2000.

Patterson, Thomas E. "The United States: News in a Free-Market Society." In *Democracy and the Media. A Comparative Perspective*, ed. R. Gunther and A. Mughan, 241–65. New York: Cambridge University Press, 2000.

Pell, John. "Mr. Hoover's Hair-Shirt." *North American Review* 5, no. 8 (1930): 4–5.

Pfiffner, James P. "Can the President Manage the Government?" In *The Managerial Presidency*, ed. James P. Pfiffner, 3–22. Pacific Grove, CA: Brooks/Cole, 1999.

——. *The Strategic Presidency: Hitting the Ground Running*. 2nd ed. Lawrence: University Press of Kansas, 1996.

Pious, Richard M. *Why Presidents Fail*. New York: Rowman & Littlefield, 2008.

Ponder, Daniel. *Good Advice: Information and Policy Making in the White House*. College Station: Texas A&M University Press, 2000.

Porter, Roger B. *Presidential Decision Making: The Economic Policy Board*. New York: Cambridge University Press, 1980.

Priess, David. *The President's Book of Secrets*. New York: Public Affairs, 2017.

Prior, Markus. *Post-Broadcast Democracy*. New York: Cambridge University Press, 2007.

Ragsdale, Lyn. *Vital Statistics on the Presidency: The Definitive Source for Data and Analysis on the American Presidency*. 4th ed. Washington, DC: CQ Press, 2014.

Reeves, Richard. *President Nixon: Alone in the White House*. New York: Simon & Schuster, 2002.

Rittel, H. W. J., and M. M. Webber. "Dilemmas in a General Theory of Planning." *Policy Sciences* 4, no. 2 (1973): 155–69.

Rockman, Bert A. "Off with the President's Head?" *Presidential Studies Quarterly* 39, no. 4 (2009): 786–94.

Roosevelt, Theodore. *Theodore Roosevelt; an Autobiography*. New York: Macmillan, 1913.

Rossiter, Clinton. *The American Presidency*. New York: Harcourt, Brace, 1960.

Rottinghaus, Brandon. *The Institutional Effects of Executive Scandals*. New York: Cambridge University Press, 2015.

——. *The Provisional Pulpit*. College Station: Texas A&M University Press, 2010.

Rudalevige, Andrew. *By Executive Order: Bureaucratic Management and the Limits of Presidential Power*. Princeton, NJ: Princeton University Press, 2022.

——. *Managing the President's Program: Presidential Leadership and Legislative Policy Formation*. Princeton, NJ: Princeton University Press, 2002.

——. "The Structure of Leadership: Presidents, Hierarchies, and Information Flow." *Presidential Studies Quarterly* 35, no. 2 (2005): 333–60.

——. " 'Therefore, Get Wisdom': What Should the President Know, and How Can He Know It?" *Governance* 22, no. 2 (2009): 177–87.

Sabato, Larry. *Feeding Frenzy: How Attack Journalism Has Transformed American Politics*. New York: Free Press, 1991.

Saunders, Elizabeth N. *Leaders at War: How Presidents Shape Military Interventions*. Ithaca, NY: Cornell University Press, 2011.

——. "No Substitute for Experience: Presidents, Advisers, and Information in Group Decision Making." Supplement, *International Organization* 71, no. S1 (2017): S219–47.

Sigelman, L., and D. M. McNeil. "White House Decision-Making Under Stress: A Case Analysis." *American Journal of Political Science* 24, no. 4 (1980): 652–73.

Simonton, Dean K. "Presidential IQ, Openness, Intellectual Brilliance, and Leadership: Estimates and Correlations for 42 U.S. Chief Executives." *Political Psychology* 27, no. 4 (2006): 511–26.

Sinclair, Barbara. *Party Wars: Polarization and the Politics of National Policymaking.* Norman: University of Oklahoma Press, 2006.

——. "Studying Presidential Leadership." In *Researching the Presidency*, ed. G. C. Edwards III, J. H. Kessel, and B. A. Rockman, 387–412. Pittsburgh, PA: University of Pittsburgh Press, 1993.

Skowronek, Stephen. "Mission Accomplished." *Presidential Studies Quarterly* 39, no. 4 (2009): 795–804.

——. *The Politics Presidents Make: Leadership from John Adams to Bill Clinton.* Cambridge, MA: Harvard University Press, 1993.

Smith, Kathryn. *The Gatekeeper: Missy LeHand, FDR, and the Untold Story of the Partnership That Defined a Presidency.* Repr. ed. New York: Atria, 2016.

Sorensen, Theodore C. *Decision-Making in the White House: The Olive Branch or the Arrows.* New York: Columbia University Press, 2005.

Sullivan, Terry. *Nerve Center: Lessons in Governing from the White House Chiefs of Staff.* College Station: Texas A&M University Press, 2004.

Thompson, Hunter S. "Fear and Loathing on the Campaign Trail '76." *Rolling Stone*, June 3, 1976.

Troy, Tevi. "Don't Worry, America: The 3 A.M. Phone Call Is a Myth." *Politico*, September 10, 2016.

——. *Fight House: Rivalries in the White House from Truman to Trump.* Washington, DC: Regnery History, 2020.

Vandenbroucke, Lucien S. "The 'Confessions' of Allen Dulles: New Evidence on the Bay of Pigs." *Diplomatic History* 8, no. 4 (1984): 365–76.

Walcott, C. E., and K. M. Hult. *Empowering the White House.* Lawrence: University Press of Kansas, 2004.

——. *Governing the White House: From Hoover to LBJ.* Lawrence: University Press of Kansas, 1995.

——. "White House Structure and Decision Making: Elaborating the Standard Model." *Presidential Studies Quarterly* 35, no. 2 (2005): 303–18.

Walker, Ronald H. "A President's Time." *The New Nixon*, February 13, 2010.

Walker, Stephen G. "The Psychology of Presidential Decision-Making." In *The Oxford Handbook of the American Presidency*, ed. W. G. Howell and G. C. Edwards III, 550–74. New York: Oxford University Press, 2009.

Warshaw, Shirley Anne. *The Domestic Presidency: Policy Making in the White House.* Boston: Allyn and Bacon, 1997.

——. *The Keys to Power: Managing the Presidency.* New York: Routledge, 2004.

Waterman, R. W., C. L. Silva, and H. Jenkins-Smith. *The Presidential Expectations Gap: Public Attitudes Concerning the Presidency.* Ann Arbor: University of Michigan Press, 2015.

Waterman, R. W., R. Wright, and G. St. Clair. *The Image-Is-Everything Presidency.* New York: Westview, 1999.

Watson, M., with S. Markman. *Chief of Staff: Lyndon Johnson and His Presidency.* New York: Thomas Dunne, 2004.

Wattenberg, Martin P. "The Changing Presidential Media Environment." *Presidential Studies Quarterly* 34, no. 3 (2004): 557–72.

——. *The Rise of Candidate-Centered Politics.* Cambridge, MA: Harvard University Press, 1991.

Weiner, Tim. "Robert S. McNamara, Architect of a Futile War, Dies at 93." *New York Times*, July 6, 2009.

Whipple, Chris. *The Presidents' Gatekeepers.* New York: Crown, 2017.

Widmer, Ted. *Listening In: The Secret White House Recordings of John F. Kennedy.* New York: Hyperion, 2012.

Wilson, Woodrow. *Constitutional Government in the United States.* New York: Columbia University Press, 1908.

Wood, B. Dan. *The Myth of Presidential Representation.* New York: Cambridge University Press, 2009.

Woodward, B., and C. Bernstein. *The Final Days.* New York: Simon & Schuster, 2005.

Zaller, John R. *The Nature and Origins of Mass Opinion.* New York: Cambridge University Press, 1992.

Zumwalt, Elmo R. *On Watch: A Memoir.* New York: Quadrangle, 1976.

INDEX

GPSR Authorized Representative: Easy Access System Europe, Mustamäe tee 50, 10621 Tallinn, Estonia, gpsr.requests@easproject.com